The Venison Sausage Cookbook

The Venison Sausage Cookbook

Complete Guide from Field to Table

Harold Webster

THE LYONS PRESS

Guilford, Connecticut

An imprint of The Globe Pequot Press

The Lyons Press is an imprint of The Globe Pequot Press.

10 9 8 7 6 5 4 3

Printed in the United States of America

Library of Congress Cataloging-in-Publication Data

Webster, Harold W.
    The venison sausage cookbook : a complete guide, from field to table
/ Harold Webster.
      p. cm.
    ISBN 1-58574-859-5 (pb : alk. paper)
    1. Cookery (Sausages) 2. Sausages. 3. Cookery (Venison) I. Title.
    TX749.5.S28 W43 2002
    641.6'91—dc21

                                                    2002152151

Dedication

To my best two hunting buds: J. and Mr. Will.

May your dog box never be empty, your Skoal can always be full,
and may you never stop exploring and dreaming
about all things being possible.

The author, J., and Mr. Will

And to Miss Anne, who was always there
and who read the same pages so many times.

Contents

About the Author

Harold Webster is the best-selling author of *The Complete Venison Cookbook.* He writes the syndicated newspaper column "Game for All Seasons" and conducts the Game for All Seasons cooking school.

He says: "I am a sportsman and a chef who enjoys the out-of-doors. When I go hunting and fishing, I am going to the market for the best that nature has to offer."

A graduate of the University of Arkansas in recreation education and a veteran of the Marine Corps, he was raised in Nelliesburg, Mississippi. He and his wife, Anne, live at "Oak Grove" outside of Cooper's Well, Mississippi. Harold comes from a family of early Mississippi settlers who have been living, hunting, and cooking wild game, fish, and fowl in Mississippi since before 1795.

Harold has hunted, fished, and cooked across the United States and overseas. He has traveled and explored the world and along the way has sampled, enjoyed, and gained an appreciation for the out-of-doors and the many ways that venison and other wild game and fish are cooked.

He has feasted on wild boar with high chiefs in the mountain forests of Pago Pago, dined on local venison with Lacadone Indians in the steamy jungles of Quintana Roo, savored Riso Niro on Napoleon's island of Elba, enjoyed smoked Prosciutto in the beautiful city of Florence, was taught to roll sushi in Tokyo, and learned the fine art of making venison and crab sausage in Dominique You's Barataria.

Besides being an outdoor writer, chef, and world traveler, the author is also an accomplished bluewater sailor, pilot and builder of experimental aircraft, competitive archer, restorer of antique sailing vessels, builder of fine

Appalachian dulcimers, skydiver, white-water kayak racer, amateur historian, competitive marksman, scuba diver, amateur marine archaeologist, and country philosopher.

Magazines and journals in North America, Europe, and the Pacific Basin have critically reviewed Mr. Webster's writings. He has appeared on the QVC Home Shopping Network, numerous radio and TV talk shows, and book-signing tours across the United States and Europe. He teaches outdoor and game & fish cooking classes at the university and local levels both in the United States and overseas and is often a featured guest chef.

Acknowledgments

My profound thanks are due to the following individuals and companies for graciously providing their advice, supplies, equipment, photographs, and other support. Without their kind and generous assistance, this book would not have been possible:

Julie Hawley and Cody Brown (Allied Kenco Sales)
Wade Bradley and Michael Tostowaryk (Bradley Technologies
    Canada, Inc.)
Helen Dunham (The Brinkmann Corporation)
Kelly Mallery (Cabela's)
Bridget Haggerty (Chaney Instrument Company)
Bryhn Craft (Craft's Custom Meats)
Tamara Lowry and Christina Contreras (DeWied International)
Scott Cain, Jaqueline Lonberger, Bodie McAuley, Vickie Secrest,
    Jason White, and Andy Wiley (Gateway)
Todd Graf (HuntingNet.com)
Ted Leemaster (KitchenAid, Whirlpool Corporation)
Sandra Zadora (Linemaster Switch Corporation)
Sarah Labensky, CCP, (Mississippi University for Women Culinary
    Arts Institute)
A. J. Miller, Linda Craght, and Mona Reinhard (Morton Salt)
William McGinnis (Outdoor and Leisure Industry Development,
    Mississippi Development Authority)
Mike and Kenny Bush (Rebel Butcher Supply)
Thomas McIntosh (The Sausage Maker, Inc.)
Pat McGlothlin (Tony Chachere's Creole Foods of Opelousas, Inc.)
Jesus Iglesias (Tor-Rey)
Van Allen and Johnny King (Van's Deer Processing)
Icey Day
Randy Hayman
George Roberts

Foreword

When my friends and I were growing up in Natchez, Mississippi, we spent countless days in the woods and on the water hunting and fishing. Everything about those days was special. From the time spent in anticipation getting everything ready to go, to the hours and miles we hiked through the river bluffs, to the meals we had from whatever we eventually brought in, each part of the experience was equally important then, and it remains the same for me today.

Whether I'm hunting with a rifle, bow, or more often, a video camera, to say I look forward to eating some of whatever we're after each day would be an understatement. It just doesn't seem like real hunting unless there's some good food on the table at the end of the day. I've had the good fortune to sample virtually every sort of wild game that can be found in North America. Some of it's good, a lot of it's great, and all of it is a blessing. While it's all worth looking forward to, some dishes are more dependable than others, and in my experience, there's nothing more dependable than venison sausage. Whether you grill it, fry it, cook it up in a gumbo, mix it in with red beans and rice, or use it in any of a hundred other ways, nothing beats it. Nothing kicks off a morning headed for the turkey woods, or wraps up an evening after a day spent on a deer stand, like venison sausage.

There are plenty of different sausage recipes out there, but, knock on wood, I've yet to try a bad one. Of all the recipes I've tried, though, some of the very best I've ever tasted were from Harold Webster. Now he's sharing those same recipes with all of us. You'll learn everything you need to know to craft your own sausage, and even invent some recipes of your own, from this book.

There's something special about making good food from the game nature provides, and that's what this book is all about. Every time I pull a pack of venison sausage out of the freezer, I think about the hunt it came from. I remember what the day was like, whom I was with and how the weather was, and I enjoy a good meal as well. Thanks to this book, now my memories will be just as sharp, and the meal even better.

—Ronnie "Cuz" Strickland

(Ronnie "Cuz" Strickland is the senior vice president of media services for Haas Outdoor, Inc., originators of Mossy Oak Camo. Cuz is nationally recognized and best known as the world-class producer and videographer of the Mossy Oak *Hunting the Country* and *Remington Country* outdoor programs, both of which are the highest-rated shows on any outdoor network. He is also the author of three books recounting his humorous times spent in the woods. Ronnie set the state record for nontypical deer and is an avid turkey hunter who enjoys camp cooking second only to being with his family and friends.)

Introduction

This book was written for those millions of hunters and families who, like me, have always wanted to learn how to make their own venison sausage so that they can:

- Make homemade venison sausage that is safe to eat, simple, and economical to produce.
- Satisfy the tastes and traditions of their family.
- Be assured that the venison sausage they and their family are eating came from their own harvest.
- Provide a unique activity that they and all members of their family can participate in and enjoy the fruits of their labor together for many years to come.

It was for these reasons that I began experimenting with converting traditional sausage recipes from around the world into venison sausage recipes that could be made at home by anyone.

Courtesy DeWied International

Up front and for the record, there is no great mystery to making delicious sausage at home. For at least 5,000 years, people from all over the world have been making sausage at home without expensive equipment.

Most of the original sausage recipes used for this book were traditionally made out of pork. Other recipes were traditionally made from veal, lamb, goat, or sheep, and came from all areas of the world.

- My first challenge was to balance the low-fat venison with a moist meat that would make sausage that tasted as it should and would hold up during the cooking process.
- My second challenge was to develop venison sausage recipes that would be easy to make at home and would make anyone proud to serve them to their family and friends.
- My third challenge was to select only those venison sausage recipes that would require no expensive equipment and would be inexpensive to make at home.

The history of sausage making dates back to some obscure moment in time when some early man discovered that his surplus of meat lasted longer when it was chopped, mixed with a little raw natural salt, and stored in the stomach or intestines of the animal. It was in medieval Europe that the art of sausage making as we know it today was developed. As the specialized trades and guilds evolved, so did the reputation of the local sausage makers.

It took the wealth of the medieval manor and the spice routes from the Orient to discover that combining the preserving characteristics of smoke, rare spices, and the natural salt containing nitrates and nitrites would make a tasty and long-lived meat product. Warmer summer temperatures dictated that sausage making be reserved for the fall. There are some areas of northern Europe where the summer temperatures are cool enough to let the making and storing of sausage be a year-round activity. The fall tradition of making sausage at home continues today.

The art of sausage making immigrated to American shores along with our immigrant ancestors. These early immigrants came from all parts of the world, and the sausage recipes they brought with them were just as diverse as their cultures. Modern refrigeration and transportation allow us to enjoy sausages made anywhere in the world and at any time of the year. Many of these traditional sausages are so familiar to us that their origins have blended into the past; many have taken new names and have crossed all ethnic, national, and culinary lines. Other great sausages are still available only within the cultural confines of the areas in which they are made.

Three examples of these regional sausages are Andouille and Boudin from Louisiana and Chorizo from Texas. The Louisiana sausages are rooted in France and migrated through Nova Scotia and deep into the Louisiana bayou county. No festive meal in bayou country would be complete without a generous portion of Boudin, and wild duck gumbo would not taste the same without smoked Andouille.

Chorizo sausage originated in Spain and traveled with the Spanish conquistadores to Mexico and then throughout the Spanish territories of Texas and the desert Southwest. Once in the Americas, Chorizo took on the flavors that we now associate with that area. When venison Chorizo sausage is cooked for breakfast, mixed with scrambled eggs, and rolled in a warm flour tortilla to make a small "Tacito," it is a complete meal—and one of the best-tasting breakfast sausages that you will ever eat.

The French carried sausage making to a higher plane of culinary expression. Beginning in the 15th century, the French term *charcuterie* came to encompass not only the making of sausage, but also all finely ground delicatessen meat products and such classic presentations as pâté and baked pasty with forcemeat filling. Some examples can be found in Chapter 20.

Back in 1994, when I began working out the sausage recipes for *The Complete Venison Cookbook*, I spent a weekend in the kitchen at the Lake-House making my first batches of hot-smoked/cooked venison link sausage and venison breakfast patty sausage. I was surprised at how easy the whole process was and even more surprised at how good the sausage tasted.

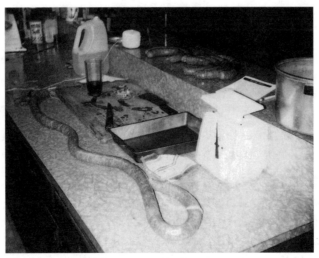

*First batch of venison link sausage made at
the Lake-House in 1994*

Since venison is so low in fat, some product must be added to hold the sausage together and prevent the sausage from tasting dry. The weekend that I made my first batches of venison sausage, I spent Friday evening searching supermarkets for pork fat or pork scraps. Instead, I purchased pork butt and pork chops with the bone removed. The difference in taste was noticed immediately. Later, when I experimented with smoked bacon ends, I found that the smoked flavor was already in my fresh sausage.

Sunday evening after I finished making my first batches of venison sausage, I invited several hunting friends over for dinner. I wanted them to sample my first efforts and give me their honest opinion. A number of them had been sending their venison to processors to be made into sausage for more than 40 years. When they had finished with dinner, I had no links and only one sausage patty left over.

I gave my recipes to my friends and asked them to see if they could replicate my sausages. During the next month, they reported back and, without exception, told me they had made venison sausage that tasted better than any they had ever eaten.

Over the next eight years, it was their continued encouragement that caused me to begin exploring all the possibilities of making venison sausage from recipes around the world that had been traditionally made with other meats.

Making your own venison sausage at home is simple, it's easy, it's inexpensive, and it's fun for not just you, but the whole family.

All the venison sausage recipes that you will find in this book are well within the abilities of the average home venison sausage maker. And every one of the sausage dish recipes can be easily made in any home kitchen.

The equipment needed to make delicious patty and link sausage is not costly—you may already have everything that you need.

- To make breakfast (fresh/bulk) venison sausage, all the equipment you need is a hand grinder, a mixing tray, a roll of plastic wrap, and cotton twine.
- Add a stuffing tube to your hand grinder, purchase an inexpensive hank of casings, and you have all you need to make link sausage.
- Seasoning and other ingredients can be found in any supermarket.

When I decided that I would begin making all of my own venison sausage, the only equipment I had was a home-style electric combination grinder/stuffer and a manufactured circular hot-smoker/cooker. With these two simple pieces of equipment, I have had no problem making all the fresh and smoked venison sausage we need and twice that amount to give away. Even today, these two pieces of equipment are all that I use to make 90 percent of my sausages.

Whenever I begin to run low on venison sausage, I place bags of raw venison chunks in the refrigerator on Thursday, shop for ingredients on Friday, spend Saturday morning making another 20-pound batch, and relax Sunday afternoon while hot-smoking/cooking the sausage links in my circular smoker.

If you have determined that you really enjoy making sausage and would like to make larger amounts at one time, you may wish to consider purchasing an electric grinder, a larger stuffer, and even go so far as to purchase a hot- and cold-smoker/cooker with an automatic smoke generator.

I have found that the larger the volume of sausage made at one time, the more hands needed. A permanent smokehouse is nice if you are going to smoke hams, bacons, and large volumes of cured and cold-smoked sausage. But for most of us a manufactured circular hot-smoker/cooker is all we will ever need.

In my travels overseas and while conducting the Game for All Seasons cooking school, hunters, friends, chefs, camp cooks, and fellow writers have all encouraged me to publish this work and to make these recipes available to all. Here they are, and I hope you will try some. Take a chance and do something you have never done before.

"Hunters for the Hungry"

The National Rifle Association supports state-level efforts through its Hunters for the Hungry Information Clearinghouse. This part of the association's hunter services division puts interested individuals in touch with programs in their area and fosters public awareness through education, fund-raising, and publicity.

How can you get involved?

If you'd like to show that you and your fellow hunters care about your community and would like to help share extra game meat with deserving families in your area, get involved today! Whether you donate meat, money, or time, your generosity is sure to have an impact.

For information about Hunters for the Hungry activities in your area, contact the NRA Hunters for the Hungry Information Clearinghouse at 800-492-4868 or via e-mail at contact@nra.org (website: http://www.nrahq.org/hunting/hungry_nat_list.asp).

PART I

Making Venison Sausage

1

Selecting Your Venison

Any cut of venison will make a fine sausage. Whether it is loin, hindquarter, or tough neck muscle, once you have ground the meat you will not be able to taste the difference. There is also no need to hang a deer in a cooler to age if the meat is to be used for sausage or ground for burgers.

When growing up, we had most of our deer made into sausage. We saved only the loins and tenderloins for kitchen use. The remainder of the deer would be taken down the road to the combination country butcher/grocery store/gas station to be made into link sausage. Looking back now, I can understand why we had most of our deer made into venison sausage.

That was in the days when the venison we ate came from deer that had been harvested on the run and with a group of deer dogs hot on their heels. The scarcity of deer in the first half of the 20th century made this type of ancient hunting the only way to obtain venison for subsistence eating. This was also the time when many people began to complain that venison was tough and had a wild taste.

You the hunter control the quality of your wild venison. It is you the hunter who controls the selection process and the harvesting method. The ancient Roman author Pliny noted in his commentary on game husbandry and the harvesting of deer, "The therapeutic value of venison only hold[s] good if the stag has been killed with a single wound."

The toughness and wild smell that many of us grew up associating with venison is not inherent to the animal and was not written about prior to the early 1900s. The toughness is the result of harvesting older deer. I believe—and many scientific studies agree—that the strong wild smell we associate with venison is the result of harvesting deer that have been chased or badly shot and those at the height of the rut. The wild smell is the result of natural chemicals that build up in the tissues of a tired and frightened animal and in animals with high levels of seasonal hormones. I enjoy listening to the sound of a chase in the cold of the early morning as much as anyone. It is a real pleasure to sit and watch an old and wise buck, with a mature set of antlers, throw all caution to the wind as he walks through a field nose-down following a doe. Beautiful as he might be, this is not the deer I seek for my table.

Mr. Will and his first deer

I remember my father telling me that he never killed a deer while he was growing up. Even the occasional sighting of a deer was an event to be remembered. Hunters in many parts of the United States and Canada who hunted deer from 1910 to 1975 could tell the same story.

Today it is not uncommon to sit in a field, over a deer trail, or in the mountains and see from 4 to 30 deer a day. While recently driving through a section of the Grampian Mountain region of Scotland in early May, I observed over 150 red deer stags and hinds gathering at a brook to drink before nightfall. In many parts of the United States and Canada, the sudden increase in deer population is causing many nonhunters to see deer as a nuisance, as it is impossible to grow a garden or to have flower beds. Unlike cattle, deer normally have one fawn the first year, then twins after that; some have an occasional set of triplets. We have effectively eliminated all the natural predators that at one time controlled the deer population. Given such a rate of increase, and the fact that some does may breed in the first year, if deer are not harvested, a population of 1 million deer can reach a potential size of over 10 million in only about three years.

J. cooking venison sausage
before the afternoon hunt

We are very fortunate in that, with the current rise in deer populations, most hunters will encounter some type of deer on almost every hunt. If you are hunting for meat, you now have the opportunity to do some degree of selective harvesting.

One of the reasons that many of us spend so much time and effort selecting and harvesting our deer is to feed our families. Venison can give us a real alternative to the chemical-infused meats sold in supermarkets. In the health-conscious world that we live in today, venison has some real benefits. On a pound-for-pound basis, depending on which meats we compare venison to, we can lower our fat intake from 18.4 to 3.3 grams per 3.6-ounce portion.

Comparative Nutritive Value

(Based on 100-gram (3.6-ounce) portions)

Type of Meat	Calories	Fat (g)	Protein (mg)
Venison, loin	150	3.30	25
Chicken, breast	159	3.42	31
Turkey, light meat	154	3.45	29
Salmon, pink	138	5.75	20
Lamb, leg roast	178	7.62	25
Beef, bottom round	214	9.76	31
Veal, cutlet	213	10.35	26
Pork, shoulder	219	10.64	29
Scallops, breaded	215	11.00	17
Ground beef, lean	265	18.40	24

Source: U.S. Department of Agriculture

There is only so far that we can lower the fat contact of venison sausage, because we still need to add a moistening agent to hold the meat together and give the sausage the taste we are accustomed to. Still, we can reduce our fat intake by a measurable amount.

Most venison sausage recipes you will find here call for a measure of pork products, but depending on the recipe, the amount of pork is reduced by 60 to 80 percent. This can make a real difference in the amount of fat we consume over a period of time.

Relative Percentage of the Types of Fat within the Muscle* Tissues of Various Mammalian Species

Species	% Fatty Acids		
	Saturated	Monounsaturated	Polyunsaturated
Beef	46.3	45.5	8.2
Buffalo	43.2	45.0	11.8
White-tailed deer	45.6	30.6	23.9
Mule deer	48.0	31.8	20.2
Elk	48.4	26.6	24.9
Antelope	41.2	27.1	31.6
Moose	36.6	24.3	39.1

*Longissimus muscle

Source: Research conducted at North Dakota State University

Several venison sausage recipes reduce fat to even lower levels, yet retain most of the qualities of traditional sausage. These recipes call for mushrooms and tofu instead of pork. You will notice a difference, but if you must reduce your fat intake, these recipes still allow you to enjoy sausage. The taste and texture will be close to what you expect, and though these low- or no-fat recipes may not taste exactly like the pork sausage you are accustomed to, they will be very tasty and enjoyable.

When I butcher a deer, I am always surprised how little the final cuts of meat weigh in relationship to the live weight. One November evening a few years ago, my niece J. and I struggled for over an hour to load an older 230-pound deer onto her four-wheeler. After three days, we were finally able to get every piece of usable meat either cubed, stuffed, or ground, and packaged for the freezer. In the end, we had only 110 pounds of deer in the freezer to show for our efforts.

If you do not have scales, this chart will assist you in determining your deer's live weight in the field and give you a very close estimate of the amount of edible meat.

Estimating Live Weight and Edible Meat

(Measure girth around the chest, just behind the front legs)

Girth (Inches)	Live Weight (Pounds)	Field-Dressed (Pounds)	Edible Meat (Pounds)
24	55	38	28
25	61	43	29
26	66	49	30
27	71	53	31
28	77	59	34
29	82	64	36
30	90	70	39
31	98	74	42
32	102	80	45
33	110	87	50
34	118	91	54
35	126	99	57
36	125	104	61
37	146	115	66
38	157	126	71
39	169	135	74
40	182	144	80
41	195	156	88
42	210	170	94
43	228	182	103
44	244	198	110
45	267	214	120
46	290	233	130
47	310	251	139
48	340	272	153

Courtesy HuntingNet.com

The author is not suggesting that you make sausage out of your whole deer. That would be a misuse of some of the finest cuts of venison. But if you have a deer that has been badly shot or the meat is likely to be tough or have a wild and gamy taste, this chart will assist you in estimating the amount of edible meat that you will have at your disposal.

If you have a fine young deer that has been cleanly harvested, you will surely want to save the loins, tenderloins, and possibly the upper half of the hindquarters to make into steaks or roasts or for broiling and grilling. After removing your selected cuts, it is time to sit down and take a short rest before you begin boning out your sausage meat. Gather enough

Mineral Content of Lean Tissue
from Domestic and Game Meats*

Species	Mineral (mg/11g)								
	K	P	Na	Ca	Cu	Fe	Mg	Mn	Zn
Pork	420	204	52	4.4	0.170	0.8	25	.028	1.50
Beef	366	172	52	4.2	0.130	1.8	23	.013	3.40
Chicken	297	180	42	4.7	0.013	0.6	28	.002	0.52
White-tailed deer	284	212	51	3.8	0.280	3.6	23	.041	2.00
Mule deer	305	166	54	3.3	0.140	2.7	25	.017	1.40
Buffalo	315	177	52	5.5	0.070	2.5	23	.003	2.40
Elk	312	161	58	3.8	0.120	2.7	23	.012	2.40
Moose	316	149	65	3.6	0.070	3.0	22	.008	2.80
Antelope	339	180	49	3.2	0.170	3.1	26	.019	1.20
Pheasant	334	219	50	5.1	0.039	1.2	32	.048	0.64
Sharp-tailed grouse	279	200	67	7.2	0.260	4.8	29	.040	0.73
Sage grouse	349	226	57	5.3	0.210	4.1	31	.035	0.71
Gray partridge	364	223	43	4.7	0.170	2.7	32	.031	.066
Dove	323	252	64	5.3	0.320	4.3	31	.043	.064

*Mammal species—longissimus muscle; avian species—breast muscle
Source: Research conducted at North Dakota State University

containers to hold the meat, as well as several sharp knives; work methodically. When you are finished, you will be happily surprised at how much venison you have recovered for your sausage making.

Before you cut off the head, pull the skin down as far as you can behind the ears, leaving as much of the neck attached to the carcass as possible, and then saw off the head. Next, cut off the belly flaps and place them in a container. Drop the forequarters. Cut up and down between each rib and remove the strips of rib meat. Take your time, work your knife around the neck bones, and remove all the meat. Step back, look over your deer, and see if there are any small pieces of red meat that you have missed.

Take your sausage meat inside and cut the meat from the bones. Carefully work over each piece of meat, removing all large pieces of fat. Small pieces of fat may not necessarily be bad, but—depending on the condition of the deer—the fat may have an undesirable taste. When you have finished removing the fat, cut the meat into 1- to 1½-inch chunks and package it into 2- to 5-pound lots. If you are not making sausage at this time, freeze the packages; when you are ready to make sausage or venison hamburger, select the number of pounds your recipe calls for.

Making and freezing sausage from previously frozen meat will have no effect on the quality of your sausage. Several days before you are ready to make your sausage, place the packages in a pan and set the pan in the refrigerator. Allow your venison to thaw slowly. Do not rush the thawing process by running the venison under warm water, as this creates the perfect environment for the growth of botulism-causing bacteria.

While your venison is thawing, assemble all of your supplies and equipment and set up in a clean and clutter-free work area. You are going to need more room than you might think. Reserve a Saturday morning for the making of your first sausage. On Friday evening, gather the children in the work area and talk them through what you and they will be doing the next morning. To whet their appetites, fry up just a small amount of pork sausage for dinner. Don't serve them very much—only a taste. You want to whet their appetites for what they will be doing in the morning.

Having Your Processor Make Your Sausage for You

When you find a recipe that you like and would like to make a larger quantity of, I have found that most venison processors will custom-make sausage to your specifications if you supply all the ingredients. Even though I supply all meat, spices, and other specialized ingredients, I expect to pay them their normal price, and sometimes I tip 10 percent more for their efforts.

As venison processors have their own proven sausage recipes that they follow, it is not a good idea to walk in and try to talk to them about making custom sausage during the busy time of the year. They just do not have the time to think about changing their procedures and routine when they have a locker full of venison that needs to be processed as soon as possible.

Most processors will be glad to oblige you if you talk to them about making your custom sausage just before the season opens or at the end of the season when they have finished with their runs. Prepare your venison and other meats by cubing, packaging, weighing, and freezing them, and assemble your seasonings and other ingredients based on the weight of the packages. When you deliver your packages to your processor, everything will be ready and your sausages can be made with a minimum of effort.

2
Making Safe Sausage

I must start this chapter with words of caution. The warning is not to scare you, but to begin your education into the enjoyable world of making your own venison sausage at home. You must know and understand this information before you begin your first sausage-making project.

Botulism is caused by a natural toxin produced by bacteria found in the air, on the ground, and on our skin. It is the most deadly form of food poisoning known in the world, and the spores which produce it are some of the most difficult of toxin-producing bacteria to kill.

Botulism Is Easy to Prevent:

- Refrigerate all foods below 36° F
- Cook all foods to an internal temperature of 160° F
- Cold-smoke only those meats that contain the proper amount of a cure specifically designated for cold-smoking

Clostridium botulinum has no odor and no taste. It multiplies rapidly when:

- The environment is moist
- It has nutrients to feed on
- The temperature is between 40° F and 140° F
- The environment is low in both oxygen and acidity

It is this critical temperature range, 40° F to 140° F, that causes so many cases of botulism during the holidays. When a turkey is stuffed and placed in the refrigerator the day before, the stuffing will stay within the deadly temperature range, and the toxin rapidly grows overnight. The next day, when you cook the turkey, you will not kill the botulism.

This is also the reason why we are warned against speeding up the thawing of food by placing it in warm water. Whether it be red meat, white meat, vegetables, fowl, seafood, or any other food—*all* types of food should be thawed only by placing them in the refrigerator.

Botulism poisoning is usually first diagnosed in less than a day by blurred vision; due to muscle failure, you may be unable to hold your head up. A little later, you may have trouble speaking because your neck and throat muscles cease to function, and you may develop double vision. The chest and diaphragm muscles no longer function, and then the heart and lungs fail. All this happens in about three days. If you are not promptly treated, death will follow.

Fresh sausages must be either cooked to over 160° F and consumed when made or packaged and frozen. All cold-smoked sausage must contain the correct amount of the proper cure before smoking. Cold-smoking temperatures sometimes do not rise out of the critical range, and the application of salt and smoke will not kill botulism in sausage. Only cures that contain sodium nitrate (Prague Powder #2) will preserve meat for the cold-smoking process.

It is true that ancient Greeks and Romans used only salt to preserve their meat. But the natural salt they used was dug out of the salt mines at Salinae, Italy, and contained impurities. One of these impurities was sodium nitrate, which preserved the meat and gave their sausages the familiar smell and distinctive red color. Every time you eat the Italian-style dry-cured raw ham Prosciutto, you step back 2,000 years into history. I have often wondered what happened to those who ate the sausage when the salt came from a new pit that either did not have enough sodium nitrate or had it in too concentrated a form.

The October 30, 1975, report of the U.S. Department of Agriculture, Animal and Plant Inspections Service, Washington, D.C. (9 CFR, parts 318, 381), *Nitrates, Nitrites, and Salt,* states: "To date, no substitute for nitrite has been discovered. No compound or treatment has been found that will produce the characteristic product that possesses nitrite's antibotulinal properties."

Safety Procedures for Making Sausage:

- Have all equipment and work areas immaculately clean
- Clean all surfaces and equipment with a solution of 1 tablespoon of chlorine bleach per gallon of water and allow to air-dry
- Do not cross-contaminate meats, supplies, and equipment
- Make sure hands and nails are clean
- Refrigerate all meat to below 36° F
- Cook all sausage to an internal temperature of 160° F
- Keep raw meat separate from other foods
- Use only freshly ground meat
- Use only the amount of meat cure specified by the manufacturer
- Package and freeze sausage immediately after making or refrigerate and use within three days
- If your sausage cannot be properly cured with nitrate, do not cold-smoke it

Curing and cold-smoking have always been the traditional way to preserve certain types of sausage. They have been used for thousands of years. Unfortunately, the process is not guaranteed to be 100 percent foolproof. I suspect that many deaths have occurred over the years and were attributed to causes other than a bad sausage. There is always the possibility of one link not getting the correct amount of cure.

That said, you are now ready to begin learning about the art of making the best venison sausage you have ever eaten.

3

Types of Sausage and Cures

Types of Venison Sausage

This book divides homemade venison sausages into four groups:

- Fresh sausage (uncured and uncooked—bulk, link, and patty)
- Cooked sausage links
- Quick-cured sausage
- Cured hot- and cold-smoked sausage links

Fresh Sausage contains no curing agent and can be made into either bulk, patties, or links and then packaged and frozen. Fresh sausage is

Fresh sausage—bulk, patty, and link

where most of us began when we make our first batch of sausage, and here is where many of us may wish to remain. That is where I started. Making fresh sausage was so easy to learn because all I had to do was mix, grind, package, and freeze the sausage. It was about this time that some of the clouds of mystery began to lift and I wondered what all the fuss regarding making fresh sausage was all about. As I became more confident, I began learning how to make my fresh sausage into links.

Link sausage is easier to make than you might think. I thought the difficult part would be finding the casings. All it took was two telephone calls and I found all of the inexpensive casings I could ever want. The tricky part was to keep the casings from getting tangled while washing the salt out.

Cooked Sausage Links open up a whole new area of easy sausage making for the home processor. Cooked sausages contain no cure and may be cooked in the oven. Others are hot-smoked/cooked using a manufactured circular hot-smoker/cooker. Still others are boiled in water.

Raw sausage links before cooking

Hot-smoked or cooked sausage links are the easiest link sausage to make. There is no cure to measure, and after cooking, the links can be eaten hot off the fire. Cooked sausage is as perishable as any other cooked meat and should be stored in the refrigerator for no longer than three days or packaged and frozen.

Quick-Cured Sausage is a type of "summer sausage"—and where I first hesitated. I had heard tales of how complicated the "curing process" was, and how if it was not done correctly you could get a very bad case of food poisoning. I was confusing quick-cured sausage with the traditional method of curing and cold-smoking sausage in a smokehouse.

Quick-cured sausage

Quick-curing is completely different from curing and cold-smoking. It is nothing more than adding a home-style preserving agent to the sausage mixture and placing it in the refrigerator to cure. Some quick-cured sausages can be eaten as is; others may need to be cooked.

For safety reasons, quick-cured sausages should also be refrigerated and packaged and frozen if they are not consumed within three days. I like to call these sausages my buffet and cold sliced appetizer sausages.

Cured Hot- or Cold-Smoked Sausage Links are the traditional country smokehouse sausages. These sausages have a nitrate preserving agent added that cures the meat and prevents the growth of bacteria. These are the types of sausages that you will find hanging from the ceilings in sausage and charcuterie shops around the world. Some are smoked until they are hard, and others are hung in the air until the surface moisture has dried and formed a hard protective surface. Technically, these sausages do not require refrigeration until the surface is broken. But as a

Cured and cold-smoked link sausage.
Courtesy DeWied International

precaution, I treat them as I would any other sausage. They are stored in the refrigerator for no more than three days or packaged and frozen.

The most difficult part of making cured and cold-smoked sausage is the need for a smokehouse in which a consistent level of cold smoke and steady temperature can be maintained over a long period of time—sometimes days, and occasionally weeks.

Types of Home-Curing Agents

Modern sausage cures are inexpensive, easy to use, and safe when the package directions are followed. Once you have learned the basics of making uncured bulk and link sausage, traditional cured cold-smoked sausages will open up a whole new area of sausage making.

It takes only a very small amount of the curing agent for a large amount of meat. There are several simple but important rules you will need to follow:

- Handle all cures carefully and follow the directions on the package exactly.
- *Meat* is defined as the total combination of all meats, both lean and fat.
- Weigh all the meat before measuring the cure.
- Be sure to measure or weigh cures accurately.
- Some recipes call for level teaspoons of cure. Do not pack the measuring spoon. Use a straight-edge knife to slide across and level the top.
- The cure should be dissolved with water.
- Thoroughly mix the cure throughout all the meat.

Home-Style Quick-Curing Products

Morton Salt makes several proven cures specifically for home use. These cures are often found in the salt or canning and freezing sections of supermarkets, large discount stores, and local butcher supply stores. If you are unable to locate a local source, several of the firms listed in the appendix carry a full line of Morton home cures.

Morton Tender Quick mix. Morton Sugar Cure mix.
Courtesy Allied Kenco

Morton Tender Quick mix is a proven product that produces consistent results. The main preserving agents are salt, sugar, both sodium nitrate and sodium nitrite (curing agents that also contribute to development of color and flavor), and propylene glycol to keep the mixture uniform.

Morton Sugar Cure (plain, not smoke-flavored) mix is a product that has been developed as a cure for meat, poultry, game, salmon, shad, and sablefish. It is a combination of high-grade salt, sugar, and other curing ingredients and can be used for both dry and sweet pickle curing.

Morton Tender Quick mix and Morton Sugar Cure (plain) mix are interchangeable.

Morton Sausage and Meat Loaf Seasoning mix is a complete mixture containing salt and spices blended to exact proportions to make breakfast sausage, meat loaf, and other meat specialties.

The Morton *"Home Meat Curing Guide"* teaches how to make pork sausage and is an illustrated guide to curing ham, bacon, and other small cuts of meat. The Morton guide is available for purchase online and from several of the mail-order firms listed in the appendix.

Hot- and Cold-Smoked Sausage Cures

To safely cure smoked sausage, the only cures that are safe to use are commercial cures, which contain nitrites and/or nitrates. These compounds are found in nature and in many of the foods you normally eat. Many of the vegetables we grow in our gardens contain these two substances. The fertilizers that we use are nitrogen-based; it is the nitrites in the fertilizer that make our plants grow, and trace amounts are transferred to the plants. Vegetables that contain higher levels of nitrites are potatoes, beets, celery, lettuce, radishes, and zucchini squash. Surprisingly, even your intestines produce a small amount of nitrites.

There are two commercial cures that are the standards of the industry, and both of them provide consistent results. They are safe to use at home when the correct cure-to-meat ratios are followed.

Although these two cures are called "commercial," they are readily available to the consumer and are easy to use by the home sausage maker. The reason for the name is that these cures are used by all volume sausage makers. There is no trick to using them—just use the amount of cure recommended on the package for a specified amount of all meats.

These two cures can be purchased from your local butcher supply company. If you do not have a local butcher supply company, they can be purchased from mail-order companies listed in the appendix.

Hot-Smoked Sausage Cure: Prague Powder #1 (also known as Insta-Cure #1, Modern Cure, TCM, FLP, and Pink Curing Salt). This cure is used only with products that do require cooking after smoking. After making, store your sausage in the refrigerator for up to three days or package and freeze. Prague Powder #1 contains 6.25 percent sodium nitrite mixed with 93.75 percent salt. As the meat temperature rises, the sodium nitrite breaks down into nitric oxide and begins to dissipate at about 130° F. When the smoking/cooking process is finished, only about 10 to 20 percent of the nitrite remains. When the product is reheated and cooked, the remaining nitrite continues to dissipate. To be safe, store cooked sausages in the refrigerator for no more than three days or package and freeze.

Cold-Smoked Sausage Cure: Prague Powder #2 (also known as Insta-Cure # 2). This cure is used only with products that are dry-cured and with products that do not require cooking or refrigeration. Prague Powder #2 contains 1 ounce of sodium nitrite and 0.64 ounce of sodium nitrate mixed with 1 pound of salt. The small amount of sodium nitrate in this cure breaks down into sodium nitrite and then into nitric oxide. This process allows you to dry-cure products that take longer to cure. To be safe, store cured sausages in the refrigerator for no more than three days or package and freeze.

Ratio of Prague Powder Cures to Meat. The correct ratio of cure to meat is the same for both Prague Powder #1 and Prague Powder #2:

1 level tsp. cure to 5 lbs. meat
2 level tsp. cure to 10 lbs. meat
3 level tsp. cure to 15 lbs. meat
4 level tsp. cure to 20 lbs. meat
5 level tsp. cure to 25 lbs. meat

For larger quantities of meat, cures should be calculated by weight and not by volume measurement:

1 oz. cure to 25 lbs. meat
2 oz. cure to 50 lbs. meat
3 oz. cure to 75 lbs. meat
4 oz. cure to 100 lbs. meat

Mythical Cures to Stay Away From

There are numerous "mythical cures" written about in old and some new books that are not recommended or are dangerous to use when making sausage.

- Some recipes recommend ascorbic acid, and others use only table salt as the curing agent. These "cures" will not add any protection in preserving the meat or preventing bacterial growth in sausage. The only thing that salt will do is help remove moisture.
- Saltpeter is an extremely dangerous and deadly poison. If you find a sausage recipe that calls for saltpeter, discard it. Saltpeter has no place in making sausage at home. Its chemical name is potassium nitrate, and it is no longer allowed in the curing of smoked meats, cooked meats, or sausages, except that trace amounts are still allowed in the making of selected commercial products under close supervision.

4

Grinding Your Sausage

There is more to grinding than just grinding up a piece of meat. Grinding is also a mixing and shaping process, and the equipment can range from the simple to the complex.

As a general rule, first chop the meats, mix them together, mix in the seasoning ingredients and appropriate cure, and grind with a coarse disc to evenly distribute the ingredients. Then grind a second time through a smaller disc to make bulk fresh sausage or shape into patties. During the second grind, you can make your link sausage. In this case you will be grinding and stuffing at the same time. Attach a stuffing tube, slip on a

Miss Anne grinding her first sausage

casing, and extrude the links. Some sausage recipes may differ from this procedure; follow the instructions in the individual recipes.

All meat grinders work on the same principle. Meat is pushed down a feeding tube with a forcing stick. The meat is sheared off by a large worm screw and forced forward and through a revolving knife that cuts the meat into small pieces as the worm screw forces the meat out through the holes in the disc.

Never push meat down the grinding tube with your fingers. The worm screw at the bottom of the tube cannot tell the difference between your finger and venison. Always use the meat plunger that comes with your grinder. If your grinder does not have a plunger, either make one out of a hardwood dowel or purchase one from a butcher supply store.

Grinding discs manufactured by different companies come with slightly different hole sizes.

Grinding Disc Sizes

Hole Size	Common Disc Terminology
⅛" (.125") = 3.18 mm	Fine
⁵⁄₃₂" (.156") = 3.97 mm	Small
³⁄₁₆" (.187") = 4.76 mm	Small
¼" (.250") = 6.35 mm	Medium
⅜" (.375") = 9.52 mm	Coarse
½" (.500") = 12.70 mm	Large
⅞" (.875") = 22.23 mm	Large

Home-style electric combination grinder/stuffers are usually supplied with two grinding discs: ³⁄₁₆ inch (small) and ⅞ inch (large). For your purposes, these two sizes will meet all of your needs. If you get to the point that you need smaller and larger grinding discs, you have progressed past the recreational sausage-maker stage and are ready to upgrade your equipment.

A small number of sausage recipes require that the meat particles be reduced to a size smaller than can be obtained with the fine grinding disc. To achieve this emulsified consistency, a food processor is needed. Commercial processing facilities have a special machine that will reduce large quantities of meat into a puree in a matter of minutes. When using a food processor, it is best to pulse the machine until the mixture is so small that it sticks to the sides of the container. Use a spatula and scrape the meat back down to the center. Keep repeating this pulsing process until you have achieved a paste-like consistency.

There is a full range of grinding tools available. My first unit was a 100-plus-year-old Universal grinder that clamped to the edge of the table, which I permanently "borrowed" from my grandmother. This piece of equipment served my grinding purposes for many years.

The standard-volume hand grinder will meet the needs of all home sausage makers; these are readily available and inexpensive. Higher-volume table-mount units are popular in locations where there is no electricity and there is a need for higher grind rates. These units are sold in many mail-order sporting goods catalogs. They work just like standard units that clamp to the side of a table.

Standard-volume and high-volume grinders. Courtesy Cabela's

For less than $120, an electric combination grinder/stuffer is well worth every cent. If you are going to make more than 30 pounds of sausage a year, this type of machine will pay for itself in a very short time. A combination electric unit can grind and stuff casings at the same time as fast as two people can comfortably work.

Home-style combination electric grinder/stuffer

These combination electrical units are my first choice; I use mine year-round. Besides making sausage, my unit makes venison hamburger for Anne, chops my tomatoes for marinara sauce, minces turnips, coarse-chops pecans, and grinds apples and fruit from the orchard to make jelly and conserves.

Foot-operated grinder switch.
Courtesy Linemaster Switch Corp.

A handy accessory is a foot-operated grinder switch. When you are grinding and stuffing, you will need to stop every now and then to load more meat or to tie/twist off links. Your hands will be greasy—and all it takes is a lift of your foot to turn the grinder off.

Another type of combination grinding/stuffing machine is a food mixer with a grinding/stuffing attachment. Several brands of mixers have these grinding/stuffing accessory packs. If you have the proper mixer, the grinding and stuffing accessories may be the way to go. These units will process meat and stuff casings at about the same rate as the home-style electric units. The accessory packs cost less than the combination home-style electric grinding units and do a very fine job if you are making no more than 40 pounds of sausage per year.

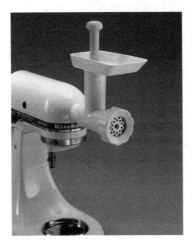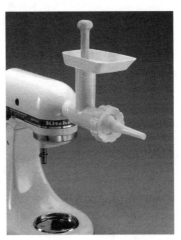

Mixer with combination grinder/stuffer attachments.
Courtesy KitchenAid

On the upper end of the home grinders is a high-volume small commercial grinder. These grinders will grind meat faster than you can push it in. This type of equipment is out of the price range of the average home venison sausage maker. If you need to grind a higher volume of sausage, you will need several sets of hands just to keep up with the volume of meat that these machines will grind out.

Over the years I have been invited to hunting lodges across the country that maintain permanent venison and game processing facilities. Members gather on a specified weekend; with all hands working, they will process 400 to 600 pounds of sausage on Friday evening.

A portion of the sausage is made into links and hung in a small commercial-style walk-in smoking unit. The remainder of the sausage is packaged into 1-pound bags of breakfast sausage and frozen. Sunday afternoon all participants are on their way back home with ice chests

Small commercial high-volume grinder.
Courtesy Rebel Butcher Supply

loaded with sausage. Only a small commercial unit such as this would meet their needs.

5

Patty Making, Casings, and Stuffing

Before you make your batch of sausage, you need to decide what form you wish the finished product to take. Making patties from bulk sausage is where most of us begin and where many of us wish to stay. The real fun begins when we successfully turn a package of raw venison into links of delicious sausage. In this chapter you will learn about:

- Making sliced or pressed patties
- Selecting the proper casing
- Types and sizes of animal casings
- Preparing casings
- Stuffing casings

Patty Making

The simplest way to make patty sausage is to either extrude or pack fresh sausage into plastic sausage tubes or roll it into logs and wrap the roll in plastic wrap. Place the fresh sausage roll in the freezer for 45 minutes to an hour; when it is "soft-frozen," slice it into patties.

To make patties from frozen sausage, place the package in the refrigerator and allow the sausage to partially thaw. When the sausage just begins to soften, take a very sharp knife and cut through the packaging to make patties.

Freezing fresh sausage into patties is simple. The trick is to keep the patties from freezing together. Place two sheets of waxed paper or precut sausage paper between each patty. The two pieces of paper will prevent the sausages from freezing together and the individual patties can be easily separated.

To make a large number of patties from freshly made sausage, an inexpensive sausage and hamburger press can be made from a tin can. Cut both ends out of the can. Place a cutout can end on the table; lay a sheet of waxed paper on top and press the can down over the paper and around the can end. Drop in the sausage mixture and lay a second piece of waxed paper on top of the can. With the other cutout end of the can, press the paper down the inside of the can. Apply gentle rocking pressure to the

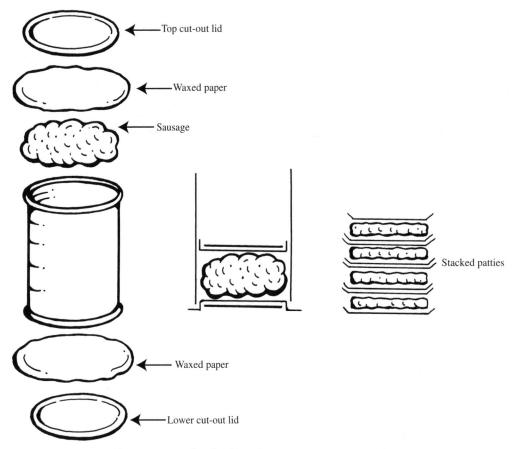

Top cut-out lid

Waxed paper

Sausage

Waxed paper

Lower cut-out lid

Stacked patties

Tin-can method of making sausage patties

sausage so that it flattens and spreads out. Continue pressing down and lift the can up and off the patty. Stack the patties in the freezer until frozen hard and then stack and wrap in plastic wrap or vacuum-pack.

If you are making several dozen patties several times a year, you may wish to make a sausage/hamburger patty press. With two people working together, you will be able to make 100 to 150 patties per hour. This spring-loaded patty press is made from three 1-inch wooden dowels, four 1-inch pieces of aluminum flat stock, a spring, a wooden base, assorted screws, and a can with both ends cut out.

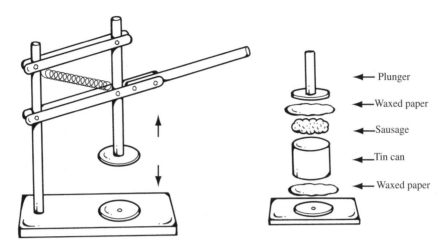

Homemade sausage patty press

Another option is to purchase a clamshell patty press. The press and the premade papers are sold by several of the mail-order firms listed in the appendix. Using a wider can, all three of these presses can also be used to make patties out of your venison burger.

Sausage press and premade sausage paper. Courtesy Cabela's

Selecting the Proper Casing

There are two basic types of casing in use today: natural casings and collagen/synthetic fibrous casings. Let us first briefly discuss collagen casings, because you will probably not wish to use them for homemade sausage.

Collagen/synthetic casings were developed to meet the institutional needs of the commercial food and restaurant industries. In these industries, portion and cost control are primary considerations. The diameter of natural casings may vary as much as 3 mm (⅛ or 0.118 inch) within any size group. This may not sound like much, but the average stuffing capacity of a hank or set of casings may vary as much as 15 pounds. You and I will not notice the irregularities, but when you are purchasing sausage in several-thousand-pound lots, the difference is considerable.

Collagen/synthetic casings are difficult to use at home because they are stuffed dry and can break while being stuffed by hand. The dry synthetic casings have no stretch and must be closely matched to the stuffing tubes. These casings have a memory and will untwist if they are twisted into links. If these man-made casings are so difficult to use, why are they made? They can be manufactured into any width or length, they are consistent in diameter and stuffing volume, and they also work extremely well with automatic, high-volume, commercial sausage-making machines.

Natural Casings are the best choice for the home sausage maker. Most natural casings come from New Zealand, Australia, or Argentina, because there are not enough sheep and hogs slaughtered in the United States to meet the demand for natural casings. Natural casings are packed in a heavy salt solution, loaded onto ships, and shipped around the world. The salt pack gives natural casings an almost indefinite shelf life.

Knife-cut, rather than hand-pulled, natural casings are the best choice for the home sausage maker because they have extra strength and are usually longer with fewer holes. The small hairlike whiskers on the outside of the knife-cut casings will disappear during the cooking or smoking process.

Even though the sausage recipes recommend a particular type and size of casing, the type and size you select will depend on what you want your finished sausage to look like. If you like a recipe and want to make sausages that are either larger or smaller in diameter, feel free to do so.

Store casings in the refrigerator at 40° F and in the original brine solution. Never freeze casings, as this will make them tough.

Bulk casings. Courtesy DeWied International

The casing hanks that you will find at your local butcher supply store are inexpensive. One hank will have many more casings than you are likely to use in a year of sausage making.

Natural casings are easy to use, and the sizes that you will need can usually be found locally. There is a good reason why the most popular sizes can be found locally; your local pork and venison sausage processing plants will be using the same size of casings that you will need.

Natural casings come in as many varieties and sizes as you can imagine. But for the home sausage maker, your casing selection problem has just been simplified, because the majority of all the sausages that you will make can be made with only two types and sizes: either 32 mm to 36 mm hog casings or 20 mm to 24 mm sheep casings. If a recipe calls for a slightly different size of casing, it will make very little difference if you use a casing one size larger or one size smaller.

Types and Sizes of Animal Casings

The common types and sizes of casings that you will need are highlighted in **bold** on the charts. Casings are measured in millimeters, but to help you estimate the size of your finished sausage, the inch equivalent is listed along with the millimeter size.

Sheep Casings

Sheep casings come from lamb and sheep and are principally used for smaller-diameter sausages such as beer or snack sticks, small breakfast sausage links, and hot dogs. Sheep and lamb casings are measured in hanks of 100 yards.

Courtesy DeWied International

Sheep Casing Sizes

Average Diameter	Average Capacity per Hank
18 mm (¹¹⁄₁₆") to 20 mm (¹³⁄₁₆")	38 to 41 lbs.
20 mm (¹³⁄₁₆") to 22 mm (⅞")	**47 to 52 lbs.**
22 mm (⅞") to 24 mm (¹⁵⁄₁₆")	**55 to 60 lbs.**
24 mm (¹⁵⁄₁₆") to 26 mm (1¹⁄₁₆")	**60 to 64 lbs.**
26 mm (1¹⁄₁₆") and over	64 to 70 lbs.

Sheep Casings for Common Sausages

18 mm to 20 mm	Snack or beer sticks, Slim Jims
20 mm to 22 mm	Breakfast sausage, small link sausage
22 mm to 24 mm	Small hot dogs, Chorizo, link sausage
24 mm to 26 mm	Larger wieners, Bockwurst, larger links

Hog Casings

Hog casings will be what you will use for most of your sausage making. These casings are used for hunter-style long-linked sausage, Italian, Polish, Boudin, Bratwurst, Andouille, large hot dogs, Kielbasa, and Pepperoni.

The largest hog casing can also substitute for recipes that call for beef rounds. Hog casings are measured in hanks of 100 yards.

Courtesy DeWied International

Hog Casing Sizes

Average Diameter	Numbered Size	Average Capacity per Hank
28 mm (1⅛") and under	#1	90 to 115 lbs.
29 mm (9⁄16") to 32 mm (1¼")	#2	95 to 120 lbs.
32 mm (1¼") to **35 mm** (1⅜")	**#4**	**115 to 140 lbs.**
33 mm (1⁵⁄16") to 36 mm (1²⁷⁄64")	#5	125 to 150 lbs.
35 mm (1⅜") to **38 mm** (1½")	**#6**	**135 to 160 lbs.**
38 mm (1½") to 42 mm (1¹¹⁄16")	#7	145 to 170 lbs.
42 mm (1¹¹⁄16") to 45 mm (1¾")	#8	175 to 200 lbs.
46 mm (1¹³⁄16") and over	#9	185 to 210 lbs.

Hog Casings for Common Sausages

29 mm to 32 mm	Hot dogs, Italian, country sausage
32 mm to 35 mm	Bratwurst, Bockwurst, Italian
35 mm to 38 mm	Polish sausage, Knockwurst
38 mm to 42 mm	Large Polish, Summer, Ring Bologna, Liverwurst

Beef Rounds

Beef rounds are sold in sets instead of hanks. These casings derive their name from their "ring" or "round" characteristic. Beef rounds are used for Ring Bologna, Ring Liver sausage, Mettwurst, large Polish sausage, Kirshka, and other large sausages. Beef rounds are measured in sets of 100 feet.

Courtesy DeWied International

Beef Round Sizes

Average Diameter	Average Capacity per Set
35 mm (1⅜") to 38 mm (1½")	55 to 65 lbs.
38 mm (1½") to **40 mm** (1¼")	**72 to 75 lbs.**
40 mm (1¼") to **43 mm** (1¹¹⁄₁₆")	**80 to 83 lbs.**
46 mm (1¹³⁄₁₆") and over	85 to 95 lbs.

Preparing Casings

Your casings will come packed in a concentrated brine solution. You will first need to wash the salt from both the outside and the inside of the casings. Once the salt has been washed from a casing, it should be discarded and not returned to the hank. Casings are supplied in hanks or sets in lengths varying from 18 inches to 12 feet.

To calculate the amount of casing that you will require, use the following as a guide:

- 2 pounds of sausage meat will stuff about 8 feet of 20 mm to 22 mm sheep casing.
- 2 pounds of sausage meat will stuff about 4 feet of 32 mm to 34 mm hog casing.
- 2 pounds of sausage meat will stuff about 2 feet of 40 mm to 43 mm beef round.

Select and remove only enough casings for one batch of sausage. Removing the salt must be done carefully to prevent tangles and knots along the long casings. The best way is to remove them one at a time by lifting all the casings out of the container by the tied end and laying them out for their full length. Select and remove one casing from the tied end and work it loose down the whole length of the casing bundle. Place the casing in a bowl of water, hanging the end of the casing over the lip of the bowl. Repeat for as many casings as you will need for this one batch. Place the casing bundle back into the original salt solution, lay the looped end on top of the bundle, and store the container in the refrigerator.

Place the drain screen in the sink drain—the casings will be slippery as you wash them and can slip down the drain before you have time to catch them. Stretch the end of a casing over the end of the faucet and slowly run a small stream of warm water through the whole length. The casings may be twisted, so it will be necessary to assist the casing to straighten out as it

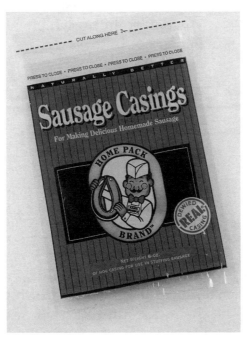

Home Pack sausage casings.
Courtesy DeWied International

fills with water. If casings are very long and will not straighten out while washing, cut them into shorter lengths.

Continue running water through the casing for a minute or so. When you have finished washing the inside, wash the outside, lower the casing into a large bowl of warm water, and lay the loose end over the edge of the bowl. Repeat the procedure for each casing.

Sheep Casings. First rinse with fresh water and then soak in 85° F to 90° F water for 30 minutes prior to use.

Hog Casings. First rinse with fresh water and then soak in 85° F to 90° F water overnight or for at least 30 minutes prior to use.

Beef Rounds. First rinse with fresh water, soak in cold water overnight, and then soak for 30 minutes in 100° F water prior to use.

Stuffing Casings

The stuffing process is the part that the children remember the most; this is when they see their efforts come together into an identifiable product.

Stuffing can be made easier if the proper stuffing tube is matched with the casing size. You can always use the next larger size of casing. Because natural casing can stretch a small amount, you may be able to use the next larger size of stuffing tube, but this is not always the case. Casings are measured in millimeters, but stuffing tubes are measured in inches. This chart will assist you in determining which size of stuffing tube is appropriate for which size of casing.

Matching Casings with Stuffing Tubes

Casing Size	Stuffing Tube Size
16 mm to 18 mm	⅜" (9.53 mm)
19 mm to 22 mm	⁷⁄₁₆" (11.11 mm)
23 mm to 27 mm	½" (12.70 mm)
28 mm to 33 mm	⁹⁄₁₆" (14.29 mm)
34 mm and over	¾" (19.05 mm)

There are two procedures for grinding/stuffing casings. One procedure calls for stuffing a preground and premixed product. The other calls for grinding and stuffing at the same time. Either way, the process is the same.

Thoroughly washing the salt from the casings and lubricating the stuffing tube with vegetable oil will allow the casings to slide on and off the tube much more easily. Slip the entire casing onto the oiled stuffing tube. Tie a knot on the end of the casing and slowly press the sausage mixture down into the grinder/stuffer. Gently hold the casing as it fills and begins to slide off the stuffing tube. Stuff the whole casing as one unit or pinch off into links as they come out and twist or tie with cotton twine.

To keep the links from unwinding, twist one link several times away from you and twist the next link several times toward you. To make sausage rings, leave 4 to 6 inches of casing at each end of the link so that the ends can be tied together to make a ring. If you see air bubbles form as the sausage is being stuffed, prick the bubble with a pin. When you have finished, look over the sausage; if you see an air bubble, prick it with the pin. Stuffing sausage is as simple as that.

Standard- and high-volume
combination grinder/stuffers.

Standard- and high-volume stuffers.
Courtesy Cabela's

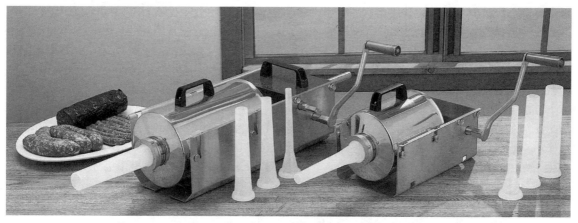

Large-volume cylinder stuffers. Courtesy Cabela's

I have stuffed hundreds of pounds of sausage by myself, and have had a lot of fun in the process. But two people will make the process go much faster. One person operates the stuffer and keeps the sausage flowing. The second person manages the casing and twists or ties off the links as they are made. After a few links are made, the person operating the stuffer will know when to stop so the link can be twisted or tied.

Whether you are using a hand-cranked combination grinder/stuffer or a large-volume drum stuffer, the procedure is the same. As you stuff and twist/tie off your links, you can stop the process at any time. You will need to occasionally re-wet the casing if it begins to stick to the stuffing tube or seems to be drying out.

There are many home-style electric combination grinder/stuffers on the market. They are economically priced and will serve you well past the sausage season. I suggest that you purchase a foot-operated switch, which is similar to the type of foot pedal used on sewing machines.

Home-style combination grinder/stuffer.

While you are loading the meat hopper or making and tying/twisting off links, your hands will become very slick. An electric foot switch will allow you to turn the machine on and off without having to fumble around with slippery hands. From my experience, these combination electrical units, along with a foot switch, are a great value for the money.

As you finish stuffing each casing, place it in the refrigerator to chill until you are finished with the whole batch. Sausages that are to be eaten shortly after making are improved if they are allowed to rest in the refrigerator overnight. Sausage can be stored for up to three days in the refrigerator before eating—or package it in meal-sized lots and freeze.

6

Packaging and Storing Your Sausage

Packaging for your sausage comes in many forms. In the beginning, animal casings, clay jars, and bags woven out of grasses and reeds were the only forms of storing sausage. Today we have a variety of ways to package and preserve sausage that were not available to sausage makers 100 years ago.

Casings are only a temporary housing material made from a meat product. They will not prevent freezer burn and they will not protect the sausage from the growth of bacteria. Casings are porous and will allow an exchange of air and the evaporation of liquids from the sausage. For our purposes, casings are used only as a means to hold the sausage product in a particular shape during the cooking or curing process.

The best thing that ever happened to the recreational sausage maker was the invention of the home-style freezer. With proper packaging and freezing, your sausage should be as good six months down the road as it was the day you placed it in the freezer. It is the packaging that gives your sausage a short or long life in the freezer. When it is properly packaged in meal-sized quantities, you will find that you will eat your sausage more often, and it will last long after the hunting season is over.

How many times have you brought your sausage home and found it frozen in 4, 6, 8, or even 10 links per package? Chances are that when you opened a package, you did not cook all the sausage at once—and when you finally cooked the last piece, it did not taste as good as the first. There have been times in my house when several packages were accidentally opened at different times, and when found months later most of the sausage was freezer-burned and had to be discarded. What a waste.

As a home processor you can change this and reduce your losses to zero. It only takes a few more minutes to package your sausages into smaller, meal-sized units. Depending on the length of the sausage, you will be well served if you package the links in one- or two-link packages. If you need more links, you can always open more packages, and you will not have to throw away any of your hard-earned harvest.

As you decide on which packaging method you will be using, think in terms of how long you will be storing your sausage before it is eaten. Unless you are planning on using all your sausage within three months, consider a packaging method that will protect your harvest until the beginning of the next hunting season. There are three types of packaging systems that you should consider:

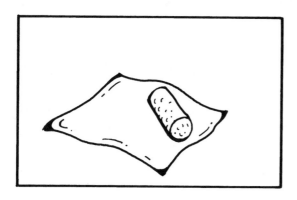

Lay sausage at one
corner of paper

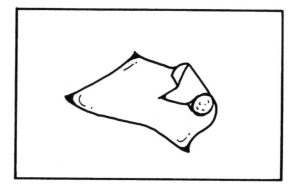

Roll tightly toward
opposite corner

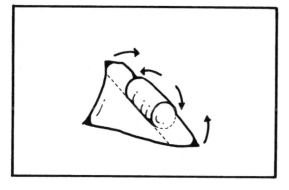

Turn ends down and
fold up

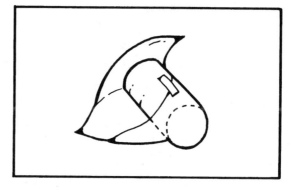

Fold ends over and
secure with freezer tape

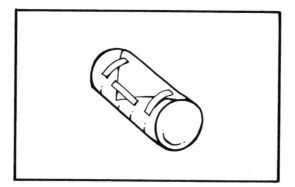

Roll sausage to end of
paper and seal with
freezer tape

Classic butcher wrap

- Short-term, 1 month
- Midterm, 6 months
- Long-term, 12 months or longer

Butcher Paper

The least effective form of packaging is butcher paper. Butcher paper works fine for short-term storage for up to three months. But no matter how careful you are in sealing the edges, butcher paper will not prevent long-term freezer burn. White wrapping paper is not butcher paper; it is very porous and should not be used for storage of more than one month. Butcher paper has a thin plastic coating on one side that helps prevent the evaporation of the moisture from within the sausage. Place the plastic side next to the meat and close with the classic butcher wrap.

Plastic Wrap

Plastic wrap should also be considered as a midterm method of storing your sausage. It works quite well when you have opened a large package of sausage and plan on using the remainder within three months. Tear off a piece of plastic wrap wide enough to wrap the edges over and long enough to wrap around twice. Lay the sausage so that you have enough wrap on the sides to fold over to the center. Roll the sausage until it is covered with two wraps, fold over the ends, and continue to roll. Place several pieces of 1-inch masking paper completely around the package and refreeze. If the sausage will be used within three days, it can be stored in the refrigerator.

Bulk sausage should be packaged in 1-pound packages. If you are unable to locate plastic 1-pound bulk sausage tubes, plastic wrap will serve you just as well. Roll out a 2-foot length of plastic wrap. Shape bulk sausage into a 2- to 2½-inch-diameter log about 6 to 8 inches long. Place the log onto the plastic wrap. Do not fold the outside edges. Roll the sausage log until the plastic wrap is wrapped around at least four times. Use a piece of cotton twine and tie off one end of the plastic wrap close to the end of the sausage log. Lift the sausage by the other open end and shake and shape to remove air. With a second piece of string, tie the second end close to the end of the sausage.

Bulk sausage in plastic wrap

When ready to serve, place the plastic-wrapped sausage roll or vacuum package in the refrigerator to thaw. When it is partially thawed, make patties by slicing through the plastic wrap.

Resealable Plastic Bags

Resealable plastic bags are also a good midrange packaging system, but they will not protect your sausage as long as vacuum-packaging. These bags do a very good job of protecting your sausage for up to five to possibly six months. Because they do not exhaust all the air, freezer burn is still a possibility with long-term storage. Have you ever brought a frozen resealable bag out of the freezer and noticed the ice crystals that have formed on the inside? This is an indication that freezer burn is occurring. When meats or vegetables are frozen, the cells swell and rupture. Over time, the fluid inside the cells evaporates and refreezes on the inside of the bag. This evaporation leaves the surface dry and with a paper-type texture. The longer the freezer burn continues, the deeper the damage.

To fill the bags, place the frozen sausage into the bag, add 2 tablespoons of water, and shake the sausage to the bottom to cover with water. Open the closure, moisten across the ridges with water, and then close tightly. Then open the center of the closure for about ¾ inch and, with your mouth, suck out the air until the plastic closes around the meat. While keeping a vacuum pulled on the bag, seal the opening. Roll up the sealed edge and secure around the bag with two separate 1-inch pieces of masking tape.

Vacuum-Packaging

The simplest and most cost-effective method of long-term packaging is a home-style vacuum-packaging machine. The initial price may discourage many people, but when you consider how many types of food and other items can be protected by vacuum-packing and the extraordinarily long time that vacuumed food will last in the freezer, these machines are well worth the price.

Besides packaging vegetables and meats, these small machines can be used to preserve documents and books, as well as to prevent silver from tarnishing; some people prevent rust on their firearms by cleaning, oiling, and vacuum-packaging them during the off season. These small vacuum

Home-style vacuum-packaging machine

machines and their special bags are available from many mail-order sporting goods companies and in some large discount shopping centers.

Vacuum-packaged food will taste fresher and last longer than food stored in conventional packaging. But because the food is not devoid of moisture or potentially lurking pathogens, it is important to remember that vacuum-packaging is not an alternative to refrigeration or freezing.

A vacuum is measured in inches of mercury. A total vacuum, or no air at all, measures 30 inches of mercury. Air or water surrounds everything on earth, so it is not possible to create a total vacuum anywhere on earth.

The FDA rates a commercial vacuum at 21 inches of mercury. At 21 inches, the residual oxygen is greatly reduced, and therefore oxidation, dehydration, and the growth of airborne microorganisms such as aerobic bacteria, mold, and yeast cease to be factors in the deterioration of food.

Insect infestation occurs either because microscopic eggs or larvae are present in the food or packaging or because the insects infiltrate the package during storage. In either case, vacuum-packing eliminates the problem by removing the air from the interior of the package. Insects and all living organisms require air for life. When the air is removed from their environment, they cannot survive.

Along with walk-in coolers, 100-pound smokers, and high-volume grinders, many deer camps have dedicated processing facilities and often utilize small commercial vacuum-packaging machines. Although these tabletop units are not inexpensive, they provide deer camps that process a large amount of meat and sausage with year-round packaging for all types of food and game.

*Small commercial-style vacuum-packaging
machine. Courtesy Allied Kenco and Tor-Rey*

If you are vacuum-sealing your fresh links, it is best that you freeze the links before sealing them in the vacuum bags. Every casing has weak spots. When you apply the vacuum, there is a chance that a hole may appear at a weak spot, and some of the sausage may leak through the hole. If this does happen, it is not a real problem, because as you cook or hot-smoke the sausage the contents will shrink and the hole will seal. Bulk sausage and sausage patties also pack better if they are frozen before packaging. The vacuum machine will cause soft patties or bulk sausage to distort and flatten as the air is pulled out of the bag.

You can also vacuum-package liquids such as soups, stocks, stews, and ice creams. Pour the liquid into a square plastic freezer container and freeze. When it is frozen, slip the frozen block out of the container and vacuum-pack the block of frozen liquid.

Home-vacuum-packed venison sausage patties

The special bagging material comes in 8-inch and 11-inch widths either as premade bags or in long rolls. Premade bags work fine for items that would normally fit into 2-quart and 1-gallon bags. Link sausages can be made either so that they will fit into the bags or cut to fit. When packaging large sausages, bulk quantities, or odd-shaped items such as long guns and clothing, the roll-type packaging material can be cut to the required lengths.

The only drawback to using vacuum-packaging is the possibility of accidentally puncturing a hole in the frozen plastic bag. Once frozen, your sausage is as hard as a block of ice. If it's dropped, a small hole may be made in the plastic, and the vacuum will be lost. When you package items that have sharp edges, such as bones, over time a sharp edge may rub a hole through the bag. To prevent this from occurring, cover the sharp edges with several layers of paper towel or waxed paper. If you see a package that has ice crystals forming inside, or the item is loose inside, you can be sure that the vacuum seal has been violated. All you need to do is remove the item, repackage it, and re-vacuum-seal the package. Of 1,000-plus items that I have vacuum-packed, only 10 or so have ever lost their vacuum. The problem is that I have either dropped the bag on the floor or allowed a small crease to remain on the edge of the plastic bag as it was stretched across the sealing element.

Labeling

We have all lost a lot of meat to non- or mislabeling. While labeling is so easy, it is always a mystery to me why I sometimes still freeze an item or two without a label. Stick-on labels don't work well: They are hard to attach to a round surface and don't always stay in place when the package is frozen. Writing on the clear package is difficult to read when frost forms on the surface. The best way to label a package is to wrap a 1-inch piece of masking tape all the way around the package and use a small-tipped black marker to record at least the date and the item name.

Freezer Dividers

When meat is stacked in one large pile, it may take several days or even a week for the packages in the center of the stack to freeze. Therefore, at first lay your sausages all over the freezer and not in one stack. After a few days, when you are sure that all the sausage packages have frozen solid, you can restack the packages together in one area.

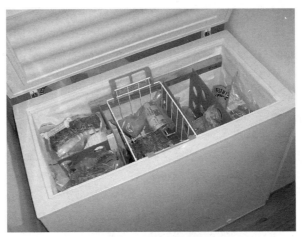

Freezer with baffle dividers

Baffle dividers and frame support

Chest-type freezers always seem to swallow up small packages, which end up lost on the bottom. The single large area of a chest-type freezer is just too large to unload when the one item that you are looking for is on the bottom. To solve this problem, break up the space into individual storage areas. Make insert dividers out of ⅛-inch Masonite sheets. The dividers should be spaced front to back every 7 to 9 inches; cut 2- to 3-inch circular holes in the dividers to allow the free flow of cold air.

To keep the dividers in place, make slotted wooden spacers that run right to left along the upper and lower sides of the freezer walls. Slip the dividers down through these slotted wooden spacers, and the dividers will hold their shape as the individual sections are filled and emptied. The dividers can be added and removed as the situation and seasons change.

When I started using these dividers, I found that we were utilizing more items because I was able to store different types of packages in different sections and we did not have to unload the whole freezer to find just one item. Another benefit was that I eliminated all the wasted upper space. I was able to fill the freezer to the top and still be able to quickly find and remove an item.

7

Operating a Smoker/Cooker and Building a Smokehouse

The word "smokehouse" conjures up images of a forbidden old wooden outbuilding sitting out back next to the corncrib. Forbidden because as a child you were threatened with life and limb if you were ever caught opening the door. Still, the sweet-smoky aroma was so overpowering that you just could not help yourself, and when you lifted the wooden latch and looked into the dark insides all you could see were dimly lit golden hams and bacon sides hanging up high from the roof.

What I remember most about Mr. Brown's smokehouse were the layers of heavy steel rods running from side to side with link after link of brownish red smoked sausages looped over the rods. The smell was debilitating. I reached up and carefully pinched off a small piece of sausage and chewed it until it was gone. I looked outside to make sure that no one was around and pinched off a larger piece and then another big piece.

Several days later Mom sent me over to Mrs. Brown's house to see if she had any fresh butter for sale. While I sat in the kitchen waiting for her to scoop up the butter, Mr. Brown came in, sat down on the bench beside me, and, looking up at the ceiling, said, "Last month, I put some rat poison on one of the sausages in the smokehouse just in case a rat was able to find his way in. When he nibbles on that sausage he is going to be one dead rat. It takes about a week or so for the poison to work. Harold Jr., tell your mother if she sees any dead rats lying around her yard, that's what happened to them."

Traditional "subsistence smokehouses" have gone the way of the family farmer, but that does not mean that you have to deny yourself the pleasures of making and cold-smoking your own cured sausage.

We all have a latent desire to build a real old-fashioned walk-in smokehouse. But the truth is, we don't need a full-time cold-smokehouse. And we do not have the time to tend a slow-burning firepit for several days or weeks. If you have the space, the time, and the desire for a walk-in smokehouse, you will find details regarding how to build one toward the end of this chapter.

What we do need is a smoking unit that will supply our family and select friends with delicious homemade and home-smoked sausage. You can either purchase a manufactured hot-smoker/cooker or build a smokepit or smokebox out in the yard. If you have to buy the materials, a manufactured smoker will be much less expensive and a lot easier to tend to.

The Smoking/Cooking Process

Contrary to common belief, smoking alone does not preserve raw meat or prevent botulism. Sausage that is hot-smoked/cooked does not require a cure. Cold-smoking does require the proper cure to be mixed in with the meat.

Hot-Smoking/Cooking

This is the process that home sausage makers are most likely to use, and it is the process that venison processors use. Hot-smoking is a cooking and flavoring process and not a preserving process. In hot-smoking, the meat is rapidly smoked/cooked at a temperature range between 180° F and 200° F. When it is finished, you can store your sausage for up to three days in the refrigerator; after that time you will either have to eat the sausage or package and freeze it. Use a thermometer to verify that each link of your sausage is cooked to at least 160° F. Even though venison processors use a curing agent mixed in with the meat, their smokers also cook the sausage; then they package and freeze it as soon as it comes out of the smoker.

Cold-Smoking

This is the process traditionally associated with the old country smokehouse. When cold-smoking, you do not want the temperature to go over 90° F to 100° F. The smoking process is finished when the meat has a deep brown color. The process may take several days to complete. Only when the meat has been cured with a nitrate curing agent should it be cold-smoked. Country-smoked hams and bacon sides are cured by either injecting or soaking the meat in a brine solution. It is the brine that keeps the meat safe. Sausages must have a nitrate cure ground in with the meat. The small stream of cold smoke flowing through the smoker is what gives the meat a mild/sweet and country-smoked flavor and a shiny protective covering. A final short burst of hot smoke is often used to finish off the meat and seal the surface. To build a smokehouse, you will need the space, time, and dedication to properly care for your meat throughout the whole process. Many cold-smoked meats may keep for months or even years when hung in a cool, dark place. An old saying states that if the cold-smoked meat lasts through the first summer, it will last forever.

Types of Manufactured Smoking Units

Manufactured Home Hot-Smoker/Cooker

Circular steel home smoker/cookers come in many shapes and sizes, and for the home smoker these units are small, easy to use, and easy to keep clean. They are affordably priced and are available from most sporting goods and discount stores and from mail-order sporting goods catalogs.

For the home smoker, these units are the best choice, and with proper cleaning they will last for many years. My first circular smoker is still working and is pressed into service whenever I am hot-smoking/cooking large batches of sausage or when friends and neighbors bring their rolled venison roasts around to me at Christmastime.

When you are hot-smoking your sausage or venison roasts, these circular smokers should be used for only hot-smoking/cooking. The only sure way to determine that your meat has reached an internal temperature over 160° F is to insert a meat thermometer into the center of the sausage.

These units are heated either by smoldering wood chips or by electricity. The units heated with wood are very good for adding a smoke flavor. But a consistent temperature is tricky to achieve, and it is difficult to keep the temperature high enough for a long enough period of time to cook raw sausage.

Electric units are your best choice. They come in two versions: those with an unregulated heating element and those that have a temperature control similar to the control on an electric skillet.

Brinkmann circular hot-smoker/cooker.
Courtesy The Brinkmann Corporation

My favorite—and a great choice for the first-time user—is the Brinkmann electric stainless-steel hot-smoker. It is virtually indestructible, easy to use, and easy to clean. Wood chips are placed in a steel pan and heated by an electric heating element. Above the wood pan is a pan that you can fill with water, beer, wine, or other liquids that will create a moist heat and give additional flavor.

The unregulated units do an outstanding job of hot-smoking/cooking a variety of meats and sausages. A 10-pound rolled venison roast or ham can be smoked and cooked in four to six hours, and a load of sausage can be finished off in two to three hours. After two hours, it is best to check the internal temperature of the meat every hour until it reaches over 160° F. A heavy steel bowl containing the wood chips is located on top of the heating element. The heating element causes the chips to smolder, and the smoke rises up through the meat. Units that can regulate and maintain a constant temperature will give you more options.

For those using manufactured smokers, the builder supplies a detailed booklet giving operating instructions and recommended cooking temperatures for different types of meat. Since each brand has its own characteristics, the directions should be read and followed.

Home-Style Combination Hot- and Cold-Smoker/Cooker

For the dedicated sausage maker, the Bradley home-style smoker with a smoke generator is a must-have piece of equipment. The temperature is easy to control, and the smoke is generated automatically by means of patented compressed-wood Bisquettes.

Home-style hot/cold smoker with automatic smoke generator.
Courtesy Bradley Technologies Canada, Inc.

The Bradley smoke generator can be used for both hot- and cold-smoking and provides up to eight hours of clean continuous smoke without supervision. The Bisquettes come in alder, cherry, apple, mesquite, hickory, and maple. These Bisquettes provide the slow, low-temperature burn required for a true cold smoke. Temperature control is easy to maintain. These units also cook at temperatures of up to 320° F.

Other manufactured smokers can range from a double-barrel 50-gallon model to a combination grill/smoker.

For camps that process their own sausages, there are several small commercial-style units available. Depending on your requirements and budget, you will not lack units to choose from.

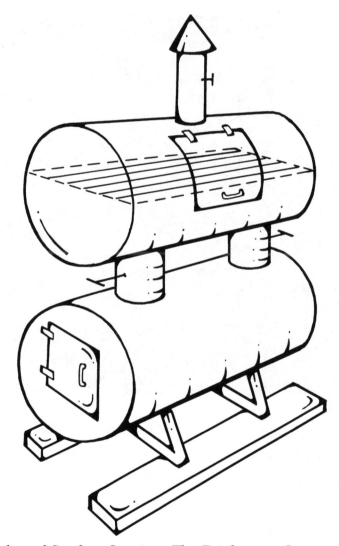

Double-barrel Smoker. Courtesy The Brinkmann Corporation

Combination patio smoker/cooker. Courtesy The Brinkmann Corporation

Small commercial-style hot- and cold-smoker/cooker (100 pounds).
Courtesy Craft's Custom Meats

Home-Built Hot- and Cold-Smoking/Cooking Systems

There is nothing quite as satisfying for you and as mystifying for your friends as for you to take them behind the house for a tour of your "old" smokehouse. For those who want to cure and cold-smoke meat and sausage in the traditional manner and have the pleasure of building their own old-fashioned smokehouse, there are several options:

- Smokepit
- Smokebox
- Walk-in smokehouse

No matter which type of smoker you choose to build, the unit should be built airtight. The smoker is a holding chamber, and when properly built it should be tight enough to prevent drafts and allow the smoke to enter at the bottom and be pulled up and out through the damper/vent openings. Any air leakage that you have through the sides will cause smoke to leak out the cracks and not completely fill the chamber. The damper/vent will allow for a draft that will pull the smoke up from the bottom and through the sausage. Half-inch steel rods are placed so that they are close to the top and run from side to side. These steel rods are strong enough that they will not sag and the sausages will not slide to the middle. This is important because the sausages should not be touching each other while they are smoking. Prewarm the smoker and rub the rods with a light coating of vegetable oil.

The first three things that you will need to consider before building a hot- or cold-smoker are:

- Will you have the time to dedicate to tending a smoldering firepit 24 hours a day?
- Do you have a piece of ground large enough and with a gentle slope?
- Will you be able to place the firepit upwind of your smokehouse?

Smokepit

In its simplest form, a smokepit may consist of a 55-gallon drum sitting over a hole in the ground. Due to the closeness of the meat to the fire, the smokepit can only be used for hot-smoking/cooking. This is fine for sausages that are eaten or packaged and frozen as soon as they are finished, but the heat will be so close to the meat that you will only be able to hot-smoke/cook. All sausage should be hung as high up as possible, and at the same level. Due to the small size of the barrel, it will comfortably hold up to 10 or 20 pounds of sausage.

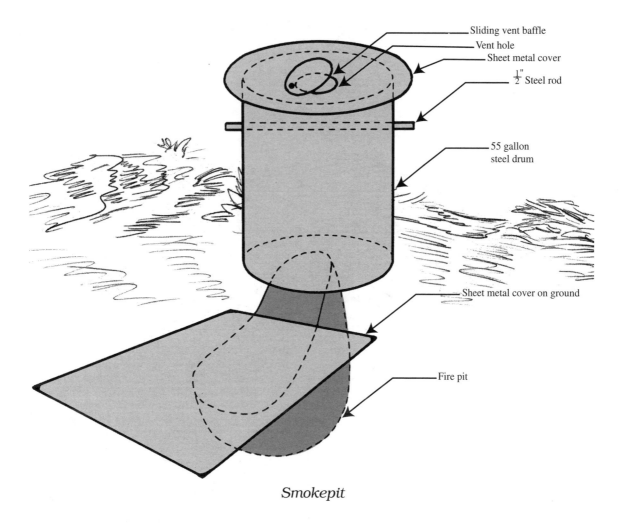

Sliding vent baffle
Vent hole
Sheet metal cover
$\frac{1}{2}$" Steel rod

55 gallon steel drum

Sheet metal cover on ground

Fire pit

Smokepit

Smokebox

In this type of unit, the fire is located some distance from the smokebox, and you will be able to either hot- or cold-smoke. When I was 14 years old, I talked my grandfather into helping me build a small smokebox out in the field behind my grandmother's garden. There was a gentle slope down from the garden that made it the perfect place for a smokebox.

When fall came, Granddad helped me make some cured venison sausage that we cold-smoked, and Grandmother treated us to a surprise breakfast consisting of her special biscuits, grits, scrambled eggs, and fried venison sausage. This feast was topped off with hand-squeezed orange juice and redeye gravy made from the sausage drippings. It is surprising what memories of our youth stay with us forever.

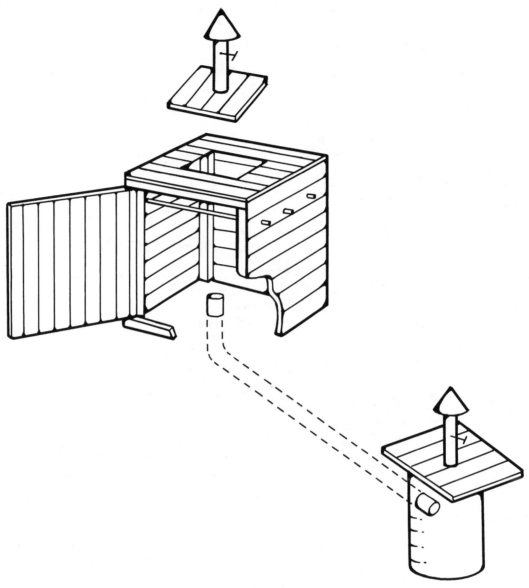

Smokebox

The smokebox differs from the smokepit in that the box that holds the sausage is located some distance away from the direct heat of the fire. With proper heat and smoke control, a fine cold-smoked product can be produced on a small budget with a smokebox. For the occasional home smoker, this type of smoker is the best option for a make-it-yourself unit. It is large enough to smoke all the sausage that your family will need, yet will be less expensive and will not take up as much space as an old-fashioned walk-in smokehouse. As with the smokepit, all sausage should be hung as high up on steel rods as possible, and at the same level.

Depending on the size of box you build, you should be able to smoke at least 40 pounds of sausage at one time.

To control the draft, cut an 8-inch hole in the top and screw a sliding metal cover in place. By opening and closing the cover, you will be able to control the draft and allow more or less smoke to escape. Even though a small stream of smoke is coming out of the hole, small animals and insects may still crawl inside. Staple a piece of screening material on top of the box and under the cover. The screen will keep out any vermin.

Walk-In Smokehouse

This is everybody's concept of what a smokehouse should look like. A walk-in smokehouse should be used only for cold-smoking meats and sausages that have had the proper cure added, or for cuts of meat that have been brine-cured.

The smaller smokebox is well suited for the family who wishes to occasionally smoke smaller batches of sausage, a few hams, or some rolled venison roasts. But if you are very serious and wish to smoke larger amounts, you will eventually want to build a "real" smokehouse.

While hunting in Indiana several years ago, I was shown a large hole in the ground that had been dug out by deer. This was where I learned that when scouting for deer, you should look for old and abandoned homesteads that may have had a smokehouse. Many years of smoking salted meat have caused the ground where the smokehouse once stood to become saturated with salt drippings. Once it is abandoned, deer will seek out the salt, dig out a sizable hole, and eat the salt-saturated dirt.

In 1974 my first walk-in smokehouse cost me $25 in materials and three weeks of labor. It was built out of recycled lumber, siding from discarded wooden shipping pallets, foundation rocks that came from a neighbor's field, and a tin roof salvaged from an old shed. The firepit and foundation were built out of the fieldstones, and the smoke tunnel and damper vent were made from pieces of salvaged 4-inch galvanized hot-water-heater air pipe. The only things I had to purchase were nails, some mortar mix, and wire screen to wrap around the frame under the siding to keep the insects and rodents out. The door hinges were made from old harness leather.

Completely wrapping around the sides, under the roof, over the smoke entry hole, and over the inside of the smoke vent with screening material is a must. Even with the smoke, a few flies might find their way in and ruin all your hard work—not to mention the rats and field mice seeking shelter from the cold.

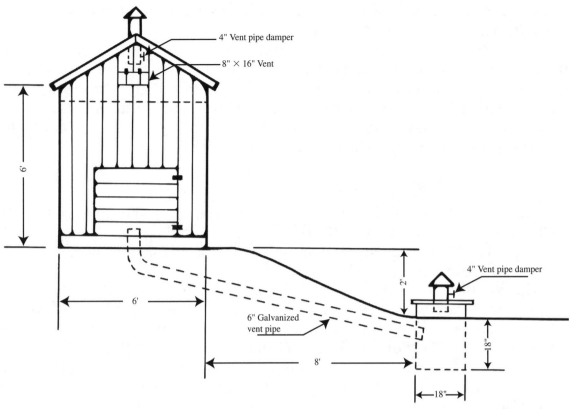

Walk-in smokehouse

Build your smokehouse door no larger than absolutely necessary and as low to the ground as possible. Some of the old smokehouses I have seen have had such small doors that you would have to squat down in order to get inside.

The drawback in using a walk-in smoker is that it can only be used for cold-smoking meat and sausages that have had a curing agent containing nitrate added to them. Cold-smoking is not a substitute for cooking. It is just another way of preserving cured meat. It is almost impossible to achieve a consistently high enough level of heat to cook the sausage to 160° F. If you want to make only smoked sausage and store it in your freezer, your least expensive way is to purchase a manufactured circular hot-smoking/cooking unit.

Refrigerator Smokers

You may have heard about converting old refrigerators into smokehouses, but converting a discarded refrigerator is not for you. Refrigerators might first appear to be the perfect candidate for a simple smokehouse. I do not recommend the use of modern refrigerators, however, because they are lined with plastic on the inside and have rubber gaskets around the door. The heat will cause the plastic to melt and give off gases that may be harmful to you and give a plastic taste to your sausage. Old refrigerators with steel on the inside might work, but they are hard to find. With even the old ones you will need to remove the rubber gaskets from around the doors and any other plastic or rubber material. In the end you may spend more time and effort converting an old steel refrigerator into a smokehouse than it is worth. A smokebox might serve you better, cost you less, be simpler to build, and be easier to use.

Smoke, Temperature, and Humidity Control

I have always found that the most difficult part of cold-smoking is maintaining a:

- Steady flow of smoke
- Constant temperature
- Acceptable level of humidity

I have built and used many types of homemade smokehouses, and each one required a period of adjustment and experimentation in order to achieve consistent results. Once you have worked out all the details, you can cold-smoke as well as any old settler. Remember, these old homesteads were lived on for 50 or 100 or more years, and the skills required to successfully operate the family smokehouse were passed down from one generation to another. By the time a young man had reached marrying age, he had helped manage the smokehouse for 16 to 20 years and knew all there was about making the old family smokehouse perform to its maximum.

Smoke Control

Being able to maintain a proper level of cold smoke 24 hours a day is mandatory. Only experience will give you a feel for the size of the wood you will need. Variations in outside temperature and wind also have to be factored in. When I built my last smokehouse, I ran a two-week test. During this time I experimented with damper settings, draft control, and the size of wood that would give me a steady stream of smoke. During the night I would set my alarm to go off every two hours so that I could get up to check on the fire. These trials gave me the confidence to know that my firepit would continue to smolder all night long. Only then was I was able to go to bed at night without waking up wondering if the fire had gone out.

My general plan of operation is to use small slivers of wood to get the fire started, then ½-inch-square pieces of dry wood until I get a good bed of coals and the temperature in the smokehouse up to 90° to 100° F. Then I place ½-inch-square pieces of green wood or wood that has been soaked overnight in water. Add more or less until you are able to maintain the temperature. In the evening I load up half the coals with hardwood sawdust that has also been soaking in water. The wet sawdust should continue to smolder all night long. Never use a flammable liquid or other fire-starting material to kindle your fire.

Common smoking hardwoods include hickory, pecan, persimmon, apple, peach, pear, plum, mesquite, alder, and the country staple, corncobs soaked in water.

Woods that are not acceptable are resinous woods, such as pine, cedar, redwood, fir, spruce, and other conifers or evergreens. Other woods that are not acceptable are poisonous woods from shrubs such as oleander or ornamental trees. That said, in Turkey they use a local resinous pinewood to smoke sausage. This is the same wood that they use to give Latikia pipe tobacco its distinctive flavor. For those who are not familiar with the flavor, the taste is definitely an acquired one in both Turkish sausage and tobacco.

Temperature Control

Control of both temperature and smoke volume is a function of the firepit. The use of a thermometer that can be read from the outside of your smokehouse will make controlling the temperature much easier. Always knowing the temperature inside the smokehouse is as important to smoking as it is to baking. I solved this problem by purchasing from a local discount store a weather thermometer that has a remote probe at the end of a 2-foot thermocouple wire. A hole was drilled through the wall, and the sensor was located in the center of the smokehouse. This arrangement allows me to check the temperature without opening the door. It takes an hour or so for the temperature to rise back to the proper level after the door is opened.

Once you have found a constant size of wood, it is a simple matter of adjusting the air vents on both the smoker and the firepit to maintain your temperature and the amount of smoke. During the night you may find that slightly closing the dampers will help keep the sawdust smoldering. Don't become overly concerned if your fire goes out. In the morning, relight the fire and get the smoke flowing again. The perfect fire is a very small one that puts out a consistent flow of smoke.

When your cured sausage or meat has reached the proper color, let the firepit go out naturally, allowing the meat to continue to hang until it naturally cools down to the air temperature and the surface skims over.

This is important because the juices on the surface need to dehydrate and seal the surface. A final burst of heavy smoke will finish the process.

Humidity Control

You might think that a dry environment is required for smoking, but just the opposite is true. A constant 75 percent humidity is ideal for dry-smoking.

You would also think that the best environment for storing smoked meats would be in the desert Southwest, but in actuality an underground root cellar makes a better alternative. Both the temperature and the humidity are perfect for storing cold-smoked meats.

The old folks didn't have hygrometers to measure humidity. This is where tradition and many years of using the same smokehouse had their benefits. The old man would stick his hand into the smokehouse and from years of smoking experience would know when it felt right. With experience you will also be able to judge when the humidity is where you want it to be.

8

Making Your First Venison Sausages

The venison sausage recipes in this book represent the best the world has to offer—and most can be made with equipment that you may already have on hand or can be borrowed from a friend. For those of you who already have experience making sausage, there are a few recipes that will challenge all of your skills.

When selecting your first sausage, you may want to consider beginning with bulk/fresh, because this can be easily packaged and frozen after making.

These sausage recipes were not traditionally made from venison. They have been converted and adjusted to utilize all types of antlered deer, whether it be an indigenous species such as whitetail, Coues, mule deer, elk, or moose, or an other world species such as red, sika, roe deer, or other Asian species.

Always store raw meat in the refrigerator below 36° F and work in small batches or with only as much meat as you will need for 15 minutes' work. When you are finished making each batch, place the sausage in the refrigerator, remove more meat, and begin with another batch.

For safety reasons, the link sausages that you get back from your processor contain a cure and are hot-smoked/cooked. You can very easily replicate this sausage by making any of the fresh link sausage recipes and then hot-smoking/cooking it in a manufactured circular smoker/cooker until it is well smoked and fully cooked.

When using one of the manufactured home smoker/cookers, always verify that each sausage has reached 160° F by inserting a meat thermometer into the center. Check every sausage, because one link may have been smaller or closer to the heat source and be fully cooked while others have not reached the proper temperature. Inexpensive dial-face thermometers can be found in the cooking accessories sections of major discount shopping centers or larger grocery stores or ordered from firms listed in the appendix.

Another good thermometer is the remote-sensing type. If you have a choice, select a model that has a 44-inch thermocouple connecting wire. By inserting the probe into a sausage in the coolest part of the cooker, you can check on the cooking process without opening the door. Once you have both of these inexpensive thermometers, you will find that you will be using them for cooking everything from turkey to steak and anything in between. The remote-sensing thermometers are often found in gourmet stores and at some discount shopping centers.

Instant-read thermometer.
Courtesy Acu-Rite

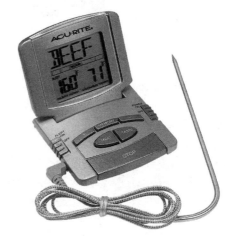

Programmable digital meat thermometer.
Courtesy Acu-Rite

Cleanliness is an Absolute Must. Small pieces of meat left in table cracks or on tools will cross-contaminate other meat and equipment. It is absolutely mandatory that all work surfaces and tools be kept immaculately clean at all times. This is not just a casual warning. Botulism will quickly multiply on one small piece of meat, and the toxins in that one small piece of meat will allow the bacteria to infect all of your meat and your other tools.

Keep All Raw Meat Chilled Below 36° F. When you are not working with your raw meat or raw sausage, place it back in the refrigerator and keep it below 36° F until you are ready to continue your processing. When you are done making sausage for the day, immediately package, label, and freeze it.

What Type of Sausage Should I Make First?

Thinking about making your first sausage is exciting and possibly intimidating, yet the whole process is so simple that after you have finished your first batch, you will wonder why you were concerned.

Working your way through making one type of sausage at a time is less confusing and a lot more fun than trying to make several types at the same time. The simplest way to begin is to start at the beginning and progress through a logical series of different sausage configurations. The first four types of sausages that you will be making are:

- Fresh bulk or patties
- Quick-cured
- Hot-smoked/cooked links
- Cooked links

When you finish making your first batch of fresh sausage, you will see that it is was not as intimidating as you had once thought, and you will be ready to move on to the next type. Along the way, you may also decide that there is one configuration that you like best. Concentrate your efforts on making that type and let others experiment with the rest.

Your First Venison Sausage: *Fresh Bulk or Patties*

You will be surprised at how good your first venison sausage will taste—as good as or better than any commercial venison sausage you have ever had someone else make for you.

Cutting "soft-frozen" bulk sausage into patties

A good choice for your first venison sausage would be a fresh bulk or patty sausage such as:

- *Hot Italian Bulk Venison Sausage (p. 81)*
- *Chorizo—Mexican Venison Sausage (p. 81)*
- *Spicy Good Venison and Honey Sausage (p. 81)*

These sausages are easy to make, and you can always make link sausages out of them on the next go-around. All the equipment you need is a hand-cranked grinder, plastic wrap, and cotton twine. Involve your children in your first sausage-making experience. They will never forget the pleasure they received when the first batch was cooked.

Your Second Venison Sausage: *Quick-Cured*

A quick-cured sausage is the next logical step in the learning process. These sausages are made into a log and rolled in aluminum foil or plastic wrap for the curing process. The Salami recipe is a typical refrigerator sausage, which is sliced and served cold. The Pepperoni recipe is also cured in the refrigerator and then baked before being served either hot or cold.

Quick-cured summer sausage

Your second effort in the art of sausage making should be one of the quick-cured sausages such as:

- *Overnight Venison Salami (p. 118)*
- *Oven-Baked Spicy Venison Pepperoni (p. 125)*
- *Easy Breakfast Venison Sausage (p. 120)*

Your Third Venison Sausage: *Hot-Smoked/Cooked Links*

These link sausages will be familiar to you because they are similar to the types that you have been getting back from your venison processor.

Don't let the casing scare you. Begin by matching the stuffing tube with the casing size. Slide the casing onto the moistened stuffing tube, tie off the end, grind out the links, and twist or tie with cotton twine between each link. When finished, take a sharp needle and prick any air pockets that may have developed.

Hot-smoked/cooked links

These sausages are cooked as they are being hot-smoked and can be eaten as is, although most of us would rather recook the sausages in a skillet or on the grill, in a tasty stew, or in a gumbo with seafood or wild goose.

You will need a grinder with a stuffing tube matched to the casing size, hog casings, and a circular home-style hot-smoker/cooker.

If you are vacuum-sealing and freezing your fresh links prior to cooking them, it is best to place them in their bags and freeze them solid before sealing them in the vacuum bags. Every casing has a few minute weak spots. When you apply the vacuum, there is a chance that a hole will appear at a weak spot, and some of the sausage may leak out through the hole. If this happens, it is not a real problem because as you cook or hot-smoke/cook the sausage, the contents will shrink and the hole will seal. When you hot-smoke your sausage, always verify that the internal temperature of each link has reached at least 160° F.

There may be times when you are hot-smoking/cooking links of several sizes. Insert a thermometer into the end of the narrowest sausage and hot-smoke/cook until the internal temperature reaches 160° F. Remove the smaller sausage and insert the thermometer into the next-larger-diameter sausage. Continue checking and removing until all sausages have been cooked and removed. Any fresh bulk sausage recipe will do for stuffing into casings and hot-smoking/cooking.

These venison sausage recipes are a good starting place for your first hot-smoked/cooked project:

- *Pennsylvania Dutch Christmas Venison Sausage (p. 105)*
- *Sicilian Venison Sausage (p. 100)*

Your Fourth Venison Sausage: *Cooked Links*

For your fourth sausage, you will need a grinder with a stuffing tube matched to the casing and 36 mm to 42 mm hog casing or beef rounds.

Cooked links. Courtesy DeWied International

Two of these link sausages are baked and the other is boiled. All are equally good:

- *Baked Kielbasi Venison Sausage (p. 132)*
- *Boiled Venison Potato Sausage Rings (p. 135)*
- *Baked Russian Venison Sausage (p. 136)*

PART II

Venison Sausage Recipes

9

Fresh Venison Sausage Recipes

Fresh venison sausage is the easiest kind of sausage to make because it requires only a simple meat grinder and contains no curing agents. As the name implies, it is made fresh.

Many home sausage makers wish to make only bulk and patty sausage and prefer not to become involved in smoking or curing processes. Because these sausages are so easy to make and package, this is completely understandable. A small amount of Liquid Smoke can be added to the sausage mixture to give it a "smoky" taste.

Because these sausages are raw and contain no cures, they should be either cooked and eaten when they are made or stored in the refrigerator for no more than three days. If it will be more than three days before they are eaten, they should be packaged and frozen. Fresh sausage should be cooked until the internal temperature reaches 160° F.

These are the best recipes to involve the children in, because they can taste the results as soon as the sausage is made. A good project for the children is to have them help make the sausage on Saturday and then cook the sausage along with pancakes and eggs for breakfast on Sunday morning. With this story, they will be the stars of Show-and-Tell on Monday morning. Chances are that they will be the only students in their class who have ever made sausage with their own hands—especially sausage made from their own deer. Be prepared, though; you may have more children in your kitchen the next Saturday than you bargained for.

The ingredients to make these sausages are readily available from any supermarket. The exceptions are the Oriental sausages. The few unique ingredients required for these sausages can be found in Oriental or Mediterranean specialty food stores.

After you have made your first sausage, form a tablespoon portion into a small patty and fry it. This testing process will allow you to adjust the spices to your individual taste. If you make a change and like it, give the sausage a new name. Don't be afraid to experiment with ingredients; that is the fun of making your own sausage.

Any of these fresh sausage recipes can also be stuffed into the casings of your choice. Except that it must be stored in the refrigerator for no longer than three days, fresh sausage doesn't have a lot of hard-and-fast rules. If you enjoy it, make some more and cook it any way that you wish.

Mild and Easy Venison Sausage

5 lbs. ground venison
3 lbs. ground pork, cubed
2 Tbsp. salt
1 Tbsp. black pepper

1 tsp. ground nutmeg
1 garlic clove, minced
hot water
32 mm to 34 mm hog casings (optional)

Mix the venison, pork, and spices and grind twice with a fine disc. Add just enough hot water to achieve a sausage consistency. Either stuff into casings or make into patties. Store in the refrigerator for up to 3 days or package and freeze.

Hunter's Venison Sausage

4 lbs. venison, cubed
4 lbs. pork, cubed
2 Tbsp. salt
2 Tbsp. black pepper
¾ tsp. ground mace
¼ tsp. ground nutmeg

¼ tsp. ground cloves
½ tsp. ground allspice
½ tsp. garlic powder
½ tsp. cayenne pepper (optional)
½ cup (approx.) hot water
20 mm to 24 mm sheep casings (optional)

Mix the venison and pork together and grind with a fine disc. Add the spices and mix well. Grind a second time. Add approximately ½ cup of hot water to the meat to achieve the desired texture. Either stuff into casings or make into patties. Store in the refrigerator for up to 3 days or package and freeze.

Portuguese Linguica Venison Sausage with Spanish Sherry

1½ lbs. ground venison
½ lb. ground boneless pork chops with fat
1 tsp. coarse salt
¼ tsp. garlic powder

4 oz. port or Harvey's Bristol Cream
2¼ tsp. paprika
32 mm to 34 mm hog casings

Mix all ingredients and grind with a coarse disc. Try a good port for a true taste of Portugal; the taste of Harvey's Bristol Cream is unique and absolutely unforgettable. Stuff into hog casings, refrigerate, and cook. Store in the refrigerator for up to 3 days or package and freeze.

Spicy Good Venison and Honey Sausage

7 lbs. ground venison
5 lbs. ground lean pork
hot water
2 Tbsp. salt
2 Tbsp. black pepper

½ tsp. red pepper
¼ tsp. cinnamon
½ tsp. sage
½ cup honey

Mix together the ground venison and pork. Mix in a little hot water if the meat seems dry. Add the spices and honey and grind through a coarse disc. Make into 4" wide × ½" thick patties. Package and freeze immediately after making, or store in the refrigerator for up to 3 days.

Hot Italian Bulk Venison Sausage

2 tsp. salt
1 tsp. black pepper
4 tsp. fennel seeds
3 Tbsp. minced fresh oregano
1 tsp. garlic powder
1 tsp. cayenne pepper, or to taste

1 tsp. finely chopped red pepper flakes, or
    to taste
6 lbs. boneless venison, cubed
2 lbs. boneless lean pork, cubed
1½ lbs. bacon or pork fat, chopped finely
32 mm to 35 mm hog casings (optional)

Sprinkle the seasonings over the meats in a large tray. Mix well. Grind once with a coarse grinding disc. Mix well and grind a second time with a fine disc. Either stuff into casings or make into patties. If freezing, wrap individual pieces in plastic wrap and freeze after making. Otherwise, store in the refrigerator for up to 3 days.

Chorizo—Mexican Venison Sausage

Chorizo is a traditional Mexican sausage. When cooked with scrambled eggs and rolled in flour tortillas, it is called Tacitos or Chorizo con Huevos.

¾ lb. venison loin, cubed
¼ lb. pork, cubed
1 tsp. salt
2 Tbsp. chili powder
¼ tsp. cumin

1 Tbsp. minced fresh oregano
3 garlic cloves, pressed
2 Tbsp. apple cider vinegar
6 eggs, beaten (optional)
flour tortillas (optional)

Mix together all the ingredients except the eggs and tortillas and grind twice through a fine disc. Cover and refrigerate overnight. Form into patties or stuff into small casings. Cook as you would any other sausage.

If you want one of the best breakfasts you have ever eaten, fry the sausage loose in a pan until it is browned, pour off half the liquid, then mix the beaten eggs into the sausage and scramble. Place 2 Tbsp. of the sausage and egg mixture on a flour tortilla and roll tightly to make a Tacito. Tacitos can be eaten as is or fried until crisp. Serve with salsa.

Store the sausage in the refrigerator for up to 3 days or package and freeze.

Sweet Spanish Venison Sausage
with White Raisins

1½ lbs. ground venison
½ lb. ground boneless pork chops with fat
1 tsp. coarse salt
½ tsp. black pepper
¼ tsp. cayenne pepper
¼ tsp. nutmeg

¼ tsp. ginger
2 garlic cloves, crushed
6 Tbsp. preferably white (sultana) or dark
    raisins
1 tsp. sugar
32 mm to 35 mm hog casings (optional)

Mix all the ingredients together and grind through a fine disc. Stuff into sheep casings or leave in bulk for patties. Package and freeze if the mix is not going to be used within 2 days. Otherwise, store in the refrigerator.

Boudin Blanc—
Venison Roast Sausage

¼ cup bacon drippings
1 cup chopped onions
1 cup chopped parsley
1 Tbsp. minced garlic
¼ tsp. onion powder
1 cup water

2 cups steamed rice
4 cups chopped leftover venison roast
ground red pepper to taste
¼ tsp. salt
32 mm to 35 mm hog casings, cut into
    3' lengths

Add the bacon drippings to a hot skillet and sauté the onions until just clear. Add the parsley, then the garlic, onion powder, and water; cook until the onions are completely cooked. Remove from the stove, add the rice, and blend well. Mix the red pepper and salt into the meat. Install the fine disc on the grinder and grind/stuff into the casings. Make Boudin into 4" to 5" lengths. To cook, add a little water to a skillet and warm the Boudin. Store in the refrigerator for up to 3 days or package and freeze.

Quick Polish Sausage

21 lbs. venison, cubed
13 lbs. lean pork, cubed
4 oz. hot water
1½ oz. allspice
½ oz. paprika

2 tsp. garlic powder or 4 tsp. onion powder
½ tsp. dehydrated onion flakes
12 oz. salt
½ lb. dry milk
35 mm to 38 mm hog casings (optional)

Grind the venison and pork twice with a fine grinding disc. Mix in the water. Combine the remaining ingredients and mix into the meat. Either stuff into casings to make a long sausage, make into individual 6" to 8" link sausages, or make into patties. Store in the refrigerator for up to 3 days or package and freeze.

Cevapcici Venison Sausage

A Central European sausage made without casings.

2 garlic cloves, minced
½ tsp. paprika
½ tsp. salt
⅛ tsp. black pepper

⅛ tsp. ground cloves
1 lb. ground venison
¼ lb. ground bacon
1½ Tbsp. flour

Mix together the garlic, paprika, salt, pepper, and cloves, and knead into the ground venison and bacon. Divide the venison into 20 equal parts. Dampen hands and roll each part into a 2" long sausage. Roll each sausage in flour, then shake off the excess. Refrigerate until firm. The sausages can also be packaged and frozen for later use. To cook, place the sausages in a wire fish cooking grill that can be turned over and grill on both sides. The sausages can also be pan-fried with a little grease or butter. Store in the refrigerator for up to 3 days or package and freeze.

Oatmeal and Venison Sausage

1 lb. pinhead oatmeal
2 cups hot venison stock or canned beef
   broth
4 lbs. venison, minced
2½ lbs. pork shoulder, minced

1½ oz. salt
1 oz. coarsely ground black pepper
½ oz. chopped fresh sage
30 mm to 32 mm hog casings

Soak the oatmeal in the hot stock or broth overnight. Mince the venison and pork as finely as you can, add the remaining ingredients, and fill the casings. Hang and allow to dry in the refrigerator for a few hours. Store in the refrigerator for up to 3 days or package and freeze.

Heart and Liver Venison Sausage

4 lbs. venison, minced
1 lb. venison heart and liver, minced
1½ lbs. pork belly or bacon
2 oz. salt
1 tsp. crushed black peppercorns

1 tsp. crushed juniper berries
1 oz. crushed garlic
red wine
32 mm to 35 mm hog casings (optional)

Mince all the meat together and stir in the rest of the ingredients. Moisten the mixture well with wine, cover, and place in the refrigerator overnight. Either stuff into casings or make into patties. This sausage takes a little longer to cook; it is also very good when baked. Store in the refrigerator for up to 3 days or package and freeze.

Syrian Venison Sausage Links with Red Wine and Pine Nuts

1 lb. venison, finely ground
1 lb. boneless lamb, finely ground
2 Tbsp. chopped fresh tarragon
2 tsp. ground coriander
1 tsp. ground allspice

2 Tbsp. dry red wine
¼ cup whole pine nuts
1 tsp. salt
½ tsp. black pepper
24 mm to 26 mm sheep casings

Combine all the ingredients and mix together in a large bowl. Mix well with your hands. Stuff into casings using a large or no disc and twist off into 3" links. Store in the refrigerator for up to 3 days or package and freeze.

Spicy Hot Thai Venison and Chicken Sausage

1¾ lbs. venison, cubed
1¾ lbs. boned chicken thighs with skin, cubed
1 Tbsp. green curry paste
1 bunch cilantro, minced
3 Tbsp. minced fresh basil
3 Tbsp. minced fresh mint
1½ Tbsp. minced garlic

1½ Tbsp. grated ginger
¼ cup *nuoc mam* (fish sauce)
1 Tbsp. kosher salt
1 tsp. red pepper flakes
1 Tbsp. black pepper
1 tsp. cayenne pepper
22 mm to 24 mm sheep casings (optional)

Grind the meats through a coarse disc and mix in the remaining ingredients. The sausage can be either cooked loose or stuffed into small sheep casings. Store in the refrigerator for up to 3 days or package and freeze.

Assyrian-Style Venison Sausage

2 lbs. venison, finely ground
1 lb. lamb, finely ground
¼ lb. beef fat, finely ground
1 Tbsp. salt
1 tsp. coarsely ground black pepper

1 Tbsp. minced fresh basil
¼ cup pomegranate juice
1 tsp. minced fresh tarragon
28 mm or smaller hog casings

Mix together all the ingredients and stuff into pork casings. Stuff into 5" long sausages and tie off on both ends. Store in the refrigerator for up to 3 days or package and freeze.

Mediterranean Herbal Venison Sausage

1 lb. venison, cubed
½ lb. lean pork, cubed
¼ lb. bacon, cubed
1 Tbsp. salt
2 tsp. white pepper

1 tsp. ground thyme
1 tsp. ground marjoram
5 pieces pimiento, minced
1 tsp. ground cinnamon
28 mm or smaller sheep casings

Grind the venison, pork, and bacon through a fine grinding disc. Mix the herbs and spices and sprinkle over the meats, mix together, and regrind through a coarse disc. Make into any length sausage. The raw sausage may be stored in the refrigerator for up to 3 days and then hot-smoked/cooked, or packaged and frozen.

Polish-Style Venison Sausage

4 lbs. venison, cubed
2 lbs. lean pork, cubed
1 cup water
2 Tbsp. black pepper
½ tsp. red pepper flakes

2 Tbsp. minced garlic
1 Tbsp. marjoram
1 Tbsp. sugar
35 mm to 38 mm hog casings (optional)

Mix together the venison and pork and grind using a coarse grinding disc. Mix in the remaining ingredients and regrind using a fine grinding disc. The sausage can be made into link sausages or patties. Store in the refrigerator for up to 3 days and then hot-smoke/cook, or package and freeze after making.

Sai Oua—
Northern Thai Venison Sausage

1 Tbsp. finely minced lemon grass
3 lbs. venison, cubed
1 lb. boneless pork chops, minced
1 tsp. salt
¼ cup minced garlic
2 Tbsp. minced coriander
2 Tbsp. minced cilantro
1 tsp. black pepper

¼ cup lime juice
1 tsp. *phom kha* (galangal or Laos powder)
1 Tbsp. minced green onion
1 Tbsp. *kapi* (fermented shrimp paste)
1 Tbsp. finely chopped *prik ki nu* (green birdseye chilies)
20 mm to 22 mm sheep casings (optional)

Chop the lemon grass in a food processor until very fine. Combine all the ingredients. Stuff into sausage casings, tying into 4" long sausages, or form into patties or meatballs. To cook, fry or broil and serve with sticky rice. Store in the refrigerator for up to 3 days or package and freeze.

Note: Lemon grass, *phom kha* (galangal or Laos powder), *kapi* (fermented shrimp paste), and *prik ki nu* (green birdseye chilies) can be found in any good Thai or Vietnamese market.

Chaurice Venison Sausage

A variation on a spicy 19th-century Louisiana Creole sausage. Cook with white or red beans. It is also good for breakfast with eggs.

4 lbs. venison, cubed
2 lbs. pork fat, cubed
2 cups minced onion
1½ Tbsp. minced garlic
1½ tsp. red pepper
½ tsp. chili powder
1 tsp. red pepper flakes

8 tsp. salt
2 tsp. black pepper
2 tsp. crushed dried thyme leaves
5 Tbsp. minced fresh parsley
3 bay leaves, finely crushed
½ tsp. allspice
22 mm to 24 mm sheep casings (optional)

Mix together the venison and pork fat and grind once with a coarse grinding disc. Add the remaining ingredients and mix thoroughly. Make into patties or stuff into sheep casings, making 6" long sausage links. Store in the refrigerator for up to 3 days or package and freeze.

Garlic Venison Sausage Patties

2 lbs. boneless venison, chopped
¾ lb. pork fat, chopped
1 small white onion, chopped
4 large garlic cloves, minced
2 tsp. salt
1 tsp. black pepper

1 tsp. ground sage
⅛ tsp. filé powder
½ tsp. ground thyme
¼ tsp. ground nutmeg
¼ tsp. ground ginger
⅛ tsp. ground allspice

Mix all the ingredients and grind once with a coarse grinding disc. Mix well and grind again with a fine grinding disc. Shape into patties or use plastic wrap and roll into a large roll. Refrigerate overnight and allow the sausage to firm. Store in the refrigerator for up to 3 days or package and freeze.

Soonday—
Korean Stuffed Venison Sausage

2 cups cooked rice
2 garlic cloves, crushed
1" fresh ginger, diced
1 tsp. salt
½ tsp. white pepper
1 Tbsp. sesame oil

1 tsp. crushed sesame seeds
5 green onions, chopped
2 cups (8 oz.) venison blood or canned
  tomato puree
28 mm to 35 mm beef rounds

Mix together the cooked rice, garlic, ginger, salt, pepper, sesame oil, sesame seeds, green onions, and either blood or tomato puree. Tie one end of the casing with cotton string. Loosely stuff the casing along its entire length—otherwise when the rice expands it will cause the casing to split. Tie the other end. Store in the refrigerator for up to 3 days or package and freeze.

To cook, place the venison Soonday in a large pan of lightly salted water. Curl around, cover, and bring the water to a boil. Cook on low for 45 minutes. Test for doneness by sticking in a skewer; when the skewer comes out dry, the sausage is done. Cut diagonally into ¼" thick slices and serve warm with boiled cabbage.

Romanian Kosher Venison Sausages

3 lbs. venison, cubed
¼ lb. lean beef, cubed
1¼ lbs. fatty beef, cubed
5 tsp. kosher salt
1 Tbsp. coarsely ground black pepper
2 tsp. ground coriander
⅛ tsp. ground allspice
⅛ tsp. ground bay leaf

⅛ tsp. ground nutmeg
1 tsp. dry mustard
2 Tbsp. whole yellow mustard seeds
2 Tbsp. minced garlic
2 tsp. sugar
½ cup water
26 mm or larger sheep casings

Grind the lean meats through a food grinder with a ⅜" disc. Grind the fatty beef through a ¼" disc. Mix the ground meats with all other ingredients except water and casings. Add just enough water to allow you to work the spices in. Knead until well blended. Stuff into casings and tie into 5" links. Store in the refrigerator for up to 3 days or package and freeze.

Cevapcici Venison Sausage with Lamb and Pork

1 lb. venison, cubed
½ lb. lamb, cubed
½ lb. pork, cubed
6 garlic cloves, minced finely
1 tsp. salt
1 tsp. baking soda

2 tsp. coarsely ground black pepper
1 tsp. red pepper
salt and pepper to taste
garlic pepper to taste
1 egg white, beaten
flour

Mix together all the ingredients except the flour and grind together using a fine disc. Dampen hands and roll into 2" long sausages. Roll each sausage into flour, then shake off the excess. Refrigerate for 2 hours or until firm. Store in the refrigerator for up to 3 days or package and freeze.

To cook, place sausages in a wire fish cooking grill that can be turned over and grill on both sides; or the sausages can be pan-fried with a little grease or butter. Serve with pita bread or hard rolls and either raw or sautéed onions.

Spiced Bratwurst Venison Sausage

½ tsp. caraway seeds
1½ lbs. venison, cubed
1 lb. lean pork butt, cubed
½ lb. pork fat, cubed
1 tsp. white pepper

¼ tsp. ground allspice
½ tsp. ground marjoram
1 tsp. salt
32 mm to 34 mm hog casings

Roll the caraway seeds flat with a heavy rolling pin and set aside. Mix together the meats and grind once using a fine disc. Mix together the caraway seeds, white pepper, allspice, marjoram, and salt. Mix the spices into the ground meat. Stuff the mixture into the casings, twist off, and tie into 6" to 8" lengths. Store in the refrigerator for up to 3 days or package and freeze. To cook, fry the Bratwurst in butter or dip in milk and broil or grill.

Sweet and Spicy Venison Sausage Patties

7 lbs. lean venison, cubed
3 lbs. pork fat, cubed
⅓ cup salt
½ cup dark brown sugar, packed

1½ Tbsp. ground sage
2 tsp. black pepper
2 tsp. red pepper

Mix together all the ingredients and grind with a fine grinding disc. Make into ½" thick sausage patties or shape into a log and roll in plastic wrap to make bulk sausage. Store in the refrigerator for up to 3 days or package and freeze.

Cajun-Style Venison Liver Boudin

A variation on a traditional Louisiana Cajun meat and rice sausage recipe

½ lb. boneless pork, cubed
⅛ lb. venison liver, sliced ½" wide
3 cups water
½ cup chopped onion
¼ cup chopped green onions
1 tsp. parsley flakes

1 tsp. celery flakes
¾ tsp. salt
½ tsp. black pepper
¾ tsp. cayenne pepper
¾ cup steamed rice
32 to 35 mm hog casings

Place the pork, venison liver, and water in a large saucepan and bring to a boil. Reduce the heat and simmer until the pork is tender. Remove the pork and venison liver; save the cooking liquid. Grind the meats with a fine grinding disc. Add the vegetables and spices to the cooking liquid and cook until the onions are tender. Add the ground meats and simmer until most of the liquid has evaporated. Gently stir in the rice. Place a coarse grinding disc on the meat grinder and stuff into 10" to 12" sausages. Hang overnight in the refrigerator to dry. Store in the refrigerator for up to 3 days or package and freeze. To cook, prick the casings several times, then simmer in water for 10 to 12 minutes before serving.

Spiced Syrian Venison Sausage

A variation on a very old Syrian sausage recipe.

1½ lbs. ground venison
1½ lbs. ground lamb
1 tsp. salt
1 tsp. coarsely ground black pepper
1 tsp. minced basil leaves

¼ tsp. cinnamon
⅛ tsp. cloves
¼ cup pomegranate juice
1 tsp. minced tarragon leaves
24 mm to 26 mm sheep casings

Mix all the ingredients and grind with a fine disc. Stuff into casings and make into 5" long sausages. Store in the refrigerator for up to 3 days or package and freeze.

Bratwurst Venison and Onion Sausage

1 cup whole milk
2 eggs, lightly beaten
¼ cup bread crumbs
3 lbs. venison, cubed
2 lbs. pork, cubed
5 tsp. salt

1½ tsp. white pepper
¼ tsp. ground cloves
1 onion, chopped
½ tsp. mace
34 mm to 36 mm hog casings

Mix the milk and eggs and soak the bread crumbs in the mixture. Combine the venison and pork and fine-grind twice. Mix the salt, white pepper, cloves, onion and mace. Mix into the bread crumb mixture. Stir the bread crumb mixture into the meat mixture with a spoon until it is light and fluffy. Grind with a fine disc and stuff the mixture into the casings. Twist off and tie into 6" to 8" links. Store in the refrigerator for up to 3 days or package and freeze. Bratwurst can be fried in butter or dipped in milk and broiled or grilled. If you do not have pork casings, the Bratwurst can be made into patties and cooked like burgers.

Yugoslavian Venison Sausage without Casings

1 lb. ground venison	½ tsp. salt
¼ lb. ground boneless pork chops	⅛ tsp. black pepper
2 garlic cloves, minced	1½ Tbsp. all-purpose flour
½ tsp. paprika	

Grind the meats through a fine disc and mix in the garlic, paprika, salt, and pepper. Divide into 20 portions. Wet hands and form each portion into a 2" long sausage. Roll each sausage in flour and then shake off the excess. Refrigerate until firm. Store in the refrigerator for up to 3 days or package and freeze. Place sausages in a metal hot dog holder and cook on a grill for 6 to 7 minutes, turning at least once. These can also be pan-fried without any additional grease.

Bangers Venison Sausage

A variation on an old and fine English sausage.

Banger Seasoning	**Sausage**
5 tsp. white pepper	2½ lbs. venison, cubed
2½ tsp. mace	1 lb. pork fat, cut into small cubes
2¼ tsp. salt	1½ cups dry unseasoned bread crumbs
2 tsp. ground ginger	1½ cups canned chicken broth
2 tsp. ground sage	3½ tsp. Banger Seasoning
½ tsp. ground nutmeg	22 mm to 24 mm sheep casings

Mix together the Banger seasoning. Grind the venison and pork together using a fine disc. Mix the ground meat together with the remaining ingredients and regrind into casings. Make sausages 4" to 6" long. Venison bangers should rest in the refrigerator overnight before cooking. The sausages can be used as you would normally use any small link pork sausage. Store in the refrigerator for up to 3 days or package and freeze.

Alsatian Christmas Breakfast Venison Sausage

1½ lbs. ground venison
½ lb. ground boneless pork chops
1 tsp. coarse salt
⅛ tsp. ground ginger
½ tsp. sugar

¼ tsp. ground cinnamon
¼ tsp. ground cloves
½ tsp. fine black pepper
⅛ tsp. ground nutmeg
26 mm or larger sheep casings (optional)

Mix all the ingredients together and grind through a fine disc. Stuff into sheep casings or leave in bulk for patties. Store in the refrigerator for up to 3 days or package and freeze.

Louisiana-Style Venison Boudin Bon Blanc

Traditionally the French made a pork blood sausage, or pudding, that was called Boudin. Boudin blanc is sausage made with pork meat instead of blood. The traditional Louisiana bayou version adds rice to the mixture, which makes it even whiter.

3 lbs. boneless venison, cubed
water
4 cups chopped white onions, divided
1 bay leaf, broken
6 peppercorns
5 tsp. salt, divided
1 cup chopped green bell pepper
1 cup coarsely chopped parsley
½ cup coarsely chopped green onions

1 Tbsp. minced garlic
¼ cup bacon drippings, rendered pork fat, or beef suet
2½ cups steamed rice
1 Tbsp. dried sage leaves
½ tsp. red pepper
½ tsp. black pepper
32 mm to 34 mm hog casings, cut into 3' lengths

Place the venison in a large pot and cover with 1" of water. Bring to a boil and skim off any foam that appears on the surface. Add 2 cups of the onions, the bay leaf, the peppercorns, and 1 tsp. of the salt. Reduce the heat and simmer, partially covered, for 1½ hours or until the venison is tender. Remove the venison and mix well with the 2 remaining cups of onions, green bell pepper, parsley, green onions, garlic, and bacon drippings. Grind with a fine disc. Mix and knead in the rice, sage, red and black pepper, and remaining 4 tsp. of salt. Place a coarse grinding disc on the grinder and make mixture into 12" to 24" long sausages; tie off after each sausage is made. Before cooking, prick the Boudin with a sharp fork in six to eight places. Melt 2 parts butter to 1 part vegetable oil in a skillet. Coil the sausage inside the skillet and cook, uncovered, until the Boudin is brown on both sides. Store in the refrigerator for up to 3 days or package and freeze.

Boerevors Venison Sausage

A variation on a traditional South African sausage.

¼ cup whole coriander
4½ lbs. boneless venison, cubed
2¼ lbs. boneless pork, cubed
½ tsp. ground cloves
½ tsp. ground nutmeg

2½ tsp. salt
1 tsp. black pepper
1 lb. bacon, cut into small cubes
½ cup rice wine vinegar
32 mm to 34 mm hog casings

Place the coriander on a baking sheet and lightly brown. Grind or process the coriander into a fine powder. Sift through a fine-screened tea strainer and regrind the larger pieces. Mix the venison and pork with the coriander, cloves, nutmeg, salt, pepper, bacon, and vinegar and grind together with a coarse disc. Regrind with the coarse disc and loosely stuff the casing into one long link. Hang the sausage in the refrigerator for about 12 hours before using or freezing. Store in the refrigerator for up to 3 days or package and freeze. Boerevors are at their best cooked on a grill.

Spicy Oriental Venison Sausage

3½ lbs. venison, cubed
1½ lbs. boneless pork chops, cubed
1 Tbsp. salt
⅛ tsp. red pepper flakes (optional)
½ cup honey

1 cup sake (Japanese rice wine)
¼ cup fresh-squeezed orange juice
1 cup teriyaki sauce
2 Tbsp. rice wine vinegar
30 mm to 32 mm hog casings

Grind the meats through a coarse disc. Mix in the remaining ingredients, stuff through a coarse disc, and tie off into 4" to 6" links. Prick the links with a sharp fork and fry. Store in the refrigerator for up to 3 days or package and freeze.

Oxford Venison Sausage

A variation on an old English sausage recipe.

½ lb. venison, ground
½ lb. lean pork, ground
6 oz. pork fat, ground
3 slices white bread with crust, cubed
1 tsp. salt
¼ tsp. black pepper
¼ tsp. cayenne pepper
⅛ tsp. freshly grated nutmeg

⅛ tsp. mace
⅛ tsp. dried thyme
⅛ tsp. dried marjoram, crumbled fine
1 tsp. dried sage
1 tsp. grated lemon peel
1 egg, lightly beaten
32 mm to 35 mm hog casings

Mix together the ground venison, pork, fat, and bread. Mix together the salt, pepper, cayenne, nutmeg, mace, thyme, marjoram, sage, and lemon peel into the egg and knead into the meat mixture. Stuff the mixture into hog casings. To cook, prick any air pockets with a pin, then poach, braise, or fry. Store in the refrigerator for up to 3 days or package and freeze.

Smoke-Flavored Andouille Venison Sausage

Andouille is a favorite Louisiana sausage.

4 lbs. boneless venison, cubed
2 lbs. pork fat, cubed
¼ tsp. hickory Liquid Smoke
3⅓ Tbsp. minced garlic
2 Tbsp. salt
½ tsp. black pepper
⅛ tsp. red pepper
⅛ tsp. chili powder

⅛ tsp. mace
⅛ tsp. allspice
½ tsp. dried thyme
1 Tbsp. paprika
¼ tsp. ground bay leaf
¼ tsp. ground sage
32 mm to 34 mm hog casings

Cut the casings into 3-yard lengths. Sprinkle the meat with the Liquid Smoke. Pass the meat once through the coarse disc. Mix together all the spices, sprinkle over the meat, and mix in well. Place the fine disc on grinder and make approximately 12" sausages. Tie off each sausage as it is made. Place in the refrigerator and allow to rest overnight. Slice ½" thick and use in gumbos or slice and cook in a skillet. Store in the refrigerator for up to 3 days or package and freeze.

Traditional Southern-Style Venison Breakfast Sausage

17 lbs. venison
8 lbs. boneless pork chops
¾ cup salt
6 Tbsp. black pepper
5 Tbsp. rubbed sage

2 Tbsp. red pepper (optional)
1 Tbsp. ground nutmeg
1 Tbsp. ground ginger
1 Tbsp. mace
29 mm to 32 mm hog casings

Cut the venison and pork into cubes and grind with a coarse grinding disc. Mix together all the ingredients and grind with a fine grinding disc. Form the sausage into patties or stuff into casings. Store in the refrigerator for up to 3 days or package and freeze.

Scandinavian Venison and Potato Sausage

4 lbs. venison, cubed
4 lbs. beef round steak, cubed
2 lbs. beef fat, cubed
5 lbs. ground raw potatoes

4 Tbsp. salt
1 Tbsp. garlic salt
3 large onions, ground
2 Tbsp. black pepper

Mix together the venison, beef, and fat and grind through a coarse disc. Mix in the remaining ingredients and stuff into casings through a fine disc, tying off into 18" to 20" links. Store in the refrigerator for up to 3 days or package and freeze. When ready to cook, place the thawed sausage in a skillet, cover with water, and cook over very low heat until the water has evaporated and the sausage browns.

Venison and Beef Chorizo Sausage

¾ lb. venison loin, cubed
¼ lb. beef fat, cubed
1 tsp. salt
2 Tbsp. chili powder
¼ tsp. cumin

½ tsp. ground oregano
3 garlic cloves, minced
2 Tbsp. apple cider vinegar
18 mm to 20 mm sheep casings (optional)

Mix together all the ingredients and grind twice through a fine disc. Wrap in plastic wrap and refrigerate overnight. Form into patties or stuff into small sheep casings. Cook as you would any other sausage. Store in the refrigerator for up to 3 days or package and freeze.

Venison, Pork, and Mutton Boerevors with Red Wine and Brandy Sausage

A variation on a traditional South African sausage.

1¼ lbs. boneless venison, cubed
1¼ lbs. boneless pork, cubed
2¼ lbs. boneless mutton, cubed
1¼ lbs. bacon, cubed
½ tsp. black pepper
¼ tsp. ground cloves

1 Tbsp. salt
¼ tsp. ground coriander
1 Tbsp. port or other sweet red wine
2 Tbsp. red wine vinegar
1 Tbsp. brandy
32 mm to 34 mm hog casings

Mix all the ingredients together and grind twice using a coarse disc. Lightly stuff 12" sausages during the second grinding. Cut in half when cooking. Place the sausages on a rack in the bottom of the refrigerator for about 12 hours before using. Store in the refrigerator for up to 3 days or package and freeze.

Basic and Mild-Flavored Venison Sausage

17 lbs. venison, cubed
8 lbs. ground pork, cubed
¾ cup salt
¼ cup fine black pepper

2 Tbsp. coarse black pepper
5 Tbsp. rubbed sage
28 mm or smaller hog casings

Cut the venison and pork into cubes and grind with a coarse grinding disc. Mix together all the ingredients and grind with a fine grinding disc. Form the sausage into patties or stuff into prepared casings. The sausage can be frozen as patties or in bulk after making. Store in the refrigerator for up to 3 days or package and freeze.

Brown Rice and Venison Boudin Sausage

This is a rather hot and spicy sausage. It is also a nontraditional Louisiana Boudin sausage recipe in that it calls for brown rice rather than white.

1 lb. venison liver, cubed
3 lbs. boneless pork butt, cubed
6 cups water
3 cups raw brown rice
2 bunches green onions, minced
4 onions, chopped fine
¼ cup minced parsley

2 Tbsp. minced garlic
2 Tbsp. salt
1 Tbsp. red pepper
2 tsp. black pepper
2 tsp. white pepper
32 mm to 35 mm hog casings

Place the venison liver and pork in separate saucepans, cover with water, bring to a boil, and reduce the heat. Simmer for 1 hour or until tender. Skim the foam and discard. Boil the water, add the rice, and stir several times. When the water begins to boil, reduce the heat to a low simmer, cover, and cook for 30 to 40 minutes or longer until all the water is absorbed. Remove the liver and pork and set aside to cool. Discard the liver cooking liquid. Save 2 cups of the pork cooking liquid. Mix together and grind the liver and the pork with a medium or coarse grinding disc.

Place the ground meat in a large bowl; add all the remaining ingredients along with the 2 cups of pork cooking liquid and mix together. Grind a second time and make into links about 1' long and tie on both ends. To serve, heat the oven to 350° F and bake for 10 to 15 minutes or until the skin begins to brown and crack. Store in the refrigerator for up to 3 days or package and freeze.

Moroccan Sausage with Currants and Venison

2½ lbs. venison
½ lb. beef fat
1 Tbsp. salt
1½ tsp. curry powder
1½ tsp. coarsely ground black pepper
½ tsp. ground cinnamon

½ tsp. ground thyme
½ cup currants
½ cup pomegranate juice
1 Tbsp. minced garlic
30 mm to 32 mm hog casings

Grind the meats through a small disc. Mix together the remaining ingredients, pour over the meat, and mix well. Stuff into casings and twist or tie into 5" lengths. Store in the refrigerator for up to 3 days or package and freeze.

Grilled Bratwurst Venison Sausage

2½ lbs. venison, cubed
½ lb. pork fat, cubed
¼ tsp. ground allspice
½ tsp. crushed caraway seeds

½ tsp. dried marjoram
1 tsp. white pepper
1 tsp. salt
35 mm to 38 mm beef rounds

Mix the meats and grind with a fine disc. Mix in the remaining ingredients and regrind with a fine disc, stuff into rounds, and tie/twist into 4" to 5" links. Store in the refrigerator for up to 3 days or package and freeze. Best cooked by pan-frying or grilling.

Grecian Loukanika Venison Sausage

1 lb. venison, ground
½ lb. fresh pork rind, boiled for 2 hours,
    drained, and ground
½ lb. pork fatback, ground
1 tsp. salt
grated rind of 1 navel orange
1 tsp. crushed dried marjoram or thyme

1 bay leaf, ground
⅓ cup red wine
1 tsp. ground allspice or coriander
1 tsp. black pepper
2 garlic cloves, minced very finely
28 mm or smaller hog casings

Grind the venison, pork rind, and fatback through a fine disc. Spread the ground meats in a large pan, sprinkle with remaining ingredients, and knead thoroughly. Grind with a medium disc and pinch every 3½" to 4", and allow a space to form between the links. The sausages can be packaged and frozen at this point. To cook, poach in water for 1 hour and fry. Store in the refrigerator for up to 3 days or package and freeze.

White Boudin Venison Sausage

2½ lbs. venison, cubed
½ lb. lean pork, cubed
water
4 cups chopped onions, divided
8 peppercorns
1 bay leaf, crumbled
5 tsp. salt, divided
1 cup chopped bell pepper

1 cup chopped parsley
½ cup chopped green onions
1 Tbsp. minced garlic
1½ cups cooked short-grain white rice
1 Tbsp. chopped dried sage leaves
1½ tsp. red pepper
½ tsp. black pepper
32 mm to 35 mm hog casings

Place the venison and pork in a large pot and cover with 1" of water. Bring to a boil and mix in 2 cups of the onions, the peppercorns, the bay leaf, and 1 tsp. of the salt. Reduce the heat and simmer for 1½ hours. Remove the meat and mix with the remaining onions, bell pepper, parsley, green onions, and garlic. Grind with a fine disc. Mix in the rice, sage, peppers, and remaining salt. Mix together and beat until smooth and fluffy. Use a coarse disc and stuff into casings. Store in the refrigerator for up to 3 days or package and freeze. To cook, prick the casings with a sharp fork every few inches. Melt butter and coil the sausage in the center of the skillet. Cook, uncovered, until both sides are brown.

Garlic and Spiced Venison Sausage

1 small white onion, chopped
2 lbs. venison, cubed
¾ lb. pork fat, cubed
4 large garlic cloves, minced
2 tsp. salt
1 tsp. black pepper

1 tsp. ground sage
½ tsp. ground thyme
¼ tsp. ground nutmeg
¼ tsp. ground ginger
⅛ tsp. ground allspice
38 mm to 42 mm hog casings (optional)

Mix all the ingredients and grind once with a coarse grinding disc. Mix well and grind again with a fine grinding disc. Stuff into casings or make into patties. The sausage can also be made in bulk and frozen by forming it into a log and rolling it in plastic wrap. Store in the refrigerator for up to 3 days or package and freeze.

Spiced Venison Breakfast Sausage

11 lbs. venison, cubed
5 lbs. pork butt, cubed
½ cup coarse salt (kosher)
5 tsp. white pepper
3 Tbsp. rubbed sage
1½ tsp. ground ginger

5 tsp. ground nutmeg
5 tsp. ground thyme
4 tsp. red pepper
3 cups ice water
22 mm to 24 mm sheep casings

Grind the venison and pork through a small disc and refrigerate for 2 hours. Mix in the remaining ingredients and grind a second time into casings. Hang the sausages in the refrigerator to dry. Store in the refrigerator for up to 3 days or package and freeze.

Frozen Hot-Sweet Italian Venison Sausage

11 lbs. venison, cubed
5 lbs. pork butt, cubed
2¾ cups very cold red wine
7 Tbsp. coarse salt (kosher)
7 Tbsp. whole fennel seeds
6 Tbsp. black pepper
1 Tbsp. ground coriander

3 Tbsp. red pepper flakes (optional)
2 Tbsp. oregano
1½ tsp. sugar
1½ tsp. caraway seeds
1 tsp. Accent (MSG)
32 mm to 35 mm hog casings (optional)

Grind the venison and pork through a ¼" disc and refrigerate for 2 hours. Mix in the remaining ingredients and grind a second time into casings. Hang in the refrigerator to dry. The sausages can also be made into patties. Store in the refrigerator for up to 3 days or package and freeze.

Sicilian Venison Sausage

4½ lbs. venison, cubed
½ lb. pork fat, cubed
2½ Tbsp. salt
3 tsp. black pepper
3 tsp. fennel seed

1 Tbsp. red pepper flakes (optional)
2 garlic cloves, minced
1 tsp. anise seeds
35 mm to 38 mm beef rounds

Grind the meats together with a coarse disc. Mix in the remaining ingredients and stuff into casings. Twist off every 4" or 6". Store in the refrigerator for up to 3 days or package and freeze.

Linked Tequila Chorizo Venison Sausage

Mexican sausage is made with fresh pork, and the Spanish version is made with smoked pork. Try using smoked, but raw, venison. Links can be fried or grilled, or the casings can be removed and the meat crumbled. This sausage can also be used in casseroles, soups, stews, and enchiladas.

2 lbs. venison, cubed	1 tsp. ground cinnamon
10 oz. pork fat or beef suet, cubed	1½ tsp. ground cumin
2 med. onions, chopped	1 tsp. ground oregano
8 garlic cloves, pressed	½ tsp. allspice
½ cup apple cider vinegar	1 Tbsp. salt
¼ cup tequila	22 mm to 24 mm sheep casings

Grind the meats with a coarse disc, mix in the remaining ingredients, grind with a fine disc, and stuff into casings, twisting off at 4" intervals. Wrap the sausages in plastic wrap and refrigerate for 24 hours. Store in the refrigerator for up to 3 days or package and freeze.

Hungarian Venison and Raisin Sausage

This is a mild and fragrant Hungarian sausage. The paprika makes it look fiery hot, but it is quite mild.

¾ lb. ground venison	¼ tsp. ground black pepper
¼ lb. ground boneless pork chops	½ garlic clove, minced finely
1½ tsp. ground nutmeg	½ garlic clove, boiled and mashed
⅓ tsp. allspice	¼ cup white raisins (sultanas)
1½ tsp. paprika	36 mm to 38 mm hog casings (optional)
⅛ tsp. salt	

Mix all the ingredients and grind together through a coarse disc. Grind a second time with a fine disc into casings or package in bulk. Store in the refrigerator for up to 3 days or package and freeze.

Chipolata Venison Cocktail Sausages

7 lbs. venison, cubed
1½ lbs. pork fat, cubed
1 Tbsp. sage
1 tsp. dried onion flakes
1 tsp. thyme
1 tsp. mace

1½ Tbsp. salt
6 oz. plain bread crumbs
1 Tbsp. black pepper
2 cups cold water
26 mm to 28 mm sheep casings

Grind the meats together with a coarse disc. Mix the remaining ingredients into the cold water. Place the meats in a food processor to emulsify and then place in the refrigerator to chill. Mix in the spices. Using a fine disc, stuff the mixture into casings and tie off into 1" links. Grill, sauté, or cook in the oven and serve at once. Store in the refrigerator for up to 3 days or package and freeze.

Sujuk Made with Venison

A spicy and sour Lebanese sausage.

cheesecloth
4 lbs. finely ground venison
2 lbs. finely ground beef chuck
⅔ cup ground cumin
5½ Tbsp. ground allspice
3½ tsp. garlic powder

3½ Tbsp. minced garlic
2 Tbsp. red pepper flakes
2½ Tbsp. paprika
2½ Tbsp. salt
cotton twine

Cut six pieces of cheesecloth into 5" × 15" pieces, fold, and sew three sides together. Place all the ingredients in a large glass bowl and mix well. Cover and refrigerate overnight. Heat a skillet. Remove the meat from the refrigerator and divide into 6 portions. Divide each portion into 8 smaller portions, and place each set of 8 in a cheesecloth bag so that the meat mixture comes to within 3" of the top of the bag. Tie the bags shut with cotton twine and flatten them with a rolling pin to smooth out the filling. Hang the bags in the refrigerator for 7 to 10 days until the meat is dried. Remove the cheesecloth, package, and freeze. To serve, place in the refrigerator overnight to thaw. Slice thin, briefly cook on both sides, and serve with wedges of warm pita bread.

Refrigerated Polish Venison Sausage Links

1½ lbs. venison, cubed
½ lb. pork fat, cubed
½ tsp. black pepper
1½ tsp. sugar
½ tsp. dried thyme
¼ tsp. dried basil

¼ tsp. garlic powder
¼ tsp. whole mustard seeds
½ tsp. dried marjoram
⅛ cup ice water, divided
35 mm to 38 mm hog casings

Mix the meats and pass through a coarse grinding disc. Mix the sugar and spices in a separate bowl and divide into 2 equal parts. Mix half of the spices into the meat, then half of the water. Mix in the remaining spices and water. Cover and refrigerate overnight. Stuff into casings, tying every 8". Store in the refrigerator for up to 3 days or package and freeze. To cook, grill, steam, or fry.

Krautwurst Venison and Sauerkraut Sausage

2 lbs. venison burger
½ jar sauerkraut, ground
4 small potatoes
3 small onions
1 cup unseasoned bread crumbs
2 eggs, beaten
1 Tbsp. salt

1 Tbsp. black pepper
1 tsp. caraway seeds
½ tsp. ground sage
½ tsp. marjoram
½ tsp. thyme
38 mm to 42 mm hog casings

Grind the venison with a medium disc. Mix all the ingredients together. Regrind through a small disc, stuff into casings, and tie off into 12" links. Store in the refrigerator for up to 3 days or package and freeze.

Luganega Venison and Parmesan Cheese Sausage

3 lbs. venison, cubed
2 lbs. pork butt, cubed
2 garlic cloves, minced
1 Tbsp. minced fresh oregano
2 tsp. black pepper

1⅓ cups grated Parmesan cheese
2 tsp. salt
¼ cup dry white wine
38 mm to 42 mm hog casings

Mix all the ingredients with the venison and pork. Grind through a small disc and stuff into two coils. Cover and refrigerate the coils overnight. Store in the refrigerator for up to 3 days or package and freeze.

Lunenburg Venison Sausage

1 deer liver
deer lights (lungs)
2 Tbsp. salt
boiling water
2 deer tongues
1 deer heart
2 deer kidneys

2" strip of pork belly fat
2 Tbsp. allspice
2 tsp. black pepper
1 cup minced fresh summer savory
4 large onions, cubed
38 mm to 42 mm hog casings

Soak the deer liver and lights in salt and water for 1 hour to remove the blood. Pour boiling water over the tongue and remove the skin. Cut all the meats and fat in small pieces and boil for 1 hour. When cooked, place the meat in the refrigerator until cool enough to handle. Grind the meats, along with the cracklings from the pork, through a coarse disc. Grind the onions through a fine disc and fry in a small amount of fat until just brown. Mix together all the ingredients and stuff into casings using a fine disc. Store in the refrigerator for up to 3 days or package and freeze.

Grilled Venison Boerevors Sausage Links

A traditional South African sausage.

3½ lbs. venison, cubed
3½ lbs. pork butt, cubed
1 lb. bacon, diced
2 Tbsp. salt
1 tsp. pepper
2 tsp. grated nutmeg
1 tsp. ground cloves

¼ tsp. ground thyme
¼ tsp. ground allspice
½ cup red wine vinegar
1 garlic clove, minced
¼ cup Worcestershire sauce
32 mm to 35 mm hog casings

Cut the meats into cubes and mix with the remaining ingredients. Grind using a medium grinding disc and stuff into casings. Grill or fry on both sides over coals. Serve warm. Store in the refrigerator for up to 3 days or package and freeze.

Pennsylvania Dutch Christmas Venison Sausage

3½ lbs. ground venison
1½ lbs. smoked bacon, ground
½ cup brown sugar
2 tsp. salt
1 tsp. garlic powder
1 tsp. onion powder
½ tsp. ground coriander

2 tsp. black pepper
¼ tsp. ground allspice
¼ tsp. ground nutmeg
¼ tsp. ground cinnamon
¼ tsp. ground savory
⅛ tsp. ground cumin

Mix the venison and bacon together and grind with a coarse disc. Shape into patties and fry. Store in the refrigerator for up to 3 days or package and freeze.

Irish-Style Venison Sausage

A variation on a traditional Irish sausage.

1½ lbs. venison, cubed
½ lb. pork fat, cubed
1 oz. unseasoned bread crumbs
½ tsp. ground allspice
1 tsp. salt
¼ tsp. black pepper
⅛ tsp. dried sage or marjoram

⅛ to ½ tsp. ground ginger
⅛ to ½ tsp. mace
⅛ to ½ tsp. ground nutmeg
⅛ to ½ tsp. ground cloves
⅛ to ½ tsp. cayenne pepper (optional)
32 to 35 mm hog casings

Fine-grind the meats once, mix in the remaining ingredients, fine-grind a second time, and stuff into casings. Store in the refrigerator for up to 3 days or package and freeze.

Sucuk—Turkish Venison Sausage

2 lbs. finely ground venison
¼ lb. beef fat
1¼ tsp. black pepper
½ tsp. paprika
½ tsp. cayenne pepper
¾ tsp. ground allspice
1¼ Tbsp. salt

⅛ tsp. ground cinnamon
⅛ tsp. ground cloves
⅛ tsp. mace
⅛ tsp. ground nutmeg
1 tsp. curry powder
¾ tsp. cumin
1½ garlic cloves, minced

Mix all the ingredients and grind through a coarse disc. Make into flat patties 2½" in diameter, place on a piece of waxed paper, and freeze. When frozen, stack in piles of four with two pieces of waxed paper between each patty. Store in the refrigerator for up to 3 days or package and freeze.

Mergeza—Spicy Tunisian Venison Sausage

2½ lbs. venison, cubed
½ lb. lean pork, cubed
1 Tbsp. salt
2 tsp. coarsely ground black pepper
1½ tsp. cayenne pepper
1½ Tbsp. cumin
¼ cup paprika

1 tsp. ground cinnamon
1 tsp. ground ginger
1 tsp. thyme leaves
1½ Tbsp. minced garlic
½ cup pomegranate juice
28 mm or smaller hog casings

Grind the venison and pork once through the ⅛" disc. Mix together all the remaining ingredients; pour over the meat and mix well. Grind through the same disc and stuff into casings. Twist or tie into 5" links. Store in the refrigerator for up to 3 days or package and freeze.

Portuguese Venison Sausage

1½ lbs. venison, cubed
½ lb. boneless pork chops, cubed
1 tsp. salt
¼ tsp. black pepper
½ tsp. red pepper flakes (optional)

8 cloves garlic, minced
⅛ tsp. paprika
¼ cup water
1 Tbsp. red wine vinegar
30 mm to 32 mm hog casings

Combine the meats in a large tray and set aside. Combine the remaining ingredients, pour over the meat, and mix in well. Cover with aluminum foil and refrigerate for 2 days. Remix twice a day. Through a fine disc, stuff into casings, making 10" links. Dry links and hang in the refrigerator for an hour. Cook or package and freeze.

Epping Venison Sausage

8 lbs. crustless bread
water
4 oz. white pepper
13 oz. salt
¼ oz. ground nutmeg

¼ oz. ground ginger
¼ oz. ground marjoram
23 lbs. venison, cubed
7 lbs. pork fat, cubed
24 mm to 26 mm sheep casings

Soak the bread in water and press to remove excess water. Mix the seasonings with the meats and grind with a fine disc. Knead in the bread. Grind through a fine disc into casings and twist off into 6" to 8" links. Store in the refrigerator for up to 3 days or package and freeze.

Yugoslavian Cevapcici Venison Sausage

1 lb. ground venison	1 tsp. paprika
1 lb. ground lamb, pork, or veal	1 large garlic clove, crushed
1 tsp. ground marjoram	1 egg, beaten
1 tsp. salt	5 to 6 drops Tabasco sauce, or to taste
⅛ tsp. black pepper	3 to 4 Tbsp. beef broth

Combine all the ingredients and grind through a fine disc. Shape into sausages about ⅜" thick and 4" long. Cook slowly until well browned. Turn the sausages often; they should be cooked until brown on the outside and slightly pink on the inside. According to tradition, these sausages are served on a bed of chopped onions, with tiny hot peppers, mixed vegetables, and heavy bread. Store in the refrigerator for up to 3 days or package and freeze.

Venison Chipolata

Chipolata is an Old World French sausage. The name means "little fingers."

7½ lbs. venison, cubed	1 tsp. ground thyme
1 lb. pork fat, cubed	1 tsp. mace
1½ Tbsp. salt	2 cups water
1 Tbsp. black pepper	6 oz. unseasoned bread crumbs
1 Tbsp. ground sage	20 mm to 24 mm sheep casings
1 tsp. onion flakes	

Grind the venison and pork fat through a ⅜" disc. Mix the spices in the water and place in the refrigerator to chill. Using a food processor, emulsify the meat, then place in the refrigerator to chill. In a mixer, add the seasonings and the water to the meat, then slowly mix in the bread crumbs. Return to the refrigerator to chill. Grind again and stuff into casings, making small 2" links. Wrap the links and place back in the refrigerator to cool. Store in the refrigerator for up to 3 days or package and freeze.

Ohio Valley Venison Sausage

1 oz. unseasoned or white bread crumbs
8 Tbsp. hot water
½ tsp. freshly grated nutmeg
¼ tsp. salt
⅛ tsp. pepper

1 lb. venison, cubed
½ side smoked bacon, cubed
6 oz. pork fat, cubed
32 mm to 34 mm hog casings

Soak the bread crumbs in water. Add the nutmeg, salt, and pepper, then mix all the ingredients together. Grind with a fine disc and stuff into one long coil. The sausage can be coiled inside a large skillet, covered, and cooked or packaged and frozen. Store in the refrigerator for up to 3 days or package and freeze.

Linguica—Portuguese Fried Venison Sausage

2 lbs. venison, cubed
2 lbs. pork fat, cubed
3 tsp. salt
6 garlic cloves, minced
5 small dried hot peppers, crushed
  (optional)
1 Tbsp. coriander

1 Tbsp. paprika
½ tsp. ground cinnamon
½ tsp. ground cloves
½ tsp. ground allspice
¼ cup apple cider vinegar
½ cup cold water
24 mm to 26 mm sheep casings (optional)

Cut the venison and fat into cubes. Grind with a coarse disc. Place the ground meat in a large pan and mix in the remaining ingredients. Cover and chill in the refrigerator overnight. Shape into patties or stuff into links. Store in the refrigerator for up to 3 days or package and freeze.

Grilled Venison Liver and Smoked Bacon Links

½ lb. venison liver, cubed
½ lb. boneless pork chops, cubed
¼ cup chopped fresh sage
2 Tbsp. minced garlic
¼ cup whole capers, drained

¼ tsp. black pepper
½ cup dry white wine
½ lb. smoked bacon, cubed
32 mm to 35 mm hog casings

Combine the venison liver and pork with the sage, garlic, capers, pepper, and white wine. Cover and refrigerate for 4 hours. Remove the mixture from the refrigerator and add the bacon. Place the mixture in a food processor and pulse until well combined but not quite smooth, or pass through a fine disc two times. Grind a third time and stuff into casings, forming one long link. Coil the sausage on a hot grill or under a preheated broiler and grill for 5 to 6 minutes on each side. Store in the refrigerator for up to 3 days or package and freeze.

Sai Grog—Thai Venison Sausages

¾ lb. venison, cubed
¼ lb. pork fat, cubed
¼ cup minced garlic
½ cup steamed rice
1 tsp. black pepper

1 tsp. salt
1 tsp. Accent (MSG)
¼ cup lime juice
2 Tbsp. *nuoc mam* (fish sauce)
24 mm to 26 mm sheep casings (optional)

Grind the meats through a fine disc. Combine the ingredients, cover, and refrigerate overnight. Stuff sausage casings, form patties, or roll into ¾" meatballs. Steam the sausages for 30 minutes or—when made into meatballs—deep-fry. Store in the refrigerator for up to 3 days or package and freeze.

Tuscan Venison Sausage

A typical sausage of northern Italy, in the area of Lucca.

2 Tbsp. kosher salt
1½ tsp. coarse black pepper
2 Tbsp. sugar
4 lbs. ground venison
1 lb. ground pork fat
1 tsp. garlic powder

¾ tsp. mace
½ tsp. ground coriander
¼ tsp. cayenne pepper
½ cup ice water
30 mm to 32 mm hog casings (optional)

Pulverize the salt, black pepper, and sugar in a food processor. In a large bowl, mix together the venison, fat, garlic powder, mace, coriander, cayenne, and ice water. Mix in the ground ingredients. Stuff the sausage mixture through a fine disc into the casings and twist off in 3" lengths. The sausage also can be formed into patties or rolled into logs. Store in the refrigerator for up to 3 days or package and freeze.

Satay—Indonesian Marinated Venison Sausage

½ lbs. venison loin
¼ lb. pork butt
2 garlic cloves, chopped
½ cup chopped green onions
1 Tbsp. chopped fresh ginger
1 cup roasted and salted peanuts
2 Tbsp. lemon juice

2 Tbsp. honey
½ cup soy sauce
2 tsp. crushed coriander seed
1 tsp. red pepper flakes (optional)
½ cup chicken broth
½ cup melted butter
24 mm to 26 mm sheep casings

Cut the meats into 1" to 2" cubes and refrigerate. Place the garlic, onions, ginger, peanuts, lemon juice, honey, soy sauce, coriander, and red pepper in a food processor and puree until almost smooth. Add the broth and butter and mix again. Place the venison in a resealable plastic bag and pour the mixture over the meat. Marinate overnight in the refrigerator. Remove the venison, pour the marinade into a small saucepan, bring to a boil, and cook for 5 minutes. Reserve ¼ cup to brush on the sausages as they cook. Stuff through a fine disc into casings. In a small saucepan, boil the remaining marinade liquid for several minutes, then set aside to cool; reserve to use as dipping sauce. Store in the refrigerator for up to 3 days or package and freeze. To cook, skewer and grill or broil the venison until brown on both sides. Turn and brush with the cooked marinade.

Sai Grog Chiang Mai—Thai Venison Sausage

4 large dried Thai chilies, soaked in water
  until soft
½ tsp. salt
1 Tbsp. minced lemon grass
1 tsp. minced cilantro roots
1 tsp. grated lime zest
½ tsp. minced galangal (Thai ginger)

2 tsp. minced garlic
2 Tbsp. minced red onions
1½ cups ground venison
½ cup ground boneless pork chops
2 Tbsp. minced cilantro leaves
2 Tbsp. *nuoc mam* (fish sauce)
22 mm to 24 mm sheep casings

Combine the softened dried chilies, salt, lemon grass, cilantro roots, lime zest, galangal, garlic, and onions in a food processor and grind to a paste. Mix together the chili paste, meats, cilantro leaves, and fish sauce. Tie a knot at one end of the casing, then use a fine disc to stuff the casing into one long link. Tie another knot to close. Prick air bubbles with a pin.

Grill or fry over medium-low heat until golden brown and fully cooked. While cooking, prick a few more holes to prevent the sausage from splitting. Slice into ½" thick pieces and serve with cooked sticky rice and raw vegetables. Store in the refrigerator for up to 3 days or package and freeze.

Note: Dried Thai chilies, lemon grass, cilantro roots, galangal (Thai ginger), and *nuoc mam* (fish sauce) can be found in any good Thai or Vietnamese market.

Lorne Sliced Scottish Venison Sausage

2 lbs. finely ground venison
2 lbs. finely ground pork fat
3 cups unseasoned bread crumbs
2 tsp. black pepper

2 tsp. ground nutmeg
3 tsp. ground coriander
3 tsp. salt
1 cup water

Mix all the ingredients. Line a 10" × 4" × 3" pan with aluminum foil so that the foil overlaps the edges. Two pans may be required. Smooth the venison into the pan and place in the freezer until just beginning to set. Lift the edges of the foil, remove the sausage from the pan, and cut into slices. Store in the refrigerator for up to 3 days or package and freeze.

To cook, fry the slices in a little oil until brown on both sides. Serve with bacon and eggs or grilled with onions on split large dinner rolls.

Red Wine and Leftover Venison Roast Sausage

2¾ lbs. venison roast, cubed
1½ lbs. bacon, cubed
¾ cup Chianti or other Italian red wine
3 Tbsp. minced fresh parsley

4 tsp. minced garlic
3½ tsp. salt
1⅛ tsp. black pepper
34 mm to 36 mm hog casings

Mix all the ingredients, grind with a coarse disc, and stuff into casings. Knot twice between links or tie with string twice at 4" intervals. Cut the sausage into links. It can be packaged and frozen at this point. To cook, prick the sausages several times with a short fork and grill on both sides for about 10 minutes. Store in the refrigerator for up to 3 days or package and freeze.

Spicy and Hot Tunisian Mergeza Sausage with Venison

2½ lbs. venison
½ lb. beef fat
1 Tbsp. salt
1½ Tbsp. cumin
2 tsp. coarsely ground black pepper
¼ cup paprika
1½ tsp. cayenne pepper

1 tsp. cinnamon
½ cup pomegranate juice
1½ Tbsp. minced garlic
1 tsp. ground ginger
1 tsp. thyme leaves
30 mm to 34 mm hog casings

Grind the meats through a medium disc. Mix together the remaining ingredients, pour over the meats, and mix in. Grind through a medium disc into casings and twist or tie into 5" links. Store in the refrigerator for up to 3 days or package and freeze.

Italian Parmesan and Venison Sausage

4 lbs. venison, cubed
2 lbs. pork fat or beef suet, cubed
1½ cups grated Parmesan cheese
¼ cup finely chopped parsley
2 tsp. cayenne pepper

1½ tsp. salt
1 tsp. black pepper
1 Tbsp. water
32 mm to 35 mm hog casings (optional)

Combine all the ingredients, except water, in a large bowl. Toss the mixture with the water to coat. Grind with a coarse disc and stuff into casings or shape into patties. Store in the refrigerator for up to 3 days or package and freeze.

Small Venison Sausages with Lemon and Spices

½ lb. venison, cubed
½ lb. pork fat, cubed
½ lb. lean veal, cubed
1 cup unseasoned bread crumbs
grated rind of 1 lemon
¼ tsp. ground sage
¼ tsp. ground marjoram

¼ tsp. ground thyme
⅛ tsp. summer savory
½ tsp. black pepper
4 tsp. salt
⅛ tsp. freshly grated nutmeg
22 mm to 24 mm sheep casings (optional)

Grind the meats twice with a fine disc. Mix the remaining ingredients together in a separate bowl. Spread out the meat, sprinkle with the spices, and mix well. Shape into a loaf, cover, and refrigerate overnight. Either make into links or shape into patties. Store in the refrigerator for up to 3 days or package and freeze.

Diet-Healthy Venison Sausage

Even though venison is very low in fat and cholesterol, it is not completely fat- and cholesterol-free. The last six recipes in this chapter are as low in fat, salt, and cholesterol as any homemade venison sausage recipe can be.

Try making other low-cholesterol/fat/salt sausage by deleting the pork or fat product and experimenting with salt and sugar substitutes and mushrooms or tofu. When experimenting with a salt substitute, begin by using an amount one quarter that of the salt recommended by the recipe.

Diet-healthy venison sausage will not taste like the country sausage that you grew up with. Traditional sausages derive much of their flavor from pork fat, and the texture and taste of pork fat cannot be completely duplicated.

If you are on a restrictive diet, these six sausages will provide you with a means to enjoy sausage and still be healthy. It is recommended that you first show the recipe to your physician or health-care professional and get his or her approval.

Because these sausages do not have added fat, they are best served as fried or grilled patties. When overcooked or stuffed into links, they have a tendency to become dry.

Low-Fat/Low-Sodium Venison and Mushroom Sausage

Similar in flavor to traditional county breakfast sausage.

2 lbs. venison, cubed	1 tsp. cayenne pepper (optional)
1 onion, chopped	1 tsp. ground marjoram
¾ lb. mushrooms, cubed	1 tsp. ground thyme
2 cloves garlic, minced	1 tsp. ground basil
1¼ tsp. salt (optional)	1 Tbsp. ground sage (optional)
1 tsp. black pepper	3 Tbsp. minced fresh parsley
1 tsp. chili powder	3 Tbsp. safflower or canola oil

Grind the venison, onion, and mushrooms separately with a medium disc. Mix all the ingredients together and pass through a coarse disc. Shape the sausage into a 3" diameter log; wrap in two layers of plastic wrap and tie off at one end. Gently bounce sausage on the tied end to remove air and tie off on the other end. Allow the sausage to rest in the refrigerator overnight. Either partially freeze and slice into patties or freeze the package. To prepare, allow to partially thaw and cut into ½" thick patties. Place the patties on a cookie sheet and place in the freezer until hard. Fry or grill the frozen patties, but do not overcook, because the moisture in the sausages will evaporate rather quickly. Store in the refrigerator for up to 3 days or package and freeze.

English Low-Fat Venison Sausage

English Sausage Seasoning:
5 tsp. white pepper
2½ tsp. mace
2¼ tsp. salt (optional)
2 tsp. ground ginger
2 tsp. ground sage
½ tsp. ground nutmeg

Sausage:
2½ lbs. venison, cubed
1 lb. mushrooms, cubed
1½ cups dry unseasoned bread crumbs
1½ cups unsalted canned chicken broth
¼ cup canola or safflower oil
3½ tsp. English Sausage Seasoning

Mix together the sausage seasoning. Grind the venison and mushrooms separately with a medium disc. Mix all the ingredients together and pass through a coarse disc. Shape the sausage into a 3" diameter log; wrap in two layers of plastic wrap and tie off at one end. Gently bounce the sausage on the tied end to remove air and tie off on the other end. Allow the sausage to rest in the refrigerator overnight. Either partially freeze and slice into patties or freeze the package. To prepare, allow to partially thaw and cut into ½" thick patties. Place the patties on a cookie sheet and place in the freezer until hard. Fry or grill the frozen patties, but do not overcook, because the moisture in the sausages will evaporate rather quickly. Store in the refrigerator for up to 3 days or package and freeze.

Syrian-Style Venison Sausage with Red Wine and Pine Nuts

1 lb. venison, finely ground
¾ lb. mushrooms, cubed
2 Tbsp. chopped fresh tarragon
2 tsp. ground coriander
1 tsp. ground allspice

2 Tbsp. dry red wine
¼ cup whole pine nuts
1 tsp. salt (optional)
½ tsp. black pepper
3 Tbsp. canola or safflower oil

Grind the venison and mushrooms separately with a medium disc. Mix all the ingredients together and pass through a coarse disc. Shape the sausage into a 3" diameter log; wrap in two layers of plastic wrap and tie off at one end. Gently bounce the sausage on the tied end to remove air and tie off on the other end. Allow the sausage to rest in the refrigerator overnight. Either partially freeze and slice into patties or freeze the package. To prepare, allow to partially thaw and cut into ½" thick patties. Place the patties on a cookie sheet and place in the freezer until hard. Fry or grill the frozen patties, but do not overcook, because the moisture in the sausages will evaporate rather quickly. Store in the refrigerator for up to 3 days or package and freeze.

Tofu Venison Sausage

This sausage has a slightly sweet taste with a soft aroma of spices. Cut cooled patties into quarters and serve as an appetizer along with a strong cheese such as Swiss, Gorgonzola, Stilton, or blue.

1½ lbs. venison
12 oz. firm tofu, chopped
1 tsp. salt (optional)
½ tsp. sugar substitute (spoon-for-spoon equivalent)
½ tsp. black pepper
⅛ tsp. ground ginger

¼ tsp. ground cinnamon
¼ tsp. ground cloves
⅛ tsp. ground nutmeg
⅛ tsp. red pepper flakes (optional)
1 Tbsp. minced fresh cilantro
3 Tbsp. safflower or canola oil

Grind the venison with a medium disc. Mix all the ingredients together and pass through a coarse disc. Shape the sausage into a 3" diameter log; wrap in two layers of plastic wrap and tie off at one end. Gently bounce the sausage on the tied end to remove air and tie off on the other end. Allow the sausage to rest in the refrigerator overnight. Either partially freeze and slice into patties or freeze the package. To prepare, allow to partially thaw and cut into ½" thick patties. Place the patties on a cookie sheet and place in the freezer until hard. Fry or grill the frozen patties, but do not overcook, because the moisture in the sausages will evaporate rather quickly. Store in the refrigerator for up to 3 days or package and freeze.

Healthy Creole Venison Sausage

4 lbs. venison, cubed
1½ lbs. mushrooms, cubed
2 cups minced onion
1½ Tbsp. minced garlic
1½ tsp. red pepper
½ tsp. chili powder
1 tsp. red pepper flakes (optional)

8 tsp. salt (optional)
2 tsp. black pepper
2 tsp. crushed dried thyme leaves
5 Tbsp. chopped fresh parsley
3 bay leaves, crushed finely
½ tsp. ground allspice
5 Tbsp. canola or safflower oil

Grind the venison, onions, and mushrooms separately with a medium disc. Mix all the ingredients together and pass through a coarse disc. Shape the sausage into a 3" diameter log; wrap in two layers of plastic wrap and tie off at one end. Gently bounce the sausage on the tied end to remove air and tie off on the other end. Allow the sausage to rest in the refrigerator overnight. Either partially freeze and slice into patties or freeze the package. To prepare, allow to partially thaw and cut into ½" thick patties. Place the patties on a cookie sheet and place in the freezer until hard. Fry or grill the frozen patties, but do not overcook, because the moisture in the sausages will evaporate rather quickly. Store in the refrigerator for up to 3 days or package and freeze.

Tofu and Garlic Venison Sausage Patties

2 lbs. boneless venison, chopped
1 lb. firm tofu, chopped
1 small white onion, chopped
4 large garlic cloves, minced
2 tsp. salt
1 tsp. black pepper

1 tsp. ground sage
⅛ tsp. filé powder
½ tsp. ground thyme
¼ tsp. ground nutmeg
¼ tsp. ground ginger
⅛ tsp. ground allspice

Mix all the ingredients and grind once with a coarse grinding disc. Shape the sausage into a 3" diameter log; wrap in two layers of plastic wrap and tie off at one end. Gently bounce the sausage on the tied end to remove air and tie off on the other end. Allow the sausage to rest in the refrigerator overnight. Either partially freeze and slice into patties or freeze the package. To prepare, allow to partially thaw and cut into ½" thick patties. Place the patties on a cookie sheet and place in the freezer until hard. Fry or grill the frozen patties, but do not overcook, because the moisture in the sausage will evaporate rather quickly. Store in the refrigerator for up to 3 days or package and freeze.

10

Quick-Cured Venison Sausage Recipes

Quick-cured sausages are easily made in your kitchen by using dependable home cures that are normally available in the salt or canning and freezing sections of major shopping markets, large discount shopping centers, and rural grocery stores. The appendix lists many mail-order companies that carry Morton cures.

Even though these sausages have a curing agent added, they are first cooked and then can be refrigerated for only up to three days. After that, they will need to be packaged and frozen.

Delicious traditional homemade venison sausages such as Bologna, Salami, Andouille, Pepperoni, and Braunschweiger are within the reach of anyone who has a hand meat grinder, a kitchen, and a desire to make their own sausage.

After you have made a few traditional sausages, try making the unique spicy Chinese bean sausage Laap Ch'eung, Saigkawk Na'am—Northern Thai/Lao Rice Venison Sausage, or Quick and Easy Venison Pepperoni.

Note: Some recipes call for "level teaspoons" of cure. Do not pack the measuring spoon. Use a straightedge knife to slide across and level the top.

Three-Day Venison Summer Sausage

5 lbs. venison burger
6 tsp. pickling salt
2½ tsp. mustard seed

2½ tsp. coarsely ground pepper
3 garlic cloves, minced
1 tsp. hickory smoke salt

Mix all the ingredients, cover, and refrigerate for 24 hours. Mix again and refrigerate for 24 hours. Shape into 5 logs, place in an ovenproof dish, and bake for 8 hours at 165° F. Turn every 2 hours. Store in the refrigerator for up to 3 days or package and freeze.

Overnight Venison Salami

¾ lb. venison, cubed
¼ lb. pork butt, cubed
1½ level tsp. Morton Tender Quick mix*
1 tsp. salt
½ tsp. black pepper

½ tsp. whole mustard seed
⅛ tsp. ground ginger
⅛ tsp. ground nutmeg
½ tsp. garlic powder
4 drops Liquid Smoke, or to taste

Mix all the ingredients and divide into two equal portions. Mold each portion into a sausage 1½" in diameter and wrap with aluminum foil. Place in the refrigerator overnight. Unwrap the sausages, lay in a shallow baking pan, and bake at 325° F until a meat thermometer inserted into the center of a sausage reads 160° F. Store in the refrigerator for up to 3 days or package and freeze.

Italian-Style Baked Venison Sausage

¾ lb. lean ground venison, cubed
¼ lb. boneless pork chops, cubed
1½ level tsp. Morton Tender Quick mix*
3 Tbsp. grated Parmesan cheese
½ tsp. finely ground black pepper
½ tsp. coarsely ground black pepper
½ tsp. whole mustard seed

1 tsp. finely crushed dry basil leaves
1 tsp. finely crushed dry oregano leaves
⅛ tsp. onion powder
¼ tsp. dehydrated onion flakes
¼ tsp. garlic powder
3 Tbsp. Chianti or other Italian dry red wine

Thoroughly mix all the ingredients and grind through a fine disc. Separate the mixture into two equal portions. Form each portion into sausages 1½" in diameter. Wrap in plastic wrap or aluminum foil and place in the refrigerate overnight. Unwrap the sausages and lay in a shallow baking pan. Bake at 325° F until a meat thermometer inserted into the center of a sausage reads 160° F. Store in the refrigerator for up to 3 days or package and freeze.

*Recipes containing Morton Salt products have not been tested or approved by Morton Salt.

Ho Yau Ch'eung Venison Sausage

Smoked Chinese venison sausage with oyster sauce.

3 lbs. venison, cubed
2 lbs. pork fat, cubed
2 level Tbsp. Morton Tender Quick mix*
¾ tsp. salt
½ tsp. sugar
¾ tsp. ground cloves

¾ tsp. cinnamon
¾ tsp. hot pepper flakes
¾ tsp. grated tangerine or orange zest
¾ tsp. oyster sauce
brandy or cognac
24 mm to 26 mm sheep casings

Grind the meats, cover, and chill in the refrigerator. Mix the remaining ingredients with just enough brandy to cover. Combine with the meats and grind through a fine disc into casings. Briefly hot-smoke/cook over a lychee, apple, orange, or hickory wood fire for 2 hours at 325° F until the links reach an internal temperature of 160° F. Place in the refrigerator to cool overnight. Store in the refrigerator for up to 3 days or package and freeze.

Note: Oyster sauce can be found in specialty foods sections of supermarkets or at Oriental markets.

Quick and Easy Venison Pepperoni

8 lbs. venison, cubed
2 lbs. pork fat, cubed
3 level Tbsp. Morton Tender Quick mix*
¾ cup powdered milk
water
2 Tbsp. sugar
1 Tbsp. finely ground black pepper

1 Tbsp. fine ground black pepper
1 tsp. ground thyme
3 Tbsp. chili powder
2 tsp. ground cumin
1 tsp. crushed oregano leaves
1 tsp. whole anise seeds
30 mm to 32 mm hog casings

Grind the venison and pork fat together through a fine disc. Spread out the meat, sprinkle with the Tender Quick mix, and mix well. Combine the powdered milk with just enough water to make a smooth paste. Mix the powdered milk paste and the remaining ingredients with the meat. Grind through a fine disc and stuff into casings. Cover and refrigerate overnight. Cook in a hot-smoker/cooker for approximately 2 to 4 hours until links reach an internal temperature of 160° F. Place in the refrigerator to cool. Slice thin and eat or add as a pizza topping. Store in the refrigerator for up to 3 days or package and freeze.

Summer Venison Sausage

5 lbs. venison, cubed
5 lbs. boneless pork chops, cubed
½ level cup Morton Tender Quick mix*
3 to 4 Tbsp. Liquid Smoke, or to taste

3 Tbsp. brown sugar, lightly packed
1 Tbsp. black pepper
1 tsp. garlic powder
1 tsp. ground ginger

Mix the meats with the remaining ingredients and grind through a medium disc. Cover and refrigerate overnight. Regrind through a small disc and form into sausages 10" long and 1½" in diameter. Wrap in plastic wrap or aluminum foil and place in the refrigerator overnight. Unwrap the sausages, lay in a shallow baking pan, and bake at 325° F until a meat thermometer inserted into the center of a sausage reads 160° F. Store in the refrigerator for up to 3 days or package and freeze.

Easy Breakfast Venison Sausage

7½ lbs. venison, cubed
1½ lbs. pork fat or beef suet, cubed
1 level tsp. Tony Chachere's Original
   Seasoning

½ level cup Morton Sausage and Meat*
   Loaf Seasoning mix

Thoroughly mix all the ingredients and grind through a fine disc. Cover and refrigerate overnight. Shape into patties and fry until done. Store in the refrigerator for up to 3 days or package and freeze.

Salami-Baked Hard Venison Sausage

4 lbs. ground venison, cubed
1 lb. pork butt, cubed
2 level Tbsp. + 2 level tsp. Morton Tender
   Quick mix*
2 tsp. coarsely ground black pepper

½ tsp. finely ground black pepper
2½ tsp. garlic salt
1 tsp. hickory-flavored salt
1 tsp. Liquid Smoke
cooking or white cotton fabric

Mix together all the ingredients and grind through a fine disc. Shape into a mound and seal in plastic wrap. Refrigerate for 3 days, mixing well once each day. On the fourth day, divide into portions and wrap in moist fabric to make sausages 1½" to 2" in diameter, tying off the ends. Lay the sausages in a shallow baking dish and bake at 325° F for 4 hours until a meat thermometer inserted into the center of a sausage reads 160° F. Turn the sausages every hour. Consume or package and freeze.

Saigkawk Na'am—
Northern Thai/Lao Rice Venison Sausage

7 lbs. venison, cubed
3 lbs. pork fat, cubed
2 lbs. cooked jasmine or other rice
3½ oz. pressed garlic cloves

2½ oz. kosher salt
½ level cup + 2 level tsp. Morton Sugar
   Cure (Plain) mix*
22 mm to 24 mm sheep casings

Mix the meats thoroughly. Mix the remaining ingredients and sprinkle over the meats. Flatten out the meat, fold several times, and knead to mix. Stuff into casings using a coarse disc and tie every 6". Place in a covered container in the refrigerator for 10 days to develop its traditional sour flavor. Do not taste before cooking. Package and freeze. Grill, broil, or bake the uncut links in a coil at 325° F until a meat thermometer inserted into the center of a link reads 160° F. Serve with sliced raw cabbage, sliced fresh ginger, and a bottle of Asian or other beer.

Spicy Venison Salami

¾ lb. venison, cubed
¼ lb. boneless pork chops, cubed
1½ level tsp. Morton Tender Quick mix*
½ tsp. pepper
½ tsp. red pepper flakes, or to taste

⅛ tsp. ground nutmeg
⅛ tsp. ground ginger (optional)
½ tsp. garlic powder
½ tsp. whole mustard seeds
6 drops Liquid Smoke, or to taste

Combine all the ingredients and divide in half. Shape each portion into a sausage 1½" in diameter and wrap with plastic wrap or aluminum foil. Refrigerate overnight. Unwrap the sausages, lay in a shallow baking pan, and bake at 325° F until a meat thermometer inserted into the center of a sausage reaches 160° F. Store in the refrigerator for up to 3 days or package and freeze.

Pecan and Sugar–Smoked Andouille
Venison Sausage

Some areas of Louisiana have a long-standing tradition of smoking their venison sausage over pecan wood and brown sugar.

10 lbs. venison, cubed
5 lbs. pork fat, cubed
3 cups ice-cold water
1 level cup + 3 level Tbsp. Morton Tender
  Quick mix*
1 cup onion powder
4½ Tbsp. kosher salt
3 Tbsp. black pepper
2 tsp. red pepper, or to taste

2½ tsp. sugar
4½ tsp. freshly ground nutmeg
2 tsp. ground allspice
2 tsp. nutmeg
2½ tsp. paprika
1½ tsp. ground bay leaf
32 mm to 34 mm hog casings
pecan chips soaked overnight in water
½ cup brown sugar, packed

Grind the meats through a fine disc and place in the refrigerator until chilled. Dissolve Morton Tender Quick mix in water, then add the remaining ingredients and combine with the chilled meat. Grind with a fine disc and stuff into hog casings. Sprinkle the brown sugar over the pecan chips and hot-smoke/cook the venison sausage until the internal temperature reaches 160° F. Remove the sausage and wash with cold water until the temperature cools to 80° F. Wipe the sausage and allow to dry for 15 minutes; place in the refrigerator to dry. Store in the refrigerator for up to 3 days or package and freeze.

Laap Ch'eung Venison Sausage

Spicy Chinese bean sauce venison sausage smoked over persimmon wood.

2 lbs. venison, cubed
2 lbs. pork fat, cubed
2 level Tbsp. Morton Tender Quick mix*
¾ tsp. salt
½ tsp. sugar
¾ tsp. bean sauce

¾ tsp. hot pepper flakes (optional)
¾ tsp. ground cloves
¾ tsp. cinnamon
¾ tangerine or orange zest
3 oz. brandy
22 mm to 24 mm sheep casings

Grind the meats through a medium disc, cover, and chill in the refrigerator. Mix the remaining ingredients and combine with the meat. Grind through a fine disc and stuff into casings, twisting off into 6" links. Smoke over a lychee, persimmon, or hickory wood fire for 2 hours until the internal temperature reaches 160° F. Place in the refrigerator to cool overnight. Store in the refrigerator for up to 3 days or package and freeze.

  Note: Bean sauce can be found in specialty food sections or at Oriental markets.

Hungarian Venison Sausage

3 lbs. venison, cubed
1 lb. beef round steak, cubed
1 lb. pork fat, cubed
2 Tbsp. minced garlic cloves
1 cup water
2 Tbsp. salt

1½ tsp. finely ground black pepper
3 Tbsp. paprika
3 level Tbsp. Morton Tender Quick mix*
¼ tsp. ground cloves
32 mm to 34 mm hog casings

Grind the meats through a coarse disc and mix in the remaining ingredients. Cover and cool in the refrigerator. Stuff the casings and twist off into 12" to 16" lengths. Place the sausages in a home-style hot-smoker/cooker and smoke until the internal temperature reaches 160° F. Remove the sausages and hang in the refrigerator to dry for 2 hours. Store in the refrigerator for up to 3 days or package and freeze.

Coarse-Ground Venison Bologna

4 lbs. venison, cubed
6 lbs. pork butt, cubed
2 cups cold water
½ level cup Morton Tender Quick mix*
3 Tbsp. brown sugar, lightly packed
1 Tbsp. ground white pepper
1 Tbsp. ground coriander

⅛ tsp. minced fresh tarragon
1 Tbsp. ground mace
1 tsp. onion powder
2 cups nonfat dry milk powder
2 Tbsp. Liquid Smoke, or to taste
46 mm or larger beef rounds

Grind the meats through a fine disc and mix in the remaining ingredients. Cover and place in the refrigerator overnight. Grind the mixture a second time with a small disc; stuff into individual 12" long beef rounds. Place the venison Bologna in a large stockpot and cover with water. Bring the water to a boil and lower to a simmer. Cook until the internal temperature reaches 160° F. Place the sausage in ice water and allow to cool for 20 minutes. Place in the refrigerator to dry. Store in the refrigerator for up to 3 days or package and freeze.

Knockpolse—
Hot-Smoked Danish Venison Sausage

26 lbs. venison, cubed
12 lbs. veal, cubed
12 lbs. lean pork, cubed
¾ cup salt
1¾ level cups Morton Tender Quick mix*
3 Tbsp. ground ginger

3 Tbsp. ground cinnamon
7 Tbsp. ground white pepper
4 garlic cloves, minced
4 green onions, minced
5 lbs. pork fat, minced
32 mm to 34 mm hog casings

Grind the venison, veal, and lean pork together with a coarse disc. Mix in the remaining ingredients, except the pork fat, and grind with a fine disc. Spread out the sausage, sprinkle with the pork fat, fold over several times, and knead until mixed. Grind through a coarse disc and fill the casings, tying or twisting into 6" to 8" links. Hot-smoke for 1 hour and then boil until the internal temperature reaches 160° F. Can be served either hot or cold. Store in the refrigerator for up to 3 days or package and freeze.

Wienerpolse—
Bavarian Venison Sausage

26 lbs. venison, cubed
12 lbs. veal, cubed
12 lbs. pork fat, minced
20 oz. salt
1¾ level cups Morton Tender Quick mix*
¼ cup ground coriander

⅛ cup powdered (confectioners') sugar
7 Tbsp. white pepper
2 garlic cloves, minced
4 green onions, minced
24 mm to 26 mm sheep casings

Mix the venison, veal, and pork fat together. Mix in the remaining seasonings. Grind through a fine disc into casings and tie or twist into 6" links. Hang the links in the refrigerator for 24 hours. Hot-smoke for 1 hour and then boil until the internal temperature reaches 160° F. Place in the refrigerator to cool. Store in the refrigerator for up to 3 days or package and freeze.

Oven-Baked Spicy Venison Pepperoni

¾ lb. venison, cubed
¼ lb. boneless pork chops, cubed
1½ level tsp. Morton Tender Quick mix*
¾ tsp. black pepper
¼ tsp. red pepper flakes, or to taste
½ tsp. whole mustard seeds

¼ tsp. garlic powder
½ tsp. rolled and crushed whole fennel seeds
¼ tsp. rolled and crushed whole anise seeds
1 tsp. Liquid Smoke, or to taste

Mix all the ingredients together and knead until thoroughly mixed. Divide the mixture into two equal portions and make sausages about 1½" in diameter. Wrap in plastic wrap or aluminum foil and place in the refrigerator overnight. Unwrap the sausages and lay in a shallow baking pan. Bake at 325° F until the internal temperature reaches 160° F. Store in the refrigerator for up to 3 days or package and freeze.

Braunschweiger Venison Sausage

9 lbs. venison, cubed
1 lb. pork fat, cubed
½ level cup Morton Tender Quick mix*
7 Tbsp. salt
5 Tbsp. dried onion
½ tsp. ground allspice
1 Tbsp. ground white pepper
½ tsp. ground marjoram

1 tsp. ground nutmeg
1 tsp. ground ginger
1 tsp. ground sage
1 tsp. ground cloves
3 Tbsp. ground mustard
2 cups ice water
40 mm to 44 mm beef rounds

Grind all the meats through a medium disc. Add the remaining ingredients and mix well. Pass through a fine disc and into casings. Fill a large pot with water, heat to 190° F, and then carefully lower the sausages into the pot. Be sure all the sausage is covered. Maintain the water at 170° F until the internal temperature of the sausage reaches 160° F. This should take from 2 to 2½ hours. Remove the sausage and place in a sink filled with water and ice. Allow the sausage to chill for 1 to 2 hours. Remove the sausage and wash with warm water to remove all the surface grease. Hang at room temperature for 45 minutes and allow the sausage to dry.

Place in a preheated smoker and hot-smoke for 3 hours until the internal temperature reaches 160° F. Maintain a heavy flow of smoke until a nice rich brown color is obtained. Place in the refrigerator and cool. Store in the refrigerator for up to 3 days or package and freeze.

Longganisa—Filipino Venison Sausage

1¼ lbs. venison, cubed
1 lb. pork, cubed
1½ Tbsp. salt
1½ Tbsp. sugar
1½ Tbsp. soy or teriyaki sauce
2 Tbsp. rice wine vinegar

2 Tbsp. red wine
1 level Tbsp. + 1 level tsp. Morton Tender
 Quick mix*
1 tsp. black pepper
2 tsp. minced garlic
24 mm to 26 mm sheep casings

Mix all the ingredients together and pass through a coarse disc. Cover, place in the refrigerator overnight, and stuff into casings. To cook, place a small amount of water in a skillet, pierce the casings with a sharp fork, and boil the sausages until the internal temperature reaches 160° F. Store in the refrigerator for no more than 3 days or package and freeze.

Mettwurst Venison Sausage

Spread on toasted bread or crackers

2 lbs. venison liver, cubed
3 lbs. pork, cubed
1 level Tbsp. + 2 level tsp. Morton Tender
 Quick mix*
1 Tbsp. salt

3 tsp. white pepper
3 tsp. coriander
1 cup reserved meat cooking water
32 mm to 34 mm hog casings

Boil the venison liver and pork until tender. Strain through a colander and reserve the water. Combine all the ingredients, except the reserved cooking water, and pulse in a food processor until smooth and pasty. Stuff into casings and tie off into 8" to 10" links. Place the links in a large pot containing the reserved water and simmer for about 20 minutes or until the internal temperature reaches 160° F. Cool in ice water and refrigerate for 24 hours before using. Store in the refrigerator for up to 3 days or package and freeze.

Easy Cured and Smoked Venison Summer Sausage

3 lbs. venison, cubed
5 lbs. pork butt, cubed
2 lbs. veal, cubed
½ level cup Morton Tender Quick mix*
6 Tbsp. salt
1 Tbsp. ground white pepper
2 Tbsp. ground nutmeg
1 Tbsp. ground allspice

1 tsp. ground marjoram
1 tsp. ground coriander
1 tsp. ground celery seeds
½ tsp. ground caraway seeds
2 tsp. whole mustard seeds
¼ cup powdered dextrose
40 mm to 42 mm beef rounds

Mix together the meats and grind through a coarse disc. Mix in the remaining ingredients. Regrind through a fine disc. Cover and place in the refrigerator for 24 hours. Stuff into beef rounds and hang in the refrigerator for 3 hours to dry. Smoke heavily in a hot-smoker until the internal temperature reaches 160° F. Remove and wash with hot water. Allow to cool to room temperature for 1 hour or until the surface water has evaporated. Hang overnight in the refrigerator. Store in the refrigerator for up to 3 days or package and freeze. To serve, allow the sausage to thaw in the refrigerator, slice ½" thick, and fry or grill.

11

Cooked Venison Sausage Recipes

Cooked sausages are ready to eat when they are made, or they can be stored in the refrigerator for up to three days or frozen, thawed, and served whenever you are ready. All you have to do is place them in the refrigerator overnight to thaw, serve as is or recook, and sit back and enjoy.

The critical temperature for cooked sausage is 160° F. To assure that your sausages have reached this temperature, a small investment in a dial or remote-sensing thermometer is in order. Besides being useful in sausage making, these thermometers will more than pay for themselves when you are trying not to go over 140° F while roasting your boneless venison hindquarter or broiling 2-inch-thick venison loin steaks.

Andouille Venison Sausage with Fresh Spices

A variation on the classic Louisiana Cajun sausage.

3 lbs. venison, cubed
2 lbs. pork fat, cubed
½ tsp. ground mace
½ tsp. ground allspice
½ tsp. ground cloves
1 Tbsp. freshly ground pepper
1 Tbsp. salt
1 tsp. chili powder
1 tsp. red pepper

2 large onions, minced
3 bay leaves, powdered
2 garlic cloves, minced
1 Tbsp. minced fresh parsley
1 Tbsp. minced fresh marjoram
1 Tbsp. minced fresh thyme
32 mm to 36 mm hog casings, cut into
   24" lengths

Mix and grind the meats with a coarse disc. Combine the remainder of the ingredients and mix together well with the ground meat. Place a fine disc on the grinder and grind the meat mixture into 12" long sausages. Take the casing off the stuffing tube and tie off each sausage. Place the sausages in the refrigerator overnight and then hot-smoke/cook until the internal temperature reaches 160° F. You can also add raw sugar, sorghum molasses, sugarcane, or dark brown sugar to the smoldering wood to give a pleasant flavor to the Andouille. Cut in ½" slices and use in gumbos or soups, or fry the slices in lard or peanut oil. Store in the refrigerator for up to 3 days or package and freeze.

Moroccan-Style Venison Sausage

2 lbs. venison, cubed
1 lb. lamb, cubed
¼ lb. beef fat or suet, cubed
1 Tbsp. salt
1½ tsp. curry powder
1½ tsp. coarsely ground black pepper

½ tsp. ground cinnamon
½ tsp. ground thyme
½ tsp. chopped fresh red currants
½ cup pomegranate juice
1 Tbsp. minced garlic
28 mm or smaller hog casings

Mix together all the ingredients and stuff through a fine disc into casings. Make into 4" to 6" long strings of sausage links. For a real Moroccan-flavored smoke, throw some moist coffee beans and a little Latikia pipe tobacco on the hot-smoking/cooking chips.

Matiti—Romanian Sausage with Venison

4 garlic cloves
water
½ cup beef stock or broth
1½ tsp. salt
½ tsp. black pepper
1 tsp. ground thyme

½ tsp. ground basil
½ tsp. baking soda
2 lbs. venison
1 lb. pork butt
30 mm to 34 mm hog casings

Process the garlic in a small amount of water to make a paste. Remove to a large bowl and mix in the beef stock, salt, pepper, thyme, basil, and baking soda. Place the meats in a separate bowl and mix in the spice and soda mixture. Stuff into casings to make 6" links. Cook until the internal temperature reaches 160° F. Store in the refrigerator for up to 3 days or package and freeze.

Klobasa—Slovak Venison Sausage

1 whole head garlic
water
4 lbs. venison
6 lbs. pork butt
1 Tbsp. black pepper

3 Tbsp. salt
1 tsp. ground marjoram
3 cups ice water
32 to 35 mm hog casings

Process the garlic in a little water and let the mixture set for 1 hour. Cut the meats into cubes and place in a large pan. Add the spices, garlic, and water and mix well. Let the meat mixture marinate in the refrigerator for an hour. Grind the meat with a medium disc and stuff the casings to make 8" to 10" links. Store in the refrigerator for up to 3 days or package and freeze.

To cook, pan-fry by putting a little water in a frying pan and adding the sausage. Cover and steam the sausage for a few minutes. Uncover and boil off the water. Brown the sausage on one side, then turn and brown the other side.

Klobasa and sauerkraut make a fine dinner. First, put a little water in a frying pan, then add the sausage. Cover and boil for about half an hour. Take the pan off the stove and drain. Add the sauerkraut to the pan, add some more water, and simmer until the sauerkraut is heated.

Lielbasi Venison Sausage

An Old World Lithuanian sausage recipe.

4 lbs. venison, cubed
1 lb. pork, cubed
1 heaping tsp. ground mustard
1 heaping tsp. ground whole allspice
½ tsp. coarsely ground black pepper

½ large onion, diced
1 large garlic clove, finely minced
1 tsp. salt
½ cup warm water
35 mm to 38 mm hog casings

Mix the venison and pork together and grind through a coarse disc. Knead in the remaining spices. Slowly knead in the water until it is absorbed. Stuff casings using a coarse grinding disc. Make into 8" to 10" sausages and tie off on both ends. Store in the refrigerator for up to 3 days or package and freeze. To cook, poach or boil for 20 minutes until the internal temperature reaches 160° F.

Hot and Spicy Tunisian-Style Venison Sausage

2 lbs. finely ground venison
1 lb. finely ground lamb
¼ lb. finely ground beef fat
1 Tbsp. salt
1½ Tbsp. ground cumin
2 tsp. coarsely ground black pepper
¼ cup paprika

1½ tsp. cayenne pepper, or to taste
1 tsp. ground cinnamon
½ cup pomegranate juice
1½ Tbsp. minced garlic
1 tsp. ground ginger
1 tsp. minced fresh thyme leaves
34 mm to 36 mm hog casings

Mix together all the ingredients. Stuff through a fine disc into long sausage rings and tie both ends together to make circles. To impart a very interesting Arabic flavor to the sausage, hot-smoke/cook it, and during the last hour of smoking throw a few small pine lighter-knot chips on the smoking grate. The pine resin will give a distinct Middle Eastern flavor to the sausage. Store in the refrigerator for up to 3 days or package and freeze.

Baked Kielbasi Venison Sausage

Kielbasi is an Old World Ukrainian sausage.

5 lbs. venison, cubed
1 lb. veal, cubed
13 lbs. lean pork butt, cubed
1 garlic head, minced
1½ Tbsp. salt
1 tsp. black pepper

2 Tbsp. mustard seeds
⅛ tsp. paprika
1 Tbsp. garlic salt
1 qt. warm water
35 mm to 38 mm hog casings

Mix the venison, veal, and pork. Place a coarse disc on the grinder and grind all the meats together. Mix the garlic, salt, pepper, mustard seeds, paprika, and garlic salt together and knead into the meat. Slowly knead in the water until all of it is absorbed. Using the coarse disc, stuff the casings. Make into sausages 8" to 10" long and tie off after each is made. Before baking, prick the casings with a sharp fork. Lay the Kielbasi on a wire roasting rack and bake at 325° F for 1 hour; add a little water to the pan and replenish as needed. Store in the refrigerator for up to 3 days or package and freeze.

Boudin Rouge Venison Sausage

Louisiana Cajun-style blood sausage. This recipe is best prepared with head-shot deer, as the blood will not be contaminated.

2 white onions, finely minced
½ lb. pork fat, finely minced
1 garlic clove, finely minced
1 lb. or 2 cups venison blood

¼ tsp. salt
¼ tsp. black pepper
½ tsp. red pepper, or to taste
32 mm to 35 mm hog casings

Lightly fry the onions in a small amount of the pork fat. Add the garlic, lightly sauté, and remove from the heat. Mix the fat with the venison blood. Mix in the onions and spices. After all the ingredients are mixed well, grind through a fine disc and make 6" to 10" links. Tie double knots between the links. Slip the casing back onto the stuffing funnel and repeat the filling and knot-tying until you have a string of about 2' to 3'.

Place the Boudin in simmering water and cook until no blood comes out when you prick the casing. Do not boil—this will cause the blood to curdle. Take the Boudin out of the water and let dry in the refrigerator. To serve, separate the links and fry in lard or broil. Store in the refrigerator for up to 3 days or package and freeze.

Spicy Spanish Venison Sausage

1¼ lbs. venison, cubed
½ lb. boneless pork chops, cubed
1 onion, quartered
2 garlic cloves, minced
2 tsp. salt

1 tsp. paprika
½ tsp. red pepper flakes
½ tsp. black pepper
¼ tsp. red pepper
30 mm to 32 mm hog casings

Grind the meats, onion, and garlic through a coarse disc. Mix in the remaining ingredients and stuff into casings, twisting off into 8" links. Place the sausage in a large pot, cover with water, and simmer until the internal temperature reaches 160° F. Add more water if needed. Remove the sausage from the water and hold it under cold running water for a few minutes to cool. Refrigerate until ready to serve.

Vegetable and Venison Liver Sausage

¼ lb. venison or other liver, cubed
2 lbs. venison, cubed
2 oz. minced frozen spinach
2 oz. minced frozen turnip or mustard
   greens

2 oz. fresh kale, minced
1 cup cooked brown rice
3 oz. egg substitute
32 mm to 34 mm hog casings

Process the liver until emulsified. Grind the venison through a fine disc. Mix together all the ingredients and stuff into casings, tying or twisting into 6" to 8" links. Hot-smoke until the internal temperature reaches 160° F. Store in the refrigerator for up to 3 days or package and freeze.

Cooked Venison Brockwurst Sausage (Large Batch)

This recipe makes a rather large quantity of Brockwurst.

19 lbs. venison
6 lbs. lean beef
¾ lb. nonfat dry milk
¾ cup salt
2 qts. ice water
3 eggs, lightly beaten

2 Tbsp. sugar
3 Tbsp. onion powder
¼ cup ground white pepper
1 Tbsp. ground mace
1 Tbsp. ground ginger
32 mm to 34 mm hog casings

Cube and mix together the venison and beef. Make the first grind using a coarse disc. Mix the remaining ingredients into the ground meat and make the second grind using a fine disc. Stuff the sausage into casings. Cook the Brockwurst in 170° F water. Insert a meat thermometer into one of the Brockwurst and cook until the internal temperature reaches 160° F. Remove and immediately immerse in ice water. Store in the refrigerator for up to 3 days or package and freeze.

Boiled Venison Potato Sausage Rings

8 lbs. venison, cubed
4 lbs. lean pork, cubed
6 medium onions, chopped
13 lbs. potatoes, peeled and cubed
2 Tbsp. sugar

⅛ tsp. ground nutmeg or cinnamon
⅓ cup black pepper
¾ cup salt
34 mm to 36 mm hog casings

Mix the venison and pork and grind finely. Mix the onions and potatoes and grind coarsely. Mix all the ingredients and stuff through a coarse disc into casings. Tie the ends of the sausages together to make rings. Prick each ring several times to release air while cooking. Place the rings in a large pot of water; bring to a boil and simmer for 5 minutes. Boiling too long can cause the sausage rings to split. Remove the rings and allow to cool in the refrigerator. Store in the refrigerator for up to 3 days or package and freeze. To eat, thaw and simmer in water for 10 minutes.

Haggis with Venison

3½ lbs. small oatmeal
5 lbs. deer hearts
3 lbs. deer liver
2 lbs. beef suet
3 medium onions, finely chopped
⅓ cup salt
2½ Tbsp. ground white pepper
2 tsp. dried thyme leaves
1 tsp. dried rosemary leaves, chopped

1 Tbsp. ground nutmeg
¼ cup Scotch whiskey (optional)
2 qts. cold water
1 cup distilled white vinegar
2 tsp. salt for soaking casings
46 mm or larger beef rounds, or 2 to 3
   cleaned deer stomachs
cotton twine

Toast the oatmeal on a cookie sheet in a 375° F oven for 10 minutes and set aside. Place the hearts and liver in water and cook on a high simmer until tender. Remove, set aside, and reserve the cooking liquid. Grind the hearts and liver with the beef suet through a ¼" grinding disc. Bring the reserved liquid to a boil and sprinkle in the oatmeal. Stir vigorously until the oatmeal has softened. Drain the oatmeal and stir in the cooked hearts, liver, and remaining ingredients, except the cold water, vinegar, 2 tsp. salt, and casings. Turn the casings inside out and soak in the cold water with the salt and vinegar for ½ hour. Drain them and rinse very well, inside and out. Stuff the Haggis and tie off the ends with cotton twine. Prick with a fork, place in a steamer, and steam for 1 hour and 20 minutes, or cook for about 3 hours in 170° F water or until the internal temperature reaches 160° F. Remove and chill in ice water until all heat is gone. Slice and serve with beef gravy. Haggis is quite perishable. Warm and eat, refrigerate for no more than 1 day, or package and freeze.

Smoked Kielbasa Venison Sausage

Also called Kielbasy or smoked Polish sausage.

4 tsp. kosher salt
1¾ tsp. black pepper
3 Tbsp. paprika
1 tsp. crumbled marjoram
½ tsp. crumbled savory
2 tsp. minced garlic

10 oz. beef, cubed
16 oz. pork fat, cubed
⅓ cup ice water, divided
1¼ lbs. venison, cubed and chilled
35 mm to 38 mm hog casings

Mix together the salt, pepper, paprika, marjoram, savory, and garlic. Mix together the beef, pork fat, half the ice water, and half the seasoning mix, and puree in a food processor. Place in a large bowl and mix in the remaining seasonings, venison, and remaining water. Divide in half and process until coarse. Mix both batches together. Cover and place in the refrigerator for 24 hours. Stuff into casings through a fine disc and tie into 20" to 30" links. Hang the sausages in the refrigerator for 12 hours. Hot-smoke/cook until the internal temperature reaches 160° F. Refrigerate for no more than 3 days or package and freeze.

Place the coil in a skillet and cover halfway with water. Bring to a simmer and cook for about 10 minutes, turn, and cook the other side for 10 minutes. Pour off the water, prick every inch or so, and brown both sides. Store in the refrigerator for up to 3 days or package and freeze.

Baked Russian Venison Sausage

4 lbs. ground venison
1 lb. ground pork fat
3 Tbsp. whole caraway seeds
2 large onions, chopped
1 Tbsp. black pepper
1 Tbsp. pressed garlic

1 Tbsp. salt
1 cup chopped fresh parsley
2 cups cold water
3 Tbsp. whole dill seeds
38 mm to 42 mm hog casings

Combine all the ingredients, pass through a fine grinding disc, and stuff into casings. Preheat the oven to 350° F and bake for 1 hour. Store in the refrigerator for up to 3 days or package and freeze.

Hawaiian Portuguese Venison Sausage

Portuguese sausage is enjoyed at any meal in Hawaii. A favorite breakfast is sliced Hawaiian Portuguese sausage served with scoops of rice and eggs.

2¼ lbs. venison, cubed
¾ lb. pork fatback, cubed
2 tsp. salt
½ tsp. Prague Powder #1
¼ cup pineapple juice
¼ cup water
6 Tbsp. dark brown sugar, packed

2 Tbsp. paprika
2 Tbsp. minced garlic
1 tsp. ground anise
3 Tbsp. teriyaki or soy sauce
1 Tbsp. Tabasco sauce
30 mm to 32 mm hog casings

Mix the meats and grind through a fine disc. Dissolve the salt and Prague Powder in the pineapple juice and water. Spread the meat and mix in the cure. Whisk together the remaining ingredients and mix into the meat. Wrap in aluminum foil and refrigerate for 12 hours. Stuff into casings, twisting off into 8" links, and hang in the refrigerator for an hour to dry. Hot-smoke/cook until the internal temperature reaches 160° F. Store in the refrigerator for up to 3 days or package and freeze.

Danish Sausage with Venison

4 lbs. venison, small-ground twice
1 lb. boneless pork chops, small-ground
   twice
1 Tbsp. powdered (castor) sugar
1 Tbsp. ground allspice
¼ tsp. ground thyme

1 tsp. ground ginger
3 Tbsp. salt
1 Tbsp. black pepper
1 cup water
30 mm to 32 mm hog casings

Mix all the ingredients, stuff into casings through a fine disc, and tie or twist off into 6" links. Store in the refrigerator for up to 3 days or package and freeze. To cook, place the sausages in a frying pan, cover with boiling water, and bring to a boil. When done, remove the sausages and discard the liquid. Melt butter in the skillet and brown the sausages on all sides.

Spanish Venison Sausage

22 oz. venison, cubed
10 oz. pork fat, cubed
1 onion, quartered
2 garlic cloves, minced
2 tsp. salt
1 tsp. paprika

½ tsp. crushed red pepper flakes, or to taste
½ tsp. black pepper
¼ tsp. cayenne pepper
24 mm to 26 mm sheep casings

Mix together the meats, onion, and garlic and grind together using a coarse disc. Add the remaining ingredients, mix thoroughly, grind with a coarse disc into casings, and tie off into 2" links. Put the sausage in a large deep pan or pot and cover with water. Cook on top of the range over very low heat for at least 1 hour or until the water evaporates, adding more water during the cooking time if necessary. The sausage is done when the casing splits. Remove the sausage from the pan and hold it under cold running water for a few minutes to cool. Store in the refrigerator for up to 3 days or package and freeze.

Kupaty Venison Sausage

Georgian beef and lamb sausage made with venison.

1½ lbs. venison, cubed
½ lb. boneless lamb, cubed
¼ lb. lamb fat, cubed
1 cup chopped onions
1 garlic clove, minced
2 tsp. salt

½ tsp. black pepper
¼ tsp. ground cinnamon
¼ cup water
2 Tbsp. barberries or 1 cup fresh pomegranate seeds
28 mm to 32 mm hog casings

Grind the meats, fat, onions, and garlic through a coarse disc. Mix in the salt, pepper, cinnamon, and water. Gently stir in the barberries. Grind through a large disc, tie, and cut off into 10" links, leaving enough casing at each end to tie together to make a ring. Blanch in boiling water for 1 minute, wipe dry, and hang in the refrigerator for 2 days. Store in the refrigerator for up to 3 days or package and freeze. To cook, fry in a little cooking oil until cooked through.

Pickled Venison Pepperoni

Pickled Pepperoni Seasoning Mixture
¾ cup powdered milk (mix in enough water
    to make paste)
2 Tbsp. sugar
1 Tbsp. coarse black pepper
1 Tbsp. black pepper
3 Tbsp. chili powder
1 tsp. ground thyme
1 tsp. chopped fresh oregano

1 tsp. whole anise seeds
1 tsp. ground cumin

Sausage
5 lbs. venison, cubed
1 lb. boneless pork chops, cubed
3 Tbsp. pickling salt
Pickled Pepperoni Seasoning Mixture
32 mm to 35 mm hog casings

Mix together the Pepperoni Seasoning Mixture and set aside. Grind the venison and pork together through a fine disc. Add the pickling salt and mix well. Then add the Pepperoni Seasoning Mixture. Fold and knead several times. Stuff the mixture into the casings through a fine disc, cover, and refrigerate overnight. Hang the Pepperoni in a smoker and cook for 2 hours until it reaches an internal temperature of 160° F. If it hasn't reached this temperature, set the oven at the lowest setting and cook until 160° F is reached.

Kolbasz—Hungarian Venison Sausage

This sausage is traditionally served with sour cream and horseradish sauce. Boiled new potatoes and sauerkraut also go well with this dish.

2 cups water
6 garlic cloves, peeled
7 lbs. venison, coarsely ground
3 lbs. pork pieces with fat, coarsely ground
⅛ cup paprika

¼ cup salt
¼ tsp. black pepper
2¼ Tbsp. ground allspice
35 mm to 38 mm hog casings

Bring the water to boil, add the garlic, and simmer for 20 minutes. Remove the garlic and mash with a little of the water. Add the mashed garlic into the remaining water and mix into the meats. Mix in the remaining ingredients. Place the meat mixture in the refrigerator for 6 hours. Grind into casings through a fine disc and hot-smoke for 3 hours until the internal temperature reaches 160° F. Store in the refrigerator for up to 3 days or package and freeze. To cook, place the sausage in a heavy pot and pour in water so the links are in ½" of water. Cover and simmer until the sausage starts to take on color. Turn the sausage over and add a little more water to keep it from burning. When both sides are brown, remove the cover and continue cooking slowly to evaporate any remaining water. The sausage should be a nice rich red brown.

Leberkaese—German Baked Venison Bologna

Serve with rye bread and mustard.

5 lbs. venison, cubed
2½ lbs. lean pork, cubed
½ lb. pork fat
1½ qts. water
½ cup salt
1 onion, ground

1 Tbsp. white pepper
1 Tbsp. ground marjoram
2 garlic cloves, mashed
2½ Tbsp. lard
1 peel of lemon, minced

Grind the meats three times through a fine disc. Place the meat, water, and salt in a mixer and mix until you have a smooth and shiny dough. You may have to work in batches. Mix all the batches together. Cover and place in the refrigerator for 3 hours and allow to cool and swell. Mix in the onion and spices and place in a baking pan, pressing the meat dough down. Bake at 325° F for 1½ hours. Store in the refrigerator for up to 3 days or package and freeze.

Lifrarpylsa—Icelandic Boiled Venison Liver Sausage

6½ lbs. venison liver, cubed
1¼ lbs. venison or other kidneys, cubed
2 cups oatmeal
¼ cup salt
1 qt. whole milk
4¼ lbs. rye meal

2 cups flour
2 lbs. pork fat, cut into small cubes
deer stomach or 46 mm or larger hog
  casings
salt
water

Grind the liver and kidneys through a fine disc. Mix in the remaining items, except the pork fat. Cover and refrigerate for 1 hour. Mix in the small-cubed pork fat. Stuff into the deer stomach and sew closed with small cotton string. If a deer stomach is not available, use hog casings. Boil for about 3 hours in salted water. The sausage can be eaten either hot or chilled, and can be cut into rice pudding with cinnamon sugar and milk. Or slice and fry it, serving with hot mashed apples or on heavy-bodied bread. Store in the refrigerator for up to 3 days or package and freeze.

Jalapeño Pickled Venison Sausage

Sausage
4 lbs. venison, cubed
1 lb. boneless pork chops, cubed
2 Tbsp. salt
4 fresh jalapeño peppers, seeded and
  minced
2 Tbsp. chopped dried bell peppers
2 Tbsp. dried parsley
1 Tbsp. paprika
1 garlic clove, minced

1 cup ice water
20 mm to 22 mm sheep casings

Pickling Solution
2 gals. white distilled vinegar, 5% acidity
3 Tbsp. prepared pickling spice per gallon
  jar of sausage
2 to 3 fresh jalapeño peppers, sliced with
  seeds, per gallon jar of sausage
  (optional)

Grind the meats through a medium disc. Mix together all the ingredients, except the Pickling Solution. Stuff through a medium disc into casings and twist off or tie into 4" to 6" links. Boil until the sausages reach an internal temperature of 160° F. Place in gallon jars, cover with the distilled vinegar, and place in the refrigerator overnight. Lift the sausages from the vinegar and set aside. Mix in the pickling spices and sliced peppers, and return the sausages to the jars. Add more distilled vinegar if needed and let stand for 4 days. Serve as an appetizer with crackers and ice-cold Mexican or other beer. For sandwiches, slice thin and layer with chopped tomato, shredded lettuce, chopped onion, and shredded mozzarella cheese.

Poached Swiss Weisswurst Venison Sausage

¾ lb. venison, cubed
1 Tbsp. salt
1 Tbsp. sugar
¾ pound pork fat, cubed
11 oz. ice
1 Tbsp. white pepper
1 Tbsp. dry mustard

¼ tsp. mace
½ tsp. ground ginger
1½ tsp. grated lemon zest
2 Tbsp. nonfat powdered milk
cotton string
32 mm to 35 mm hog casings

Combine the venison with the salt and sugar. Grind the venison and pork separately through a fine disc. Place in individual bowls and chill well. Place the ground venison in a food processor, add the ice, and sprinkle with the spices. Process the mixture until very cold (34° F). Stop processing and scrape down the sides. Continue processing until the temperature rises to 40° F. The mixture should resemble cake batter. Add the fat and process. Add the nonfat powdered milk and mix in well. Stuff the casings through a fine disc and tie off the links with cotton string. Poach in a shallow pan of 165° F water until the internal temperature reaches 160° F. Be careful not to let the water boil. Remove the sausages to an ice-water bath for 1 hour. Fry or grill and serve. Store in the refrigerator for up to 3 days or package and freeze.

Baked Oriental Venison Sausage

1¾ lbs. venison, finely ground
¼ lb. pork fat, finely ground
¼ cup minced water chestnuts
3 Tbsp. sliced shiitake mushrooms
3 Tbsp. rice wine vinegar
2 Tbsp. sesame oil
2 Tbsp. soy or teriyaki sauce

1½ Tbsp. nonfat powdered milk
1 Tbsp. white sesame seeds
2 tsp. salt
1½ tsp. black sesame seeds
¾ tsp. grated fresh ginger
1½ garlic cloves, finely chopped
¼ cup chopped green onion

Mix all the ingredients well. Divide into 12 patties, 3 oz. each. Place the patties on a lightly oiled baking sheet and bake at 350° F for about 15 minutes or until an internal temperature of 160° F is reached. Store in the refrigerator for up to 3 days or package and freeze.

Swedish Venison Korv

9 lbs. potatoes
2 Tbsp. salt
3 lbs. ground venison
1½ lbs. ground boneless pork chops
1 large onion, chopped

1½ Tbsp. black pepper
1½ tsp. white pepper
1 tsp. allspice
36 mm to 38 mm hog casings

Peel the potatoes, boil in salted water for about 10 minutes or until they are still very firm in the center, and chop. Mix the potatoes and all the other ingredients together and grind through a fine disc and into casings. Make 12" links and tie off with two knots between the links; cut between the knots and tie to make a ring. Package and freeze.

To cook, fill a pot large enough to comfortably hold the rings and boil for 45 minutes. Prick the sausage skins with a sharp fork. Serve with boiled potatoes, green peas, and a generous amount of real salted butter; homemade butter would be even better.

Hot Smoked Venison Pastrami

large needle
heavy cotton twine
1 (4 lb.) boneless venison roast
½ cup kosher salt
2 Tbsp. dark brown sugar, packed

1 Tbsp. ground ginger
1 Tbsp. coarse black pepper
4 garlic cloves, minced
2 Tbsp. coriander seeds, cracked
hickory or mesquite chips

Thread a large needle with heavy cotton twine and pass it through the large end of the venison roast. Tie both ends of the string together to make a 3" long loop. Mix together the salt, brown sugar, ginger, pepper, garlic, and coriander. Rub the mixture into every part of the meat's surface and work it into every crack and crevice. Pat the remaining seasonings over the surface, wrap the venison roast in aluminum foil, and then place it in a 2 gallon resealable plastic bag. Place the bag in a large tray and refrigerate for 10 days, turning the package daily.

Remove the venison from the package, patting back on any seasonings that have fallen off. Hang and let dry for 30 minutes. Preheat the smoker and add a panful of presoaked hickory, mesquite, or other hardwood chips. When smoke begins to emerge, hang the Pastrami in the smoker, close the door, and smoke steadily for 3 hours. Smoke/cook until the internal temperature of the meat reaches 160° F. Remove the venison Pastrami and allow to cool. Wrap in aluminum foil and refrigerate overnight or for up to 3 days before cooking. The Pastrami can be packaged and frozen at this point.

To cook, thaw the frozen venison Pastrami in the refrigerator. Cover with cold water and simmer very gently until completely tender, at least 2 hours. When it is finished cooking, allow to cool in the cooking water and serve at once, store in the refrigerator for up to 3 days, or package and freeze. To reheat cooked venison Pastrami, slice thin and briefly steam.

12

Cured and Smoked Venison Sausage Recipes

If you have or want to build a traditional smokehouse and think that you might enjoy maintaining a constant flow of smoke and an even temperature in a smokehouse for several hours or days, these sausages are what you have been looking for.

Cold-smoking alone will not preserve these sausages. It is the nitrate in the Prague Powder #2 and the sealing properties of the smoke that allow the sausages to stand on their own.

Errors have been known to occur in the mixing process, however, and not every piece or every link of sausage receives the correct amount of cure. For safety, it is recommended that these and all other sausages be packaged and frozen after making.

If you find a recipe that you like and would like to make a larger batch, the correct ratios of cure to meat for Prague Powder #2 are:

- 1 level tsp. cure to 5 lbs. meat
- 2 level tsp. cure to 10 lbs. meat
- 3 level tsp. cure to 15 lbs. meat
- 4 level tsp. cure to 20 lbs. meat
- 5 level tsp. cure to 25 lbs. meat

For quantities larger than 25 pounds, cures should be weighed at the rate of:

- 1 oz. cure to 25 lbs. meat
- 2 oz. cure to 50 lbs. meat
- 3 oz. cure to 75 lbs. meat
- 4 oz. cure to 100 lbs. meat

Items such as Prague Powders #1 and #2, Fermento, powdered dextrose, corn syrup solids, and gelatin can be purchased from a local butcher supply store or from many companies listed in the appendix. Kosher (pure) salt can be found in the salt section of your supermarket.

Pepperoni Venison Sausage

20 lbs. venison, cubed
5 lbs. beef round steak, cubed
15 oz. salt
2¼ oz. sugar
5 level tsp. Prague Powder #2, dissolved in 1 cup water

¾ cup cayenne pepper, or to taste
¾ cup ground allspice
1 Tbsp. garlic powder
5 Tbsp. whole fennel seeds
26 mm or larger sheep casings

Grind the venison with a coarse disc. Mix together with the seasonings and ground beef and grind a second time with a fine disc. Seal in plastic wrap and refrigerate for 2½ days. After refrigerating, stuff into casings and smoke at 100° F for 2 days. Store in the refrigerator for up to 3 days or package and freeze.

Venison Sopressata

6½ lbs. venison, cubed
3½ lbs. boneless pork chops, cubed
½ cup plus 1 Tbsp. salt
1 oz. powdered dextrose
2 Tbsp. whole black pepper
2 Tbsp. ground black pepper

1 Tbsp. hot cayenne pepper, or to taste
3 oz. corn syrup solids
2 level tsp. Prague Powder #2, dissolved in ½ cup water
32 mm to 34 mm hog casings

Grind all the meat through a large disc. Mix together all the ingredients, pack the meat tightly in a tub not over 6" to 7" high, and refrigerate for 48 hours. Remove the meat and grind through a small disc, then stuff into casings, making 8" to 10" links. Maintain the temperature at 55° for 48 hours, then cold-smoke until the sausage begins to take on a deep brown color. Remove from the smoker and store in a cool place for 2 months. The sausage will be finished when it weighs about 60 percent of its original weight. Store in the refrigerator for up to 3 days or package and freeze.

Salami-Cooked Venison Sausage

16 lbs. venison, cubed
9 lbs. lean beef, cubed
1 cup salt
½ cup sugar
1 qt. cold water
¼ cup black pepper
3 Tbsp. garlic powder

3 Tbsp. whole coriander seed
4 tsp. ground mace
4 tsp. ground cardamom
5 level tsp. Prague Powder #2, dissolved
   in 1 cup water
46 mm or larger hog casings or 46 mm or
   larger beef rounds

Mix the venison and beef and grind through a coarse disc. Combine the remaining ingredients and add to the meat. Grind a second time through a fine disc. Stuff into casings and hang in a 180° F smokehouse. Insert a meat thermometer; when the temperature reaches 160° F, remove the sausage and chill in cold water. Refrigerate before slicing. Store in the refrigerator for up to 3 days or package and freeze.

Venison Frankfurters

17 lbs. venison, cubed
8 lbs. ground beef
1 qt. ice
1 cup salt
¾ lb. nonfat dry milk
3 Tbsp. sugar

5 level tsp. Prague Powder #2, dissolved
   in 1 cup water
8 tsp. ground coriander
5 Tbsp. white pepper
22 mm to 24 mm sheep casings

Mix the venison and beef and grind with a coarse disc. Combine the remaining ingredients and mix into the ground meat. Grind two times through a fine grinder. Stuff into casings and twist off into 6" links. Hang in a smokehouse heated to 180° F; the frankfurters can also be cooked by boiling. In either case, insert a meat thermometer and cook until the internal temperature reaches 160° F. Then chill in an ice-water bath. Refrigerate for 8 hours before slicing. Store in the refrigerator for up to 3 days or package and freeze.

Wiener Wuerstchen—
Venison Vienna Sausage

4 lbs. venison, cubed
4 lbs. lean veal, cubed
2 lbs. lean pork, cubed
2 level tsp. Prague Powder #2, dissolved in ½ cup water
1 oz. powdered dextrose
2¾ oz. wheat flour

3½ oz. salt
1 Tbsp. ground nutmeg
1 tsp. ground coriander
½ tsp. ground cardamom
½ tsp. ground cloves
2 cups ice water
24 mm to 26 mm sheep casings

Grind the meats through a fine disc. Add the remaining ingredients, except the water, and mix thoroughly. Place the meat in a meat processor and emulsify, adding the water slowly. Through a small disc, stuff into casings and twist off into 6" to 8" links. Place in the refrigerator for 30 minutes until dry. Preheat a smoker to 150° F and cook for 1 hour. Raise the temperature to 165° F and cook until the internal temperature of the sausages reaches 160° F. Store in the refrigerator for up to 3 days or package and freeze. These sausages can also be baked in the oven.

Kabanosy Venison Sausage

A very slim and tasty sausage similar to Slim Jims.

7 lbs. venison, cubed
3 lbs. fatty pork, cubed
3½ oz. salt
¾ oz. black pepper
1 Tbsp. ground caraway seeds
1 Tbsp. ground nutmeg

1 clove garlic, minced
1¾ oz. corn syrup solids
2 level tsp. Prague Powder #2, dissolved in ½ cup water
1 oz. powdered dextrose
18 mm to 20 mm sheep casings

Mix the meats and grind through a medium disc. Spread out the meat and spread on the remaining ingredients; fold and mix well. Regrind through a small disc. Stuff into casings and tie off in 6" links. Hang the links at room temperature for 2 hours. Preheat a smoker to 140° F. Hang the sausages and give them a quick burst of heavy smoke. Maintain the temperature for an hour and then raise it to 190° F for half an hour until the internal temperature of the meat reaches 160° F. Remove the sausages and hang at 60° F to 65° F for 7 days. Maintain relative humidity at 70 to 80 percent. When the sausage size is reduced to 50 percent, it is ready. Store in the refrigerator for up to 3 days or package and freeze.

Venison Sausage Snack Sticks

18 lbs. venison, cubed
2 lbs. pork fat, cubed
4 Tbsp. paprika
6 Tbsp. ground mustard
1 tsp. ground black pepper
1 tsp. ground white pepper
1 tsp. ground celery seeds
1 Tbsp. mace

1 tsp. powdered or granulated garlic
3½ oz. kosher salt
4 level tsp. Prague Powder #2, dissolved
    in 1 cup water
1½ oz. powdered dextrose
6 oz. Fermento
18 mm to 20 mm sheep casings

Mix all the ingredients together, grind with a fine disc, and stuff into casings. Smoke at 100° F for 8 hours. Maintain the temperature for another 12 hours so that the traditional tangy flavor develops. Raise the temperature to 165° F and maintain until the meat's internal temperature reaches 160° F. Remove the sausage and wash with cold water until it reaches 75° F. Place in the refrigerator to dry. Store in the refrigerator for up to 3 days or package and freeze.

Mortadella Venison Sausage

Mortadella is a smoked sausage originating in Bologna, Italy. The Italian version is not imported, because it requires additional cooking.

6 lbs. venison, cubed
3½ lbs. pork butt, cubed
½ lb. pork snout, cubed
1 Tbsp. ground mace
1 Tbsp. ground coriander
½ tsp. ground cinnamon
⅛ tsp. ground nutmeg
6 Tbsp. kosher salt
½ oz. Chianti or other red wine

2 Tbsp. gelatin
2 level tsp. Prague Powder #2, dissolved
    in ½ cup water
2 cups ice water
2 cups nonfat dry milk
½ cup corn syrup solids
2 garlic cloves, minced
1 Tbsp. black pepper
40 mm to 43 mm beef rounds

Grind all the meats through a large disc. Boil all the spices, except the garlic and pepper, in the wine for 20 minutes. Allow the wine mixture to cool and mix in the meats. Dissolve the gelatin and Prague powder in the water and mix into the meat with the remainder of the ingredients. Grind through a small disc, cover, and refrigerate overnight. Stuff into rounds using a large disc. Preheat a smoker to 120° F. Place the sausage into the smoker and raise the temperature to 170° F. Maintain this temperature until the internal temperature of the links reaches 160° F. Rinse the sausage with hot water and then cool in ice water. Place in the refrigerator overnight. Store in the refrigerator for up to 3 days or package and freeze.

Jagdwurst Venison Sausage

German hunter's sausage.

4½ lbs. venison, cubed
1½ lbs. fresh ham, cubed
4 lbs. fresh bacon, cubed
1 Tbsp. white pepper
3½ oz. salt
1 Tbsp. ground coriander
1 garlic clove, minced
1 Tbsp. ground ginger

¾ oz. ground mustard seeds
1 Tbsp. ground nutmeg
½ oz. powdered dextrose
2 level tsp. Prague Powder #2, dissolved
    in ½ cup water
42 mm to 46 mm hog casings or 40 mm
    to 43 mm beef rounds

Grind the venison and ham through a small disc. Grind the fresh bacon through a medium disc. Add the remaining ingredients and mix thoroughly. Stuff into casings through a large disc, place in the refrigerator, and cool for 30 minutes. Preheat a smoker to 130° F and smoke for an hour. Raise the temperature to 165° F and smoke for no longer than 30 minutes or until the internal temperature of the links reaches 160° F. Store in the refrigerator for up to 3 days or package and freeze.

Sweet and Extra-Spicy Dried
Venison Sausage Snack Sticks

10 lbs. venison, cubed
2 level tsp. Prague Powder #2, dissolved in ½
    cup water
¼ cup paprika
6 Tbsp. mustard powder
1½ tsp. red pepper, or to taste
1 tsp. black pepper
1 tsp. white pepper
1 tsp. ground celery seeds
1 Tbsp. mace

1 tsp. powdered or granulated garlic
1 Tbsp. powdered or granulated onion
2½ oz. salt
½ tsp. ground marjoram
1 tsp. ground ginger
¼ cup sorghum or blackstrap molasses or
    dark syrup
6 oz. Fermento
18 mm to 20 mm sheep casings

Grind the venison through a medium disc and mix in the remainder of the ingredients. Regrind through a small disc and stuff into casings. Preheat a smoker to 100° F, hang the sausages from a steel rod, and smoke for 8 hours. Raise the temperature to 170° F and maintain until the internal temperature of the links reaches 160° F. Remove the sausages and wash with cold water until they reach 75° F. Place in the refrigerator to dry. Store in the refrigerator for up to 3 days or package and freeze.

Large Bologna Venison Sausage

17 lbs. venison, cubed
8 lbs. lean beef, cubed
1 qt. ice
1 cup salt
¾ lb. nonfat dry milk
3 Tbsp. sugar

5 level tsp. Prague Powder #2, dissolved
  in 1 cup water
8 tsp. ground coriander
5 Tbsp. white pepper
46 mm or larger hog casings or 46 mm or
  larger beef rounds

Mix the venison and beef and grind with a coarse disc. Combine the remaining ingredients and mix into the ground meats. Grind two times through a fine disc, then stuff into casings through a fine disc and make into 12" links, tying off at each end. Smoke in a smokehouse heated to 180° F; the sausage can also be cooked by boiling. In either case, insert a meat thermometer and cook until the internal temperature reaches 160° F. Chill in a cold-water bath. Refrigerate for 8 hours before slicing. Store in the refrigerator for up to 3 days or package and freeze.

PART III

Venison Sausage Dishes

13

Breakfast—Beginning the Day with Venison Sausage

All these delicious breakfast dishes are designed for the appropriate venison sausage. The dishes are prepared in the traditional manner; the difference is that they all incorporate a sausage made with venison. They will work equally well when commercial pork or other sausages are substituted. Whether you make your own venison sausage, have your venison sausage made by a processing plant, or purchase pork sausage at the grocery store, you and your family are sure to enjoy each and every one of them.

Bring your children into the kitchen with you. One of my earliest childhood memories was the day I talked my mother into teaching me how to make chocolate éclairs. She stood me on a stool and let me get my hands into all the makings.

The memories that your own children will have of cooking with you will last them a lifetime. When they get older and prepare the recipes by themselves, they will remember the happy times they spent in the kitchen with you. I wouldn't trade my own memories for anything on this earth.

Cheese and Venison Sausage–Stuffed French Toast with Maple-Pecan Syrup

½ lb. fresh venison sausage
1 loaf French or Italian bread (approx 16"
    long)
¼ lb. Muenster cheese, sliced
5 eggs
1 cup milk

1 Tbsp. sugar
1 Tbsp. olive oil
1 cup maple syrup
3 Tbsp. butter
½ cup pecan pieces

Shape the venison sausage into eight ¼" thick wide patties and sauté until done. Slice the bread diagonally into 1½" thick pieces. On one side, cut a deep and wide pocket into each slice. Insert a slice of cheese and a sausage patty into each piece of bread. Gently press the bread down onto the filling. Whisk together the eggs, milk, and sugar. Lay each stuffed bread slice into the egg mixture and coat both sides. Heat the olive oil in a large skillet and brown each piece of stuffed toast on both sides. Mix the syrup, butter, and pecans together and warm. Serve stuffed toast with the pecan syrup. Serves 8.

Sour Cream and Venison Sausage Omelets

½ lb. link venison sausage, casings removed,
  cut into bite-sized pieces
2 Tbsp. chopped green onions
½ cup sour cream

4 eggs, beaten
2 Tbsp. water
½ tsp. celery salt
1 Tbsp. canola oil

Cook the sausage and onions in a skillet until the sausage is browned, stirring frequently for 8 to 10 minutes. Remove the sausage mixture and drain on paper towels; leave the drippings in the skillet. Place the sausage in a bowl and mix in the sour cream. Whisk the eggs with the water and celery salt until well blended. Heat the sausage drippings over medium-high heat. Pour half of the egg mixture into the skillet. Using a spatula, lift the eggs as they cook, letting the uncooked part run underneath until the omelet is cooked but still creamy. Spoon half of the sausage mixture over half of the omelet. Slide onto a plate, folding the omelet over the filling. Keep warm. Heat the oil in the same skillet and repeat the process for a second omelet. Serve immediately. Serves 2.

Apple Pancakes with Small Venison Sausages

Pancakes, apples, and venison sausages in one dish makes a perfect brunch for two on the patio.

4 oz. flour
¼ tsp. salt
1 egg
10 oz. milk

½ lb. small venison sausages
2 apples, peeled, cored, and sliced
1 oz. sugar
¼ cup apple cider or juice

To make pancake mix, sieve the flour and salt together. Add the egg and beat. Slowly add the milk while stirring to make a smooth batter. Place the batter in the refrigerator to cool for 30 minutes. Cook the venison sausages on the grill or in the oven. Gently sauté the apples, sugar, and cider until the apples are just tender. Keep warm until ready to serve. While the sausages are cooking, cook the pancakes in a frying pan. Place some of the apple mix and sausages on each pancake and roll up. Serves 2.

Tomato Frittata with Venison Italian Sausage

1 Tbsp. cooking oil
¼ cup seasoned bread crumbs, divided
½ lb. venison Italian sausage, casings
  removed
2 cloves garlic, minced
1 (14½ oz.) can diced tomatoes with pepper,
  celery, and onion

10 large eggs, beaten
1 cup shredded Asiago or Parmesan
  cheese
2 Tbsp. chopped fresh parsley

Heat the oil in a skillet; add ¼ cup of the bread crumbs and lightly brown. Remove from the skillet and set aside. In the same skillet, brown the venison sausage and garlic; stir in the tomatoes. Simmer for 3 to 4 minutes. Add the eggs; cook over medium heat until the eggs are almost set. Sprinkle on the cheese, cover, and cook until the cheese melts and the egg is firm, 2 to 3 minutes. Sprinkle the remaining bread crumbs and parsley on top. Serves 6.

Puffed Venison Sausage Tarts

¼ cup sour cream
½ tsp. lemon pepper
½ tsp. ground cumin
½ lb. ground venison sausage
2 large eggs
½ cup milk
½ cup flour

¼ tsp. dried oregano
salt to taste
nonstick spray
½ cup diced green onions, divided
1 cup shredded Cheddar cheese
salt and pepper to taste
½ cup cubed tomatoes

Mix together the sour cream, lemon pepper, and cumin. Cover and chill until ready to serve. Fry the venison sausage until done, breaking up as it cooks. Drain off the excess fat. Combine the eggs, milk, flour, oregano, and salt, and beat until smooth. Spray four ½" deep tart pans with nonstick spray. Equally divide the batter, sausage, and green onions among the tart pans. Bake, uncovered, in a 425° F oven for 10 to 30 minutes or until puffed and the tops begin to tan. Top with the cheese and salt and pepper to taste and return the pans to the oven for 1 minute or until the cheese melts. Spoon the sour cream mixture over each tart. Garnish with fresh tomatoes and the remaining green onions. Serves 4.

Eggs Benedict with Venison Sausage and Cilantro Cream

Cilantro Salsa

1 bunch cilantro, chopped
2 garlic cloves, chopped
1 large tomato, peeled and chopped
½ medium onion, chopped
½ cup olive oil

3 tsp. lime juice
¼ tsp. red pepper or to taste
½ tsp. ground coriander
salt and pepper to taste
¼ cup water

Cilantro Cream

¼ cup sour cream
3 Tbsp. whipping cream

2 Tbsp. Cilantro Salsa

Sausage and Eggs

1½ lbs. bulk hot Italian venison sausage
4 garlic cloves, peeled and minced
2 Tbsp. chopped green onions
1 Tbsp. chopped fresh parsley
1 Tbsp. chopped fresh thyme
salt and pepper to taste

2 Tbsp. olive oil
water
¼ cup white wine vinegar
8 large eggs
4 flour tortillas, warmed

For Cilantro Salsa. Place all the ingredients in a blender and pulse until mixed together.

For Cilantro Cream. Combine all the ingredients in a small bowl and let sit at room temperature for 45 minutes before serving. Stir well.

For Sausage and Eggs. Combine the venison sausage, garlic, onion, parsley, and thyme in a medium bowl. Season with salt and pepper to taste and form into eight ½" thick patties. Heat the olive oil in a heavy large skillet over medium heat. Brown the venison sausage patties 2 minutes per side; cover the pan, lower the heat, and cook for about 10 minutes until the sausage is cooked. Meanwhile, bring a saucepan of water to boil over high heat. Add the vinegar. Crack the eggs and gently slide into the water; reduce heat and simmer about 3 minutes to set whites. Lift with a slotted spoon and transfer to paper towels. Place one egg on each tortilla. Place two sausage patties on top of each. Top with the remaining eggs and the Cilantro Cream; drizzle on the salsa. Serves 4.

Spicy Hot Venison Sausage Gravy

1 lb. bulk venison sausage
1 onion, minced
1 green bell pepper, minced
1 tsp. crushed red pepper flakes (optional)
2 Tbsp. minced garlic
¼ cup butter
salt and pepper to taste

¼ cup flour
1 Tbsp. minced fresh sage
1 tsp. minced fresh thyme
2 cups milk, divided
2 cubes chicken bouillon, crushed
¼ cup minced fresh parsley

In a skillet on medium heat, cook the venison sausage, onion, green pepper, red pepper flakes, and garlic until the sausage is crumbly. Drain off all but 2 Tbsp. of fat. Combine the butter, salt, and pepper with the sausage mixture and stir until the butter melts. Slowly sift the flour over the top. Mix gently and allow the mixture to cook for 5 minutes; frequently scrape the bottom of the pan to prevent burning. Sprinkle with the sage and thyme. Slowly stir in ½ cup milk. When the mixture thickens, add more milk. Do not let it boil. Add the crushed chicken bouillon and let cook for 5 minutes. If the mixture thickens too much, add more milk. Just before serving, add the parsley and about a ¼ cup more milk, because the gravy will thicken quickly as it cools. If the gravy is to be served later, add more milk to thin. Serves 4.

The first record of sausage was in Homer's *Odyssey*, written in the eighth or ninth century B.C.

The name "sausage" comes from the Latin word *salsus*, meaning salted or preserved meat.

Buttermilk Biscuits
with Breakfast Venison Sausage Gravy

Biscuits

2 pkgs. active dry yeast

¼ cup warm water

2 cups warm buttermilk

5 cups flour

⅓ cup sugar

1 Tbsp. baking powder

1 tsp. baking soda

1 Tbsp. salt

1 cup shortening

flour

shortening

2 Tbsp. butter, melted

Gravy

1 lb. ground breakfast venison sausage

2 Tbsp. finely chopped onion

1 Tbsp. flour

1 cup milk

½ tsp. nutmeg

½ tsp. poultry seasoning

¼ tsp. salt

dash Worcestershire sauce

dash hot pepper sauce

To Make Biscuits. Dissolve the yeast in the warm water and let stand for 10 minutes. Stir in the warm buttermilk and set aside. Sift together, into a large bowl, the flour, sugar, baking powder, soda, and salt. Cut in the shortening with a pastry blender until it is the size of coarse meal. Stir in the yeast/buttermilk mixture and mix well. Turn out onto a lightly floured surface and knead gently 3 to 4 times. Roll out to ¾" thick and cut with a 2½" biscuit cutter. Place the raw biscuits on a lightly greased baking sheet. Cover and let rise in a warm place for 1½ hours. Preheat the oven to 450° F and bake for 8 to 10 minutes or until golden. Remove from the oven and brush the tops with melted butter.

To Make Gravy: Crumble the venison sausage in a skillet and cook over medium-low heat. Add the onion, cook until clear, and drain off the fat. Stir in the flour, a little at a time, for about 6 minutes or until the mixture is bubbly and begins to brown. Slowly stir in the milk. Mix in the remaining ingredients and stir until thick. Serves 4 to 6.

> Many sausage recipes have become very popular in a particular region or in the city in which they were first made—and thus have taken that place's name, such as Genoa or Bologna.

Breakfast Venison Sausage Cake

1 cup raisins
3 cups boiling water
1 lb. ground venison sausage
1½ cups white sugar
1½ cups brown sugar
2 eggs, lightly beaten
3 cups all-purpose flour
1 tsp. ground ginger

1 tsp. baking powder
1 tsp. pumpkin pie spice
1 tsp. baking soda
1 cup cold coffee
1 cup chopped walnuts
shortening
flour

Preheat the oven to 350° F. Place the raisins in a bowl, cover with the boiling water, and set aside for 10 minutes. Then place the raisins in a colander to drain and set aside. Cook the sausage until lightly browned. Drain, crumble into small pieces, and set aside. In a large bowl, combine the sausage and sugars, stirring until mixed. Add the eggs and beat well. In a separate bowl, sift together the flour, ginger, baking powder, and pumpkin pie spice. Stir the baking soda into the coffee. Add the flour mixture and coffee alternately to the meat mixture, beating well after each addition. Fold the raisins and walnuts into the cake batter. Pour the batter into a well-greased and floured bundt cake pan. Bake for 75 to 90 minutes until done. Allow to cool for 15 minutes before removing from the pan. Serves 12.

Breakfast Venison Sausage and Cheese Casserole

shortening
4 cups cubed bread
2 cups shredded sharp Cheddar cheese
2 (12 oz.) cans evaporated milk
10 large eggs, lightly beaten
1 tsp. dry mustard

¼ tsp. onion powder
black pepper to taste
1 (12 oz.) pkg. fresh venison breakfast sausage, cooked, drained, and crumbled

Grease a 13" × 9" baking dish with shortening. Place the bread in the dish and sprinkle with the cheese. Combine the evaporated milk, eggs, mustard, onion powder, and pepper. Pour evenly over the bread and cheese. Sprinkle with the sausage. Cover and refrigerate overnight. Preheat the oven to 325° F and bake for 55 to 60 minutes or until the cheese is melted and begins to brown. Cover with foil if the top browns too quickly. Serves 8 to 10.

Spicy Venison Sausage Egg Muffins

12 paper muffin cups
½ lb. ground venison sausage
12 eggs, beaten
½ (4 oz.) can chopped green chili peppers,
    drained

1 small onion, chopped
1 tsp. garlic powder
salt and pepper to taste

Preheat the oven to 350° F. Insert the paper muffin cups in a 12-muffin tray. Place the venison sausage in a large skillet and cook over medium-high heat. Drain and set aside. In a large bowl, mix together the eggs, chilies, onion, garlic powder, salt, pepper, and sausage. Spoon ¼ cup of the mixture into each paper muffin cup. Bake for 15 to 20 minutes or until the eggs have set and a toothpick inserted into each muffin comes out clean. Makes 12.

Mushroom and Venison Sausage Quiche

1 lb. small button mushrooms
1 lb. ground venison breakfast sausage
½ cup chopped fresh parsley
3 eggs, beaten
1 cup half-and-half

½ cup grated Parmesan cheese
¼ tsp. salt
1 (9") frozen or unbaked piecrust

Preheat the oven to 400° F. Remove the stems from the mushrooms. Crumble the venison sausage in a large skillet, add the mushrooms, and cook on medium-high heat until the meat and mushrooms are lightly browned. Remove from the heat, drain off the grease, and mix in the parsley. In a large bowl, whisk together the eggs, half-and-half, cheese, and salt. Pour the egg mixture into the mushroom/sausage mixture and blend well. Pour into the unbaked pie shell. Bake for 25 to 30 minutes until the crust is browned and the filling is set. Let stand for 10 minutes before serving. Serves 6.

The hotter climates in southern Europe led people to develop dry sausage, which does not need refrigeration.

Apple and Venison Sausage Breakfast Omelet

½ lb. fresh venison sausage
½ cup applesauce
3 eggs, lightly beaten
1 Tbsp. sausage drippings

1 tsp. pimiento, chopped
½ tsp. chopped parsley
2 Tbsp. chopped apple

Cook the venison sausage in a skillet until browned. Drain, reserving 1 Tbsp. of the drippings. Crumble the sausage with the applesauce and set aside.

Make a French omelet using the reserved sausage drippings instead of butter. While the top is still moist and creamy, spread half the sausage/applesauce mixture over half of the omelet. With a pancake turner, fold the omelet, cut it in half, and place on serving plates. Sprinkle on the remaining sausage. Garnish with the chopped pimiento, parsley, and apple. Serves 2.

14

Seafood and Venison Sausage— The Best of Both Worlds

Sausage is the perfect foil for seafood, and the combination of both is the perfect complement for either small or large gatherings.

The flavor of the sausage adds a special touch to food that nothing else can. Sausages that have not been smoked or are only lightly smoked work best; heavily smoked venison sausage has a tendency to overpower the delicate taste of many seafoods.

It is the balance of tastes and textures that makes the combination of seafood and sausage so enjoyable.

Smoked Venison Andouille and Shrimp Jambalaya

2 Tbsp. cooking oil, divided
12 oz. smoked venison Andouille, sliced
  ½" thick
2 chicken breasts, deboned and skinless
1 medium onion, diced
2 stalks celery, diced
1 small clove garlic, minced
1 small bell pepper, diced

1 (28 oz.) can diced, peeled tomatoes
1 tsp. Worcestershire sauce
1 tsp. filé powder
1 tsp. Cajun spice blend
10 oz. raw shrimp, peeled
½ tsp. Tabasco sauce, or to taste
cooked rice for 4 to 6

Heat 1 Tbsp. of the oil in a large skillet over high heat and brown the venison sausage. Remove the sausage from the pan and reserve the drippings. Cut the chicken into ½" cubes and brown in the remaining oil. Return the sausage to the pan and add the onion, celery, garlic, and bell pepper. Sauté until the vegetables are tender. Stir in the tomatoes (with liquid) and Worcestershire sauce. Stir in the filé powder and Cajun spices, simmering over low heat for 45 minutes. Add the shrimp and cook until just firm. Season to taste with Tabasco sauce. Serve with the cooked rice. Serves 4 to 6.

Shrimp, Venison Sausage, and Couscous Stuffing

¼ cup olive oil
1 large onion, finely chopped
3 cloves garlic, finely chopped
4 celery stalks, finely chopped
1 green bell pepper, seeded and finely chopped
1 red bell pepper, seeded and finely chopped
1½ lbs. frozen or peeled fresh shrimp
2 cups coarsely chopped cooked ham
1 stick (8 oz.) hard venison sausage such as Pepperoni, sliced thin diagonally

4½ cups chicken broth
¼ cup butter
16 oz. instant couscous
2 cups crumbled corn bread
¼ cup tomato paste
2 Tbsp. chili powder
2 tsp. cumin
1 bunch parsley, finely chopped
salt and pepper to taste

Heat the oil in a very large skillet over medium-high heat. Sauté the onion, garlic, celery, and peppers until soft. Stir in the shrimp and continue to sauté until the shrimp are halfway cooked. Add the ham and venison sausage, cook over low heat for 5 minutes, and set aside. In another pot, bring the chicken broth to a boil, add the butter, and stir until the butter is melted. Quickly stir in the instant couscous, cover, remove from heat, and set aside for 5 minutes. Uncover, fluff the couscous with a fork, and spoon into a large mixing bowl. Mix the ham and venison sausage into the couscous. Mix together the corn bread and tomato paste. Mix in the remaining ingredients. If the dressing seems too dry, moisten with a little more chicken broth. Stuff the turkey or crown roast at once. Do not stuff the turkey or roast and place in the refrigerator overnight—stuff just before placing in the oven. Makes enough stuffing for a 20- to 24-pound turkey or a crown roast.

The pig, which was the main source of most sausages, was domesticated about 5000 B.C. in Egypt and China, and pig-raising spread quickly throughout the Near East, Europe, and Asia.

Shrimp and Smoked Venison Andouille Sausage with Mushroom Cream Sauce

2 Tbsp. olive oil
20 large raw shrimp, peeled
12 oz. venison Andouille sausage, sliced
16 large mushrooms, quartered
1 cup whipping cream

4 tsp. Worcestershire sauce
salt and pepper
chopped fresh parsley
cooked rice for 4

Heat the olive oil in a skillet. Add the shrimp and venison sausage and sauté until the shrimp just turn pink but are still soft. Remove the shrimp and venison sausage and set aside. Add the mushrooms to the skillet and sauté until just tender. Stir in the whipping cream and Worcestershire sauce. Simmer until the sauce begins to thicken. Return the shrimp and sausage to the skillet and simmer until the shrimp are just cooked, about 1 minute. Season with salt and pepper. Place the cooked rice on a serving platter; then spoon on the sausage and shrimp. Pour the mushroom sauce over top. Sprinkle with the parsley and serve. Serves 4.

Easy Italian Venison Sausage Paella

¼ cup olive oil
1 small onion, peeled and cut into thin strips
2 garlic cloves, minced
1 red bell pepper, seeded and diced
2 cups uncooked rice
2 cups chicken broth
1 tsp. saffron or turmeric

salt and pepper to taste
1 lb. cooked smoked Italian venison sausage links, cut into ½" slices
1 cup frozen artichoke hearts, thawed and halved
½ lb. large raw shrimp
1 cup frozen peas

Heat the oil in a large skillet; add the onion, garlic, and bell pepper. Sauté over medium heat until the onion is just clear. Add the rice, stir, and cook until the vegetables begin to brown, about 4 minutes. Add the saffron to the chicken broth and bring to a boil. Add to the rice mixture and bring back to a boil. Add the sausage and artichoke hearts; cover and cook until heated. Arrange the shrimp around the edges of the skillet and pour the peas in the center. Cover and cook for 4 to 5 minutes until the shrimp are just pink. Serves 6 to 8.

Smoked Venison Sausage and Clam Pasta

6 oz. smoked venison sausage, cooked and sliced
6 oz. cooked clam meat
¼ pound shredded ham

½ pound chopped fresh tomatoes
⅓ cup thinly sliced basil leaves
12 oz. beef broth
cooked pasta for 2

Combine all the ingredients, except the pasta; bring to a simmer and remove from the heat. Add the cooked pasta and serve. Serves 2.

Chinese Turnip, Shrimp, and Venison Sausage Cake

3 Tbsp. vegetable oil, divided
½ pound dried mushrooms, soaked in water overnight
⅓ cup dried shrimp, soaked in water overnight and drained
1 lb. small venison link sausage, sliced
2 slices fresh gingerroot

3 turnips, shredded
1½ tsp. Chinese five-spice powder
2 tsp. salt
½ tsp. chicken bouillon granules
1 Tbsp. white pepper
⅔ lb. white rice flour

Heat 2 Tbsp. of the oil in a wok or large skillet over high heat. Add the mushrooms, shrimp, and venison sausage and sauté for 30 seconds. Remove from the wok or skillet and set aside. Heat the remaining Tbsp. of oil in the wok or skillet. Add the ginger and sauté for a moment. Add the shredded turnips and stir-fry for about 3 minutes; do not remove the turnip water. Add the five-spice powder, salt, chicken bouillon, and white pepper and toss together until mixed. Remove the ginger slices. Turn off the heat. Sprinkle the turnip mixture with the rice flour and toss until mixed. Add the reserved sausage mixture and mix in. Remove from the wok or skillet and place into a 9" × 2" deep round cake pan. Wipe the wok or skillet clean, fill with water, and bring to a boil. Place the cake pan on a round wire rack over the boiling water. Reduce the heat to a simmer and steam the ingredients for 45 minutes. When the sausage cake is steamed through, remove from the wok or skillet and slice. Serve hot or cool on a wire rack. Serves 6 to 8.

Cataplana

A warm and spicy fish and venison sausage stew.

1 garlic clove, minced
1 medium onion, chopped
2 Tbsp. cooking oil
2 cans tomatoes, chopped
1 cup dry white wine
1 lb. mussels in shells, or a mixture of
    mussels or clams, or 2 doz. raw oysters

¾ lb. any firm fish fillets, skinned and cut
    into ¾" cubes
¼ lb. venison Chorizo sausage or any link
    sausage, sliced

Make tomato sauce by frying the garlic and onion in a little oil until just soft. Add the tomatoes and white wine and simmer, uncovered, for 15 minutes. Wash the shellfish in cold water, add to the sauce, and cook for 5 minutes until the shellfish open. Discard any shells that stay closed. Heat the venison Chorizo in the saucepan for a few minutes until oil begins to run. Drain the sausage and discard the oil. Add the sausage and fish to the sauce and cook for another few minutes or until the fish is firm. Serves 4.

Shrimp and Venison Sausage Jambalaya

2 Tbsp. cooking oil
1 lb. venison Andouille, Chorizo, or other
    smoked sausage, sliced ¼" thick
2 cups chopped onions
¾ cup chopped bell peppers
¾ cup chopped celery
salt and red pepper to taste
1 cup rice

1 (14½ oz.) can whole tomatoes, chopped,
    with juices
1 Tbsp. minced garlic
4 bay leaves, halved
2 cups water
¼ tsp. dried thyme
1 lb. medium shrimp, peeled
¼ cup chopped green onions

Heat the oil in a large pot. Add the venison sausage and cook for 2 minutes. Add the onions, bell peppers, and celery. Season with salt and red pepper to taste. Sauté for 6 to 8 minutes or until the onions are just clear. Stir in the rice. Add the tomatoes (with the liquid), garlic, bay leaves, water, and thyme. Cover and cook over medium heat for 20 minutes. Season the shrimp with salt and cayenne, add to the mixture, and cook for 10 more minutes until the rice is tender, the liquid is absorbed, and the shrimp are just pink. Remove from the stove, cover, and let stand for 10 minutes. Remove the bay leaves. Stir in the green onions and serve. Serves 6.

Portuguese-Style Venison Sausage and Fish Chowder

2 Tbsp. olive oil
2 bay leaves
1 Tbsp. minced garlic
2 medium onions, chopped large
1 medium green bell pepper, seeded and
   chopped large
¼ tsp. ground allspice
2 lbs. potatoes, peeled and sliced ¼" thick
4 cups fish stock or chicken broth
2 cups canned whole tomatoes with juice,
   cut into ½" chunks

6 oz. venison Chorizo or venison
   Andouille sausage, casings removed,
   sliced ¼" thick
salt and black pepper to taste
2 lbs. skinless firm-fleshed fish, whole
   fillets
¼ cup finely chopped cilantro
2 Tbsp. coarsely chopped parsley

Heat a large cooking pot and add the olive oil and bay leaves. When the bay leaves turn brown, add the garlic and cook until just beginning to brown. Add the onions, green pepper, and allspice. Sauté, stirring occasionally, for about 8 minutes or until the onions are just clear. Add the potatoes with just enough stock or broth to cover. Cover and boil for 10 minutes or until the potatoes are almost tender. Reduce the heat, add the tomatoes and sausage, and simmer for 5 minutes. Season with salt and pepper. Add the fish fillets, cook for 5 minutes, and remove from the heat. Gently stir in the cilantro and allow to stand for 10 minutes. Allow the chowder to mellow at room temperature for 1 hour before serving. Heat and sprinkle with the parsley before serving. Serves 8.

Husbandry methods vary worldwide. In many parts of the world, deer are raised on either native ranges or improved pastures. Where land costs are high and available parcels small, deer are hand-fed in open or covered enclosures.

Christmas Paella with Clams and Venison Sausage

2 lbs. small pieces of firm-fleshed fish,
    shrimp, crab claws, lobster, and/or
    mussels
12 cherrystone clams
½ lb. venison sausage links
water
2 chickens, cut into pieces
2 tsp. salt, divided
black pepper to taste
½ cup olive oil, divided
paprika

½ cup chopped onion
2 garlic cloves, minced
3 large tomatoes, finely chopped
⅛ tsp. red pepper flakes (optional)
3 cups long-grained rice
⅛ tsp. minced saffron
6 cups boiling water
1 small can English peas (or equivalent
    amount of frozen peas)
2 lemons, cut in wedges

Scrub the mussels and clams, cover, and set aside. Place the sausage links in a pan, pierce several times with a sharp fork, add enough water to completely cover the links, and bring to a boil. Reduce the heat and simmer, uncovered, for 5 minutes. Drain on paper towels. When cool, slice into ¼" pieces. Season the chicken with 1 tsp. of the salt and pepper. Heat ¼ cup of the olive oil in a skillet, add the chicken, and brown on all sides. Remove the chicken, sprinkle with the paprika, cover, and set aside. Wipe the fat from the skillet and add the remaining ¼ cup of olive oil. Heat the oil and add the onions, garlic, and tomatoes, stirring constantly. Sprinkle on the crushed pepper flakes. In a paella pan, skillet, or deep casserole dish, add the vegetables, rice, remaining 1 tsp. of salt, and saffron. Pour the boiling water over the mixture while stirring. Place the chicken, fish, and venison sausage on top of the rice. Bake for about 1 hour or until all the liquid is absorbed by the rice. In the 10 minutes before removing it from the oven, sprinkle the peas over the top. Remove and let rest for several minutes before serving. Garnish with the lemon wedges. Serves 8 to 10.

Man has hunted deer since prehistoric times. They were an important source not only for food but for tools and weapons, which were fashioned from the deer's antlers.

Com Chien Thap Cam

A traditional Vietnamese fried rice, shrimp, and crabmeat dish made with venison sausage.

6 qts. water
1⅔ cups long-grained white rice
6 dried Chinese mushrooms
1½ cups hot water
1 medium onion
2 large green onions
¼ lb. (21 to 25 per lb.) raw shrimp, peeled

2 Chinese venison sausages or other
   small sausages
¼ cup vegetable oil
1 Tbsp. *nam pla* or *nuoc mam* (fish sauce)
½ lb. lump crabmeat
2 eggs

The day before, bring a large pot of unsalted water to a boil. Stirring constantly, slowly pour in the rice. Reduce the heat and gently boil the rice, uncovered, for about 15 minutes, or until the grains are almost tender but still slightly firm. Drain the rice and fluff with a fork. Remove the rice to a large bowl, cover tightly, and allow to cool. Refrigerate overnight or for at least 12 hours. The next day, place the dried mushrooms in a small bowl containing the hot water. Soak for 30 minutes, then drain. Rinse with warm water and cut off the stems. Slice each mushroom into ½" strips. Slice the onion into ¼" strips. Slice the green onions lengthwise into ¼" strips and cut into 1" long pieces. Chop the shrimp into ¼" pieces and set aside. Cut the venison sausage into 1⅛" slices.

    Fry the sausages in a skillet or wok over moderate heat, stirring constantly, for about 2 minutes, or until the slices are crisp and browned on both sides. Remove and drain. Heat half the oil in the skillet or wok. Add the onions, stir constantly, and cook for 2 to 3 minutes or until they are just clear. Reduce the heat, add the mushrooms and chilled rice, and cook, stirring constantly, until the rice is heated through. Stir in the fish sauce. Push the rice to the edge of the skillet or wok. Pour in the remaining oil and place the shrimp in the center. Without touching the rice, cook the shrimp until they are pink and just firm. Mix the shrimp into the rice. Continue stirring and cook over medium heat for 5 minutes. Do not let the rice brown. Mix in the crabmeat and sausage and cook for 2 minutes. Break the eggs one at a time and mix in. Stir in the green onions. Taste and add more salt or fish sauce if needed. Remove to individual serving plates. Serves 6.

There are now approximately 250,000 wild
Red deer in Scotland.

Shrimp and Smoked Venison Sausage Louisian

1 lb. smoked venison Andouille sausage,
  sliced thin
6 Tbsp. olive oil, divided
1 large onion, chopped
1 large green pepper, chopped
5 stalks celery, chopped
2 Tbsp. olive oil
1 garlic clove, minced
1 hot jalapeño pepper, seeded and minced

1 Tbsp. oregano
1 Tbsp. chili powder
1 Tbsp. cumin
salt to taste
1 (28 oz.) can whole peeled tomatoes,
  drained (reserve liquid)
16 (1 lb.) raw shrimp, shelled
4 boneless chicken breasts, cubed
4 cups cooked brown rice

Sauté the venison sausage in 2 Tbsp. of the olive oil until brown and set aside. Sauté the onion, green pepper, and celery in 2 more Tbsp. of the oil until soft. Add the garlic, jalapeño, oregano, chili powder, cumin, and salt; sauté for another minute. Add the tomatoes and reserved venison sausage. Stir, adding some of the reserved tomato liquid if needed. Set aside until ready to serve. Sauté the shrimp and chicken in the remaining 2 Tbsp. of olive oil until just cooked and add to the sausage mixture. Serve over the brown rice. Serves 8.

Whitetail deer were first introduced into New Zealand in 1901.

The largest living deer is the Alaskan moose, which can weigh more than 1,700 pounds.

Saffron, Seafood, and Venison Sausage Paella

Shrimp
1 cup dry white wine
2 cherry tomatoes, seeded and chopped
2 Tbsp. olive oil
2 garlic cloves, finely minced
1½ tsp. finely minced saffron
black pepper
1½ lbs. large raw shrimp, unpeeled

Rice
¼ cup olive oil, divided
1½ cups chopped white onion
4 garlic cloves, minced
6 cups canned chicken broth

1½ tsp. finely minced saffron, divided
1 bay leaf, halved
3 cups raw long-grained rice
mesquite or hickory chips, soaked
    overnight in water
1 large red bell pepper, quartered and
    seeded
1 large green bell pepper, quartered and
    seeded
1 lb. smoked venison sausage links
1 (8 oz.) pkg. frozen peas, briefly boiled
1 lb. steamed mussels
fresh parsley, minced

For the Shrimp. Mix together all the ingredients except the shrimp and bring to a simmer in a large casserole dish. Add the shrimp and place in the refrigerator overnight. Turn the shrimp several times.

For the Rice. Heat 3 Tbsp. of the oil in a large pot. Add the onions and garlic and sauté until the onions are just clear. Add the chicken broth, saffron, and bay leaf and bring to a boil. Stir in the rice, reduce the heat to low, cover, and cook for about 15 to 20 minutes or until all the liquid is just absorbed. Place the rice in a large bowl. Cool completely and fluff several times.

Heat a barbecue grill to high heat and add the wood chips. Brush the peppers with the remaining 1 Tbsp. of oil. Place the peppers, skin side down, on the grill and cook just until the skin begins to darken in spots. Remove from the grill and when cool cut into ¼" strips.

Remove the shrimp from the refrigerator and skewer. Reserve the marinade. Place the shrimp and venison sausage on the grill and cook until the sausage is cooked through and the shrimp are just pink. Remove the shrimp first, because they will cook more quickly than the sausage. Allow the shrimp and sausage to slightly cool, then peel the shrimp and return them to the marinade. Cut the sausage into 1" thick rounds. Add the sausage and peas to the rice and toss gently. Set aside 6 shrimp. Toss the remaining shrimp and marinade with the rice mixture. Transfer to a large platter. Arrange mussels on the half shell around the edge. Place the roasted peppers in the center. Top with the reserved shrimp. Sprinkle with the minced parsley and serve. Serves 6.

15

One-Dish Venison Sausage Casseroles

Casseroles are known for being easy and quick to prepare. By making and freezing your own sausage, you add a convenience to cooking casseroles that you can't get anywhere else.

Place the frozen sausage in the refrigerator for an hour or so. It will already be soft enough for you to use when you are in a hurry yet still need to serve something different.

Venison casseroles are the ideal way to introduce venison to those who have not had the pleasure of enjoying it before.

Baked Almond, Venison Sausage, and Rice Casserole

1 lb. venison sausage links, sliced ¼" thick
½ onion, chopped
1 stalk celery, chopped
1 green bell pepper, chopped
½ cup raw long-grained white rice

2 cups hot water
1 (4½ oz.) pkg. chicken noodle soup mix
shortening
½ cup slivered almonds

Preheat the oven to 350° F. In a large skillet, combine the venison sausage, onion, celery, and green bell pepper and sauté for 5 minutes. Drain away the excess fat. Stir the raw rice into the sausage and vegetables. Stir in the water and the soup mix. Transfer this mixture to a lightly greased 2-quart casserole dish, cover with the almonds, and bake for 1½ hours. Serves 4 to 6.

Unless disturbed, deer tend to travel along
the lines of least resistance.

Baked Spinach, Italian Venison Sausage, and Cheese Casserole

1 lb. bulk Italian venison sausage
1 (8 oz.) can tomato sauce
2 (10 oz.) pkgs. frozen chopped spinach, thawed
1 tsp. fennel seeds

2 cups cottage cheese
½ cup grated Parmesan cheese
1 egg, beaten
2 cups shredded mozzarella cheese

Preheat the oven to 350° F. Brown the venison sausage in a skillet over medium-high heat. Drain the fat from the skillet and stir in the tomato sauce. Set the mixture aside. In a large bowl, combine the spinach, fennel, cottage cheese, Parmesan cheese, and egg. Mix well and spread in the bottom of a 9" × 13" baking dish. Spoon the sausage mixture over the spinach mixture and top with the mozzarella cheese. Bake for 40 minutes. Serves 8.

Fried Venison Sausage Casserole

2 lbs. venison sausage links
1¼ cups sifted all-purpose flour
1 tsp. salt

2 large eggs
1½ cups milk

Preheat the oven to 425° F. In a hot skillet, fry the venison sausages until brown on all sides. Remove and reserve the drippings. Cut crosswise in half. In a bowl, sift the flour and salt. Gradually add the flour mixture into the milk. While beating, add the eggs; beat until smooth. Pour 2 Tbsp. of the hot sausage drippings into a 12" × 8" × 2" baking dish. Arrange the sausage pieces over the bottom of the dish and pour the egg mixture over top. Bake for 25 minutes or until it puffs and browns. Serves 6.

During the Middle Ages, practically every nation in Europe manufactured some type of sausage.

Mushroom and Venison Sausage Casserole

shortening
2 cups seasoned croutons
1 cup shredded Cheddar cheese
1 (4 oz.) can mushroom pieces, drained
1½ lbs. bulk fresh venison sausage, crumbled
½ cup chopped onion

6 eggs
2½ cups milk, divided
½ tsp. salt
½ tsp. pepper
½ tsp. dry mustard
1 (10¾ oz.) can cream of mushroom soup

Place croutons in a greased 13" × 9" × 2" pan or casserole dish. Cover with the cheese and mushrooms. Brown the venison sausage and onion; drain and spread over the cheese. Beat the eggs with 2 cups of the milk, the salt, the pepper, and the mustard; pour over the sausage. Cover and refrigerate overnight. Mix the soup with the remaining ½ cup of milk and spread on top of the casserole. Bake at 325° F for 60 minutes. Serves 6.

Spicy Venison Chorizo and Cheese Casserole

shortening
¼ lb. Chorizo sausage, cooked and drained
¼ cup chopped mild green chilies
¼ fresh jalapeño pepper, minced (optional)
¼ lb. Monterey Jack cheese, cubed
3 cups cubed French bread
4 eggs

¾ tsp. cumin powder
½ tsp. salt
½ tsp. pepper
2⅔ cups milk
¼ cup butter, melted
chunky salsa
sour cream

Grease one 2 quart casserole dish or four individual ovenproof ramekins. Equally spread the venison Chorizo over the bottom of each casserole; top with the chilies and jalapeños. Sprinkle the casseroles equally with the cubed cheese, then with the French bread cubes. In a medium mixing bowl, whisk the eggs; add the cumin, salt, pepper, and milk. Pour the melted butter over each casserole. Pour the egg mixture over top. Chill for at least 2 hours or overnight.

Preheat the oven to 300° F. Place the casseroles or ramekins in a pan of hot water and bake for 45 to 50 minutes, or until puffed and set. Serve with chunky salsa and sour cream. Serves 4.

Hot Venison Sausage Links
and Baked Bean Casserole

2 Tbsp. olive oil, divided
2 garlic cloves, minced
1 cup chopped onion
1 tsp. dried oregano
1 Tbsp. chopped fresh parsley
¼ tsp. salt
½ tsp. black pepper

4 potatoes, peeled and sliced
½ lb. venison link sausage, sliced
½ cup brown sugar, packed
2 cups baked beans
¼ cup barbecue sauce
1 cup shredded Cheddar cheese

Preheat the oven to 350° F. In a medium skillet, heat 1 Tbsp. of the olive oil over medium heat. Add the garlic and cook for 30 seconds. Stir in the onion, oregano, parsley, salt, and pepper. Cook for 1 minute and remove from the heat. Spread the remaining 1 Tbsp. of olive oil over the bottom of an 8" × 8" × 2" baking dish. Layer the sliced potatoes and top with the onion mixture. Evenly distribute the sliced sausage links on top of the onion. In a small bowl, combine the brown sugar, baked beans, and barbecue sauce. Pour evenly over the sausage and top with the shredded Cheddar cheese. Place in the preheated oven for 45 minutes. Serves 6.

Swiss Venison Sausage Casserole

shortening
6 slices bread
2 lbs. mild bulk venison sausage
1 tsp. prepared mustard
1 (6 oz.) pkg. Swiss cheese slices
2½ cups milk

¼ tsp. salt
⅛ tsp. black pepper
⅛ tsp. ground nutmeg
1 tsp. Worcestershire sauce
3 eggs

Lightly grease a 13" × 9" casserole dish and layer with the bread. Sauté the venison sausage and drain. Mix the mustard into the sausage and spoon over the bread. Layer with the cheese. Whisk together the remaining ingredients and pour over the cheese. Cover with aluminum foil and place in the refrigerator for 4 hours. Remove from the refrigerator, bring to room temperature, and bake at 350° F for 30 minutes or until the cheese begins to melt. Serves 4 to 6.

Smothered Venison Sausage

1 large onion
3 green peppers
6 celery stalks
2 garlic cloves
1 lb. smoked small venison sausage links

1 large sprig fresh thyme or large pinch
   dried thyme
4 oz. dry white wine or chicken stock
½ cup chopped fresh parsley

Preheat the oven to 350° F. Cut the vegetables into thick slices. Place the sausages in a single layer into a casserole or baking dish. Add the vegetables, thyme, and wine. Cover the casserole or dish. Cook in the center of the preheated oven for 45 to 90 minutes. Sprinkle the parsley over top before serving. Serves 4.

Italian Venison Sausage, Peppers, and Onions

2 Tbsp. olive oil
4 green peppers, seeded and cut into strips
2 onions, cut into strips

salt and pepper to taste
8 Italian venison sausages (hot or mild)

Preheat the oven to 350° F. Coat the bottom of a frying pan with the olive oil. Add the green peppers, onions, salt, and pepper. Place the Italian sausages on top of the peppers and onions. Cover lightly with foil and bake for 45 minutes. Remove the foil and bake for another 7 to 8 minutes. Turn the sausages and bake for another 7 to 8 minutes. Remove from the oven and serve on soft French rolls. Serves 4 to 6.

If you are lucky enough to watch a buck working a scrape, pay particular attention to the time of day as well as his direction of travel. Deer often have a very precise schedule and can be found at a particular scrape at the appointed time.

Thick-Cut Venison Chops
with Italian Venison Sausage Casserole

4 thick-cut venison chops
salt and pepper to taste
1 Tbsp. olive oil
¼ lb. sweet Italian venison sausage
1 onion, slivered

¼ lb. mushrooms, sliced
1 garlic clove, minced
¼ cup dry red wine
1 (8 oz.) can tomato sauce
½ tsp. Italian seasoning

Preheat the oven to 375° F. Sprinkle the venison chops with salt and pepper. Heat the olive oil in a skillet and brown the chops on both sides. Remove the chops and set aside. Pour off the drippings, reserving 1 Tbsp. of liquid. Remove the casings from the sausage and crumble into the same skillet. Mix in the onion and mushrooms. Cook until the onion and sausage brown slightly. Mix in the garlic. Place the venison chops in a casserole dish. Spoon the sausage mixture over the chops and pour in the wine and tomato sauce. Sprinkle with the Italian seasoning. Cover with foil and bake for 45 minutes. Serves 4.

Mozzarella and Venison Sausage Brunch Casserole

1½ lbs. ground venison sausage
shortening
1 (8 oz.) pkg. refrigerated crescent roll
   dough

2 cups shredded mozzarella cheese
4 eggs, beaten
¾ cup milk
salt and pepper to taste

Preheat the oven to 425° F. Cook the venison sausage in a large skillet. Drain, crumble, and set aside. Lightly grease a 9" × 13" baking pan. Lay the crescent rolls flat in the bottom of the pan. Combine the cooked sausage, cheese, eggs, milk, salt, and pepper and pour over the crescent rolls. Bake for 15 minutes, or until bubbly and the rolls are baked. Serves 12.

About 79 percent of pregnant whitetail does carry twins or triplets, while only 52 percent of pregnant mule deer does have multiple births.

Vegetable and Venison Sausage Casserole

shortening
5 potatoes, sliced
1 onion, sliced
1 (15 oz.) can whole-kernel corn, undrained

1 (14½ oz.) can diced tomatoes
1 lb. venison sausage links, sliced
salt and pepper to taste

Preheat the oven to 350° F. Place the potato slices in the bottom of a lightly greased 9" × 13" baking dish. Add the onion slices, corn (with liquid), and tomatoes (with liquid). Top with the sausage slices and season with salt and pepper. Bake for about 1 hour or until the sausage is cooked. Serves 4 to 6.

Baked Smoked Venison Sausage Casserole

8 cups cubed raw potatoes
1 lb. smoked venison sausage links, sliced
1 (10¾ oz.) can condensed cream of
  mushroom soup

1 (10¾ oz.) can condensed vegetable beef
  soup

Preheat the oven to 350° F. In a 4 quart casserole dish, add the potatoes, venison sausage, mushroom soup, and vegetable beef soup and mix together well. Bake for 1½ hours. Serves 6.

   This recipe can also be made in a Crock-Pot. Place all the ingredients in the Crock-Pot and cook on low for 6 to 8 hours.

Most deer associate in groups, although a few are solitary, usually during the nonmating season. Typically, male deer gather a harem during the breeding season. Some, such as the reindeer, migrate.

Baked Venison Sausage and Potato Casserole

aluminum foil
3 large baking potatoes, peeled and sliced
  thin
black pepper to taste
1 cup shredded Cheddar cheese

1 lb. venison Kielbasa sausage or other
  sausage, sliced thin
½ tsp. dried dill
¼ tsp. caraway seeds
⅔ cup milk

Preheat the oven to 375° F. Cut two long sheets of aluminum foil and lay on top of each other; fold one long edge together and open out to make a large sheet of foil. Lay the folded foil on a 13" × 9" cookie sheet and allow the edges to hang outside the pan. Arrange the sliced potatoes on the pan, slightly overlapping the slices. Add pepper to taste. Top the potatoes with half the cheese. Lay the venison sausage slices on top and cover with the remaining cheese, dill, caraway seeds, and milk. Fold the sides of the aluminum foil over and seal all edges tightly. Bake for 1 hour. Serves 6.

Spicy Venison Sausage and Broccoli Casserole

2 cups cooked rice
1 lb. venison bulk sausage, cooked and
  drained
1 can sliced water chestnuts, drained

1½ cups cooked chopped broccoli
1 lb. (4 cups) shredded sharp Cheddar
  cheese, divided

Preheat the oven to 375° F. Layer the rice, sausage, water chestnuts, broccoli, and 1 cup of the cheese in a baking dish. Sprinkle with the remaining cheese. Bake for about 30 minutes or until the cheese is bubbly. Serves 6 to 8.

The "lost" fawns people pick up in late summer are not really lost at all. They were simply hidden while the mother browsed or rested nearby. Young whitetail fawns should never be picked up and tamed as pets.

Sweet Potato, Venison Sausage, and Fı

4 large sweet potatoes, boiled, divided
shortening
1 lb. Small Venison Sausages with Lemon
    and Spices (page 112) or any fresh
    venison sausage
2 large apples, pared and cut in thick slices

6 slices canned pineap
2 Tbsp. crumbled cooke
salt
3 Tbsp. dark brown sugar,
    divided
milk

Preheat the oven to 350° F. Peel and slice the boiled sweet potatoes ⌐nin slices. Grease a baking dish. Cover the bottom with half of the sweet potatoes. Shape the venison sausage into four flat patties and brown lightly in a skillet. Lay the sausage patties on top of the sweet potatoes. Cover with the fruits and bacon bits. Sprinkle lightly with salt and half of the brown sugar. Add the remaining sweet potatoes on top of the fruit. Brush with milk. Sprinkle with the remaining brown sugar. Bake for about 45 minutes. Serves 4.

Baked Bean and Venison Sausage Casserole

½ lb. fresh, ground venison sausage
1 small onion, chopped
2 (16 oz.) cans baked beans with pork
½ tsp. mustard powder
½ cup brown sugar, lightly packed

¼ cup white sugar
2 Tbsp. ketchup
2 Tbsp. barbecue sauce
2 Tbsp. Worcestershire sauce

Preheat the oven to 350° F. Cook the venison sausage and onions in a skillet until the sausage is browned. Drain off the excess fat. Add the remaining ingredients to the browned sausage; mix well. Pour into a casserole dish and bake for 40 to 50 minutes. Serves 5.

16

Old World Pasta and New World Venison Sausage

With all the wonderful Italian dishes that call for sausage, you would think the Italians invented sausage.

There is just something about pasta and sausage that brings to mind large family gatherings, long tables covered with steaming dishes of vegetables, and pastas with chunks of sausage and melted cheese.

Since most pasta dishes are either made from boiled pasta or baked in the oven, you can choose between a dish that is quick and easy and one that's straight from the oven, steaming, and with touches of crunchy topping.

Ziti Pasta with Italian Venison Sausage

1 lb. Italian venison sausage, casings
  removed
½ cup diced celery
½ cup diced onion
1 (14½ oz.) can peeled and diced tomatoes
1 (15 oz.) can tomato sauce
¼ tsp. garlic powder
1½ tsp. salt

1 tsp. dried oregano
salt
1 lb. dry ziti pasta
2 (4½ oz.) cans sliced mushrooms,
  drained
8 oz. shredded mozzarella cheese
¼ cup grated Parmesan cheese

Preheat the oven to 350° F. Sauté the venison sausage over medium heat with the celery and onion until the sausage is brown. In another skillet, combine the tomatoes, tomato sauce, garlic powder, salt, and oregano, and simmer while the pasta is cooking. Bring a large pot of lightly salted water to a boil. Add the pasta and cook for 8 to 10 minutes or per package directions. In a 3 quart baking dish, divide the cooked ziti pasta, mushrooms, venison sausage, and mozzarella cheese, layering twice. Top with the grated Parmesan. Bake for 45 minutes, until browned and bubbly. Serves 8.

Lasagna with Venison Sausage and Italian Cheeses

3 Tbsp. olive oil
1 large onion, chopped
4 garlic cloves, chopped and divided
1½ lbs. sweet or hot venison sausage,
    crumbled
1 large red bell pepper, chopped
1 (28 oz.) can tomato sauce
½ cup Chianti wine

1 large egg, beaten
15 oz. ricotta cheese
salt and pepper to taste
12 (7" × 3½") no-boil lasagna pasta
    sheets
12 oz. mozzarella cheese, grated, divided
¼ cup grated Parmesan cheese

Preheat the oven to 375° F. Sauté the onion and three-quarters of the garlic in the olive oil until softened. Add the venison sausage and bell pepper, and cook for 2 minutes. Break up the sausage as it cooks. Add the tomato sauce, wine, and remaining garlic. Simmer for 10 minutes. Stir together the egg, ricotta, salt, and pepper. Pour 1 cup of the sauce into a 13" × 9" × 2" baking dish and cover with 3 lasagna sheets. Spread 2 cups of sauce over the pasta. Sprinkle a third of the ricotta mixture onto the sauce and spread. Sprinkle a quarter of the mozzarella over the ricotta mixture. Make two more layers in the same manner, beginning and ending with pasta. Spread the remaining sauce evenly over the top, making sure the pasta is completely covered. Sprinkle on the remaining Parmesan and mozzarella. Cover the dish tightly with foil and bake in the middle of the oven for 20 minutes. Remove the foil and bake the lasagna for 10 minutes more, or until the top is bubbling and beginning to brown. Remove the lasagna and let it stand for 10 minutes before serving. Serves 8.

Pumpkin and Venison Sausage Pasta Salad

3 Tbsp. olive oil
1 garlic clove, minced
½ tsp. dried basil leaves
¼ tsp. dry mustard
½ tsp. salt
2 cups carrots, cut into ¼" strips
6 small venison sausages, cooked and sliced

½ lb. pumpkin-shaped holiday pasta,
    cooked
1 cup black olives, sliced
leaf lettuce
¼ tsp. freshly ground pepper
grated Parmesan cheese to taste

In a skillet, heat the oil over medium heat. Add the garlic, seasonings, and carrots. Sauté the carrots until tender-crisp, about 3 minutes. Remove from the heat. Toss the venison sausage slices with the carrot mixture, pasta, and olives. Chill and serve on a bed of lettuce, topping with grated Parmesan cheese. Serves 6.

Pizza Venison Sausage Dogs

nonstick spray
2 refrigerator pizza dough tubes
1 jar pizza or pasta sauce, divided
8 small venison sausages, cooked
optional chopped pizza toppings: onions,
    green peppers, olives, etc.

1 Tbsp. Italian herb seasoning mix
1 cup shredded mozzarella cheese
¼ cup grated Parmesan cheese

Preheat the oven to 300° F. Spray a cookie sheet with nonstick spray. Place the pizza dough on the sheet and cut into eight squares; press the dough thin with your fingers. Spoon pizza sauce onto each square. Lay on venison sausages, other pizza toppings, and Italian herb mix to taste. Sprinkle with the cheeses. Wrap the sausages completely in the dough and pinch the ends closed. Bake for approximately 15 minutes or until the crust begins to brown. Serve with warm pizza sauce for dip. Serves 6.

The red deer stag has a deep throaty bellow that can signal females or a challenge to a fight.

Hunters in the U.S. harvest approximately four million deer each year.

Penne with Cabbage, Italian Venison Sausage, and Marinara Sauce

Marinara Sauce

2 (28 oz.) cans Italian plum tomatoes with basil
¼ cup fine-quality olive oil
2 oz. salt pork
3 Tbsp. minced onion

2 garlic cloves, peeled and minced
salt to taste
6 fresh basil leaves, minced
⅛ tsp. dried oregano
pepper to taste

Pasta with Venison Sausage

¼ cup olive oil
4 garlic cloves, peeled and mashed
1 lb. Italian venison sausage, cut into bite-sized pieces
1 lb. cabbage, cooked and chopped into bite-sized pieces

salt and pepper to taste
3 cups Marinara Sauce
1 lb. dry penne pasta
salt
freshly grated Romano cheese

For the Marinara Sauce. Remove the tomatoes from the can and reserve the liquid. Using your hands, crush the tomatoes, gently removing and discarding the hard core from the stem end. Remove and discard any skin and tough membrane. Set aside. Put the oil in a large saucepan and heat over medium-low heat. Cut the salt pork into small pieces and add to the pan. Sauté for about 5 minutes. Remove and discard the salt pork, then add the onion. Sauté for 3 minutes or until clear and just beginning to brown. Stir in the garlic and sauté for 30 seconds or until just softened. Stir in the tomatoes and salt. Raise the heat and bring to a boil. Immediately reduce the heat to a very low simmer and cook for about 1 hour until the sauce is thickened. Stir in the basil, oregano, and pepper, and cook for an additional minute. Remove from the heat and serve. Makes approximately 7 cups.

For the Pasta. Heat the oil and garlic in a large sauté pan over medium heat. Add the venison sausage and sauté until the meat is cooked. Add the cabbage, salt, and pepper and sauté for an additional 1 to 2 minutes. Stir in the Marinara Sauce and cook for 3 to 5 minutes. Cook the penne per package directions in a large, deep pot of boiling salted water. Drain the pasta and return it to the pot with ½ cup of sauce. Stir for 1 minute over high heat, place the sauced pasta on a serving platter, and pour the remaining sauce on top. Serve with a sprinkle of Romano cheese. Serves 4.

Herbed Smoked Venison Sausage with Egg Noodles

½ cup chopped onion
½ cup chopped green bell pepper
2 Tbsp. butter or margarine
1 (14 oz.) can stewed tomatoes, chopped
1 (6 oz.) can tomato paste
1 tsp. salt
½ tsp. dried basil
½ tsp. paprika

¼ tsp. black pepper
¼ tsp. nutmeg
¼ tsp. garlic salt
1 lb. Kielbasa venison sausage, sliced
1 cup apple cider
2 cups raw egg noodles, cooked as
    directed

Cook the onion and green pepper in the butter until soft. Add the stewed tomatoes, tomato paste, and spices, and simmer for 10 minutes. Simmer the sausage in the cider for 10 minutes. Drain, discarding the apple cider. Combine the sausage with the cooked egg noodles and serve on a large platter. Serves 4.

Chicken and Spicy Italian Venison Sausage with Penne Pasta

2 skinless, boneless chicken breasts
1 lb. spicy Italian venison sausage
1 Tbsp. olive oil
2 garlic cloves, sliced
1 (14½ oz.) can crushed tomatoes

½ cup dry Italian red wine
2 Tbsp. chopped fresh basil
1 tsp. dried rosemary
salt and pepper to taste
1 lb. penne pasta, cooked and drained

Wash the chicken breasts and cut into large bite-sized pieces. Remove the casing from the venison sausage, cut into large pieces, and set aside. In a large, deep skillet, heat the oil and sauté the garlic. Remove the garlic from the oil. Add the chicken and sausage to the skillet and brown both lightly. Add the tomatoes and wine. Bring to a boil and simmer for 20 minutes. Season the sauce mixture with basil, rosemary, salt, and pepper. Add the cooked, drained pasta to the skillet mixture. Toss and serve. Serves 4 to 6.

Bulk Venison Sausage and White Cheese Pizza

12 oz. bulk Italian venison sausage
1 Tbsp. butter
1 cup chopped onion
1 (12") prepared pizza crust

1¼ cups pizza sauce
12 oz. mozzarella cheese, shredded
½ lb. cooked venison sausage links, sliced
12 oz. shredded Monterey Jack cheese

Preheat the oven to 350° F. Place the Italian venison sausage in a large, deep skillet. Cook over medium-high heat until browned. Drain, slice, and set aside. Over medium-low heat, melt the butter in a large saucepan. Add the onions and cook slowly, stirring occasionally, until just clear. Place the prepared crust on the pizza pan. Spread the pizza sauce over the crust and add Italian sausage. Cover with the mozzarella cheese and arrange sliced venison links over the cheese. Spread Monterey Jack cheese on top of the sausage. Bake for 20 to 25 minutes, until golden. Serves 12.

Broccoli Cavatelli with Venison Sausage

1 lb. spicy Italian sausage, crumbled
½ cup olive oil
4 garlic cloves, minced
salt
1 (16 oz.) pkg. cavatelli pasta

1 lb. frozen broccoli
½ tsp. crushed red pepper flakes
   (optional)
¼ cup grated Parmesan cheese

In a medium skillet over medium heat, fry the venison sausage until done; drain and reserve. In a small skillet, warm the olive oil and sauté the garlic until just beginning to brown. Bring a large pot of lightly salted water to a boil. Add the cavatelli and cook for 8 to 10 minutes or per package directions; drain. Three minutes before the end of the cooking time, add the broccoli and drain with the pasta. In a large serving bowl, place the pasta and broccoli; mix in the sausage mixture and red pepper flakes. Toss with the cheese and serve. Serves 4.

Rotini Pasta with Chicken and Venison Sausage

1 (16 oz.) pkg. rotini pasta
4 (3½ oz.) Italian venison sausage links,
   sliced
2 skinless, boneless chicken breast halves,
   cubed
1 onion, chopped
1 clove garlic, minced

1 green bell pepper, diced
1 tsp. Italian seasoning
salt and pepper to taste
1 (14½ oz.) can diced tomatoes
1¾ cups spaghetti sauce
1 (4½ oz.) can sliced mushrooms
3 zucchini, thickly sliced

Cook the rotini pasta per package directions in a large pot of lightly salted boiling water and drain. In a large skillet, cook the sliced Italian sausage until brown. Add the cubed chicken and cook until no pink remains in either meat. Add the onion, garlic, green bell pepper, Italian seasoning, salt, and pepper, and stir together. Cover and simmer until the vegetables are tender. Stir in the tomatoes, spaghetti sauce, mushrooms, and zucchini. Simmer until the zucchini is tender yet crisp. Toss the cooked pasta with the sauce. Serve warm. Serves 6.

Fettuccine Alfredo with Venison Sausage

8 oz. raw fettuccine pasta
½ lb. sweet Italian venison sausage, casings
   removed
½ cup butter

1 cup whipping cream
⅝ cup Pocatello or Romano cheese
3 Tbsp. minced fresh parsley

Boil the fettuccine in a large pot of salted water per package directions and drain. In a large skillet, cook the venison sausage until done. Drain and set aside. Make Alfredo sauce by melting the butter in a medium saucepan over low heat. Add the cream and cheese. Cook, stirring frequently, until the mixture comes to a gentle boil. Pour the Alfredo sauce over the fettuccine noodles and top with the cooked venison sausage. Sprinkle with the parsley and serve immediately; the sauce will separate as it cools. Serves 2 to 3.

Pastitso with Béchamel Sauce

A Greek-style pasta dish.

Venison Sausage Sauce

¼ cup olive oil
2 (2¼ lb.) pkgs. Greek Loukanika venison or
    other sausage, casings removed
1 large onion, chopped
1 large garlic clove, minced
2 Tbsp. chopped parsley

1 tsp. cinnamon
1 tsp. nutmeg
salt and pepper to taste
½ cup dry white wine
1½ cups tomato spaghetti sauce

Cheese Pasta

1 lb. elbow macaroni or penne noodles
⅓ cup butter, melted
3 eggs, beaten

1 cup grated Parmesan, Feta, Asiago, or
    Romano cheese

Béchamel Sauce

¼ cup butter
3 to 4 Tbsp. flour
2 cups milk

1 cup grated Parmesan, Feta, Asiago, or
    Romano cheese

For the Venison Sausage Sauce. In the olive oil, sauté the venison sausage, onion, and garlic until the sausage is crumbled and brown. Add the parsley, cinnamon, nutmeg, salt, pepper, wine, and tomato sauce. Simmer for approximately 30 minutes.

For the Pasta. Cook the pasta according to package directions; rinse and drain. Place in a large bowl, adding the melted butter, beaten eggs, and cheese. Mix well.

For the Béchamel. Melt the butter, add the flour, and stir until smooth. Cook for several minutes and gradually mix in the milk, stirring constantly until thickened. Mix in the cheese.

Putting It Together. Preheat the oven to 350° F. Spread half the pasta mixture on the bottom of a greased 9" × 13" baking pan. Cover evenly with meat sauce and sprinkle with some grated cheese. Cover with the remaining pasta. Sprinkle with cheese. Pour over with Béchamel Sauce. Sprinkle lavishly with cheese and bake for about 45 minutes. Allow to cool for 10 minutes and cut into squares. Serves 12.

Hot and Spicy Venison Sausage Linguine

2 tsp. olive oil
½ lb. hot Italian venison sausage links, casings removed, cut into ½" pieces
1 small green or red bell pepper, cut into ¼" strips
1 (14½ oz.) can pasta-ready chunky tomatoes
1 (9 oz.) pkg. refrigerated linguine
¼ cup grated Parmesan cheese

Heat the olive oil in a large skillet. Add the venison sausage and cook, stirring occasionally, until done; drain. Add the bell pepper and cook, stirring occasionally, until tender. Reduce the heat to low. Stir in the tomatoes and cook, stirring occasionally, for 10 to 15 minutes. Cook the linguine according to package directions, top with the sauce, and sprinkle with the cheese. Serves 4.

Vegetable and Venison Sausage Spaghetti

1 lb. sweet Italian venison sausage, casings removed
1 lb. lean ground beef
¼ cup olive oil
1 large onion, diced
1 green bell pepper, diced
1 red bell pepper, diced
1 zucchini, quartered and sliced
12 oz. mushrooms, sliced
2 carrots, shredded
4 oz. fresh basil, sliced thin
1 (10 oz.) pkg. frozen chopped spinach, thawed
1 Tbsp. chopped fresh thyme
1 Tbsp. minced fresh oregano
4 cloves garlic, crushed
1 Tbsp. sugar
salt and pepper to taste
3 (28 oz.) cans peeled and diced tomatoes
cooked pasta for 10

In a medium skillet over medium heat, cook the venison sausage and ground beef until brown. Drain, reserving 2 Tbsp. of drippings. In a large stockpot, cook the onion in the olive oil until clear. Stir in the green and red bell peppers, zucchini, mushrooms, and carrots, and cook until just tender. Stir in the basil, spinach, thyme, oregano, garlic, sugar, salt, and pepper. Cook for 5 minutes. Pour in the tomatoes, stir well, reduce the heat, cover, and simmer for 3 hours, stirring occasionally. Serves 10.

Pasta Sauce with Italian Venison Sausage

1 lb. Italian venison sausage links
½ lb. ground beef
1 Tbsp. olive oil
1 onion, chopped
1 garlic clove, chopped
1 (16 oz.) can tomatoes
1 (15 oz.) can tomato sauce

1 tsp. salt
¼ tsp. pepper
1 tsp. dried basil
1 tsp. dried oregano leaves
1 bay leaf
cooked pasta for 6

Remove the casings from the sausage links and cut into ½" thick slices. In a large skillet, brown the sausage over medium heat for about 10 minutes. Remove from the skillet and set aside. In a large skillet, heat the ground beef and olive oil, add the onion and garlic, and cook over medium heat until the beef is browned. Drain off the grease. Pour in the tomatoes and tomato sauce; mix in the salt, pepper, basil, oregano, bay leaf, and cooked venison sausage. Simmer, uncovered, for 1 hour. Stir occasionally. Remove the bay leaf, mix the cooked sauce with the hot pasta, and serve. Serves 6.

Green Pea and Venison Sausage Rigatoni with Cream Sauce

salt
1 lb. rigatoni pasta
2 Tbsp. olive oil
1 garlic clove, minced
1 lb. sweet Italian venison sausage, casings
   removed

12 oz. frozen green peas
1½ cups heavy cream
¼ cup butter
2 Tbsp. grated Parmesan cheese

Bring a large pot of lightly salted water to a boil. Add the rigatoni pasta, cook for 8 to 10 minutes or per package directions, and drain. In a skillet, heat the oil and sauté the garlic over medium heat. Brown the venison sausage in the skillet. Add the frozen peas and simmer for 5 minutes. Slowly add the heavy cream and butter to the skillet; bring to a gentle boil. Add more cream if needed. Cook for 5 minutes. Toss with the cooked pasta and sprinkle with the Parmesan cheese. Serves 4.

Cheddar Cheese and Venison Sausage Spaghetti

salt
2 Tbsp. olive oil
1 (16 oz.) pkg. spaghetti
1 lb. ground venison sausage

2 tomatoes, chopped
1 (6 oz.) can black olives, drained and
  sliced
4 cups shredded Cheddar cheese

Bring a large pot of lightly salted water to a boil and mix in the olive oil. Add the spaghetti and cook for 8 to 10 minutes or per package directions. Place the venison sausage in a large skillet, cook until done, and drain. In a large serving bowl, mix together the cooked sausage, spaghetti, tomatoes, olives, and shredded cheese. Serves 7.

Angel-Hair Pasta with Shrimp, Andouille Venison Sausage, and Creamed Mustard Sauce

salt
3 Tbsp. olive oil
1 (12 oz.) pkg. angel-hair pasta
½ lb. Andouille venison sausage, sliced
¾ lb. raw medium shrimp, peeled
¼ cup chopped green onions
½ cup sliced fresh mushrooms

1½ Tbsp. minced fresh garlic
½ cup white wine
2 cups whipping cream
1½ Tbsp. coarse-grained prepared
  mustard
1 tsp. Worcestershire sauce
salt and pepper to taste

Bring a large pot of lightly salted water to a boil. Stir in the olive oil. Add the angel-hair pasta and cook for 5 to 6 minutes or per package directions. Drain and set aside. Place the venison sausage in a large skillet and cook until done. Mix in the shrimp, green onions, mushrooms, and garlic, and sauté for 1 minute until the shrimp just begin to firm. Remove the shrimp mixture from the skillet and set aside. Pour the wine into the skillet and scrape up the browned bits. Reduce the wine by about half. Mix in the cream and continue cooking until reduced by about a third. Stir in the mustard and Worcestershire sauce. Season with salt and pepper. Return the sausage mixture to the skillet and mix into the wine mixture. Cook and stir until heated through. Place the angel-hair pasta in a large serving dish and work in the shrimp and sausage mixture. Serves 6.

Spaghetti with Tomato
and Venison Sausage Wine Sauce

1 lb. venison sausage links
1 onion, minced
2 cups sliced fresh mushrooms
¼ cup olive oil
2 (6 oz.) cans tomato paste
1 (46 oz.) can tomato juice
1 (16 oz.) can crushed Italian tomatoes
1 cup Italian or dry red wine

1½ Tbsp. dried oregano
1 Tbsp. dried basil
2 Tbsp. dried parsley
1 Tbsp. minced garlic
2 Tbsp. garlic salt
½ cup sugar
2 lbs. raw spaghetti

Preheat the oven to 350° F. Sauté the venison sausage links on both sides until done. Slice into bite-sized pieces and set aside. In a large skillet, sauté the onion and mushrooms in the olive oil until tender. Remove with a slotted spoon and set aside. Stir into the skillet the tomato paste, tomato juice, Italian tomatoes, and wine. Stir until smooth. Mix in the oregano, basil, parsley, garlic, garlic salt, and sugar. Return the sausage and onion/mushroom mixture to the tomato sauce. Bring to a boil, reduce the heat, and simmer on very low heat for at least 3 hours. Cover the pot if the sauce becomes too thick.

Cook the pasta according to package directions. Drain. Serve the sauce over the pasta. Serves 12 to 16.

17

Garden Vegetable and Venison Sausage Dishes

You do not have to be a vegetarian to love vegetables. Venison sausage combined with fresh vegetables will convert the pickiest of eaters in the family to vegetable lovers. They may still push their boiled green peas and carrots to the side of the plate, but when combined with venison sausage, the vegetables seem to disappear along with the sausage.

Instead of using just ham hocks or salted meat when cooking up a batch of turnip greens or spinach, try adding an equal amount of sliced smoked venison link sausage. When you have done this once, it will be hard to go back to the old way.

Baked Acorn Squash with Venison Sausage Filling

3 medium acorn squash
½ tsp. salt
boiling water

1½ lbs. bulk venison sausage
6 Tbsp. packed brown sugar, divided
3 Tbsp. butter, divided

Preheat the oven to 375° F. Cut the squash in half lengthwise and remove the seeds; sprinkle with salt. Place cut-side-down in a shallow baking dish, and pour in ½" of boiling water. Bake, uncovered, for 35 minutes; drain.

Cook the venison sausage in a large skillet over medium heat until browned. Crumble the sausage while stirring. Remove the sausage and drain off the drippings. Place 1 Tbsp. of the brown sugar and 1½ tsp. of the butter in each squash cavity. Spoon the sausage evenly into the six squash halves. Bake, uncovered, at 350° F for 25 minutes or until the squash are tender. Serves 6.

Grilled Venison Sausage with Wilted Vegetables

32 oz. Balsamic vinegar
1 lb. venison, cubed
½ lb. boneless pork chops, cubed
¼ lb. Pancetta (Italian salt-cured sausage roll), cubed
1 tsp. cumin seeds
1 tsp. cinnamon

1 tsp. salt
¼ lb. pork caul (lacelike intestine lining)
¼ cup olive oil
2 garlic cloves, thinly sliced
2 cups (½" slices) kale or spinach
salt and pepper to taste

Reduce the Balsamic vinegar to a syrup, cover, and set aside. Mix the venison, pork, and Pancetta, and pass through a medium disc. Sprinkle with the cinnamon, cumin, and salt; mix. Divide into 8 portions, shape into ½" thick patties, and wrap each patty in a piece of caul. Broil or grill for about 5 minutes on each side and set aside. Heat the olive oil in a large skillet and sauté the garlic until it just begins to brown. Mix in the kale and sauté until just wilted. Place the patties on serving plates, cover with wilted vegetables, and spoon over with reduced vinegar. Serves 4.

Red Cabbage with Apples and Venison Link Sausage

¼ cup bacon fat
2 Tbsp. sugar
1 small yellow onion, coarsely chopped
4 cups shredded red cabbage
2 tart red apples, cored and sliced unpeeled
2 Tbsp. apple cider vinegar

½ tsp. caraway seeds
1½ lbs. smoked Polish venison sausage links
1 lb. new potatoes
salt and pepper to taste
1 cup beer

Melt the bacon fat over medium heat. Add the sugar and cook, stirring often, until the sugar begins to brown. Reduce the heat to a simmer, add the onion, and sauté until it just begins to brown. Stir in the cabbage, apples, vinegar, and caraway seeds. Place the venison sausage links and potatoes on top of the cabbage and season with salt and pepper. Pour over with the beer. Over high heat, bring the mixture to a boil; reduce the heat to a simmer, cover, and cook for 40 to 45 minutes. Serves 4 to 6.

Lima Beans and Smoked Venison Sausage Links

water
4 cups fresh lima beans
2 Tbsp. bacon drippings
2 cups smoked venison sausage, sliced ¼"
   thick

¾ cup finely chopped onion
1 tsp. salt
½ tsp. black pepper

Place the beans in a large pot and cover with water. Bring to a boil and cook until just tender. Heat the bacon drippings in a skillet and sauté the sausage and onion until the sausage is brown and the onion just clear. Add the onion, sausage, salt, and pepper to the beans and cook for 10 minutes. Serves 4 to 6.

Baked Italian Venison Sausage

4 large red bell peppers, seeded and cut into
   eighths
4 large green bell peppers, seeded and cut
   into eighths

2 large onions, cut into thin rings
3 lbs. bulk Italian venison sausage

Preheat the oven to 350° F. Grease a deep 9" × 13" ovenproof dish or pan. Spread the peppers, onions, and venison sausage in the pan and bake for 15 minutes. Stir to coat with the sausage grease. Bake for another 30 minutes, or until the sausage is cooked. Serve hot on a large platter. Serves 8.

Vegetable Stir-Fry with Polish Venison Sausage

nonstick cooking spray
½ lb. Polish venison sausage, sliced
2 cups chopped broccoli

2 cups sliced carrots
steamed rice for 4

Spray a pan with cooking spray, add the venison sausage, and sauté. Add the vegetables, stir, and cover. Simmer for 5 to 7 minutes until the vegetables are just tender. Serve over rice. Serves 4.

Baked Beans with Venison Hot Dogs

1½ Tbsp. yellow mustard
⅓ cup ketchup
¼ cup dark brown sugar, packed

½ tsp. onion powder
2 (16 oz.) cans baked beans
6 venison hot dogs, cut into 1" slices

Preheat the oven to 350° F. Mix all the ingredients together in an ovenproof 2 quart casserole dish. Bake for 20 to 25 minutes or until the hot dogs are done. Serves 8 to 10.

Black Bean and Venison Sausage Tamale Pie

shortening
1 lb. bulk venison sausage
⅔ cup chopped onion
½ cup chopped green bell pepper
1 (15 oz.) can black beans, drained
1½ cups picante sauce
1 (8½ oz.) pkg. corn muffin mix

2 cups shredded sharp Cheddar cheese, divided
¼ cup half-and-half
1 large egg, lightly beaten
1 cup sour cream
¼ cup finely chopped fresh cilantro
¼ cup sliced black olives

Preheat the oven to 375° F. Grease a 10" glass pie plate. In a large skillet, crumble the venison sausage and brown. Drain the excess fat. Add the onions and green pepper and continue cooking until the vegetables begin to crisp. Stir in the drained black beans and picante sauce and set aside. In a medium bowl, combine the corn muffin mix, 1 cup of the Cheddar cheese, the half-and-half, and the egg. Stir until moistened. Press the corn muffin mixture on the bottom and up the sides of the greased pie plate. Spoon the sausage mixture into the crust. Bake for 25 minutes or until the mixture is set. Remove from the oven; sprinkle with the remaining cup of Cheddar cheese. Bake for 5 more minutes or until the cheese is melted. Remove and allow to rest for 5 minutes. Cut the pie into 6 wedges and serve each slice with a spoonful of sour cream, a sprinkle of fresh cilantro, and black olives. Serves 6.

One venison processor in the southern U.S. makes sausage out of 20,000 deer each year.

Baked Venison Sausage and Cabbage Pie

1 lb. smoked venison sausage links, cut
    into 1" pieces
6 red potatoes, thinly sliced
3 Tbsp. flour
1½ tsp. salt

¼ head cabbage, coarsely chopped, divided
2 cups corn kernels, divided
½ cup diced red bell pepper, divided
pepper to taste
1½ cups milk

Preheat the oven to 375° F. Brown the venison sausage in a frying pan until cooked. Place half of the sausages into a deep ovenproof pie dish. Add half of the sliced potatoes and sprinkle with the flour and salt. Add half of the cabbage, corn, and bell pepper. Repeat to make a second layer. Season with pepper and pour over with the milk. Baked, uncovered, for 1¼ hours. Serves 4.

Portuguese Bean Soup with Venison Sausage

2 cups dry kidney beans
1 cup dry great northern beans
2 smoked ham hocks
4 cups chicken broth
1½ cups chopped cilantro
6 to 7 cups water
10 oz. Hawaiian Portuguese Venison
    Sausage (page 137) links
2½ cups peeled and diced raw potatoes

2½ cups (cut 1" thick) carrots
1½ cups diced onion
½ cup diced celery
16 oz. tomato sauce mixed with 3 Tbsp.
    cornstarch
1 tsp. salt
½ tsp. black pepper
Tabasco sauce to taste

Soak the beans in water overnight and drain. In a large soup pot, add the beans, ham, chicken broth, cilantro, and enough water to cover. Bring to a boil, reduce the heat, and simmer until the ham hocks and beans are tender. Remove the skin and bones from the meat and return the meat to the soup. Slice the Hawaiian Portuguese Venison Sausage into ½" slices and fry on all sides until done; remove and drain. Add the remaining ingredients and simmer until the potatoes are tender. Serves 4 to 6.

Sausage was probably the first
convenience food, predating the TV dinner
by many centuries.

Grilled Venison Sausage Kabobs

2 lbs. spicy Italian venison sausage, sliced
    ¾" thick
1 large red bell pepper, cut into 1" squares
¼ lb. jalapeño peppers, cut into ¾" squares

1 large red onion, cut into chunks
1 (12 oz.) can beer
nonstick cooking spray
½ lb. provolone cheese, sliced

Place the venison sausage, red bell pepper, jalapeño peppers, and red onion in a large bowl. Pour in the beer. Cover and refrigerate for 2 hours. Spray a grill with nonstick spray and preheat to high. Alternately skewer the sausage, red pepper, jalapeños, and onion. Cook the kabobs until the sausage is evenly browned and the vegetables are tender. Turn several times. Lay provolone cheese on the kabobs for the last few minutes and cook until it begins to melt. Serves 8.

Three Venison Sausage and Sauerkraut Platter

2 (32 oz.) jars sauerkraut
1 medium onion, coarsely chopped
3 potatoes, pared and diced
3 carrots, pared and sliced
1 (10½ oz.) can chicken broth
1 cup Rhine wine or other white wine

1½ lbs. venison Bratwurst links
1¼ lbs. venison Knockwurst or Ring
    Bologna
½ lb. venison Pepperoni, cut into 1½"
    lengths
paprika

Preheat the oven to 350° F. Drain the sauerkraut and rinse with cold water. Squeeze out the excess water. Combine the sauerkraut, onion, potatoes, carrots, chicken broth, and wine. Place in a large pot; add the venison Bratwurst, venison Knockwurst, and venison Pepperoni on top. Cover and bake for 2 hours. Arrange the sauerkraut and sausages on a hot platter and sprinkle with paprika. Serves 6 to 8.

> A deer's most developed sense is that of smell. Hearing and sight follow in close order.

Guisado de Cerdo with Venison Sausage

1 lb. dry garbanzo beans
1 pig's tail, cut into 1" pieces
2 pig's ears, chopped
1 lb. venison Chorizo sausage, sliced into chunks
½ lb. pork shoulder, cubed
6 oz. Pancetta or other bacon, diced

1 onion, chopped
3 carrots, coarsely chopped
4 celery stalks, chopped
6 garlic cloves, chopped
1 red bell pepper, chopped
1½ tsp. paprika
salt and pepper to taste

Place the garbanzo beans in a large container and cover with water. Let soak overnight. Drain the beans and place in a large stockpot. Add the pig's tail, pig's ears, venison Chorizo, pig's shoulder, Pancetta, onion, carrots, celery, garlic, bell pepper, paprika, salt, and pepper. Fill the pot with water to cover and bring to a boil. Reduce the heat and let simmer until the beans are tender, about 1½ hours. Skim the fat from the liquid's surface. Serves 8.

Cabbage Stuffed with Venison Sausages

1 Savoy or other cabbage
salt
1 lb. small link venison sausages
1 tsp. paprika
¼ cup sour cream

salt and pepper to taste
1 (8 oz.) can crushed tomatoes
1 Tbsp. cooking oil
1 garlic clove, minced
1 tsp. caraway seeds

Preheat the oven to 350° F. Remove one large cabbage leaf for each sausage link and blanch in boiling salted water until just soft. Drain well and cut away the thick part of the center rib of each leaf. Place one sausage on each leaf and sprinkle with paprika, 2 Tbsp. of the sour cream, salt, and pepper. Roll up and pack into a baking dish. Pour the crushed tomatoes over to just cover the cabbage. Cover and place in the oven for an hour or until the sausages are thoroughly cooked. Roughly chop the remaining cabbage and stir-fry in the oil with the garlic and caraway seeds. Serve the cabbage and sausages together on a warm serving plate. Serves 2.

Broccoli and Venison Sausage Platter

1 bunch broccoli rabe or other broccoli, trimmed
1 Tbsp. salt
6 Tbsp. olive oil, divided

1 lb. Italian sausage links, cut into 1" pieces
2 garlic cloves, chopped
¼ cup fresh lemon juice, divided

Place the broccoli rabe and salt in a large pot of boiling water. Cook for 12 minutes or until the stems are tender. Drain and reserve 1 cup of the liquid. Heat 3 Tbsp. of the olive oil in a skillet and cook the sausage over medium-high heat for 10 minutes, or until evenly browned. Remove the sausage from the skillet. Stir the garlic into the skillet and cook for approximately 30 seconds. Place the broccoli rabe and reserved cup of liquid in the skillet and mix in half the lemon juice. Return the sausage to the skillet and allow the mixture to simmer for approximately 10 minutes. Mix in the remaining olive oil and lemon juice before serving. Serves 8.

Italian Zucchini with Venison Sausage and Cheese Stuffing

butter
12 oz. bulk venison sausage, crumbled
2 large zucchini
3 eggs, beaten
1 cup shredded Colby cheese
2 cups cottage cheese
1½ cups shredded Italian cheese mix

½ cup chopped onion
2 Tbsp. Italian seasoning
½ tsp. salt
½ tsp. black pepper
shortening
⅛ tsp. garlic salt
½ cup chopped fresh tomatoes

Preheat the oven to 350° F. Butter a baking dish. Place the crumbled bulk venison sausage in a large skillet. Cook over medium-high heat until evenly brown. Drain and set aside. Partially cook the zucchini in the microwave on high for 5 minutes. Remove from the microwave and let cool for about 10 minutes. Meanwhile, combine the eggs, Colby cheese, cottage cheese, Italian cheese mix, onion, Italian seasoning, salt, and pepper. Slice the zucchini in half lengthwise, scoop out the seeds, and rinse. Place the halves in the greased baking dish and sprinkle with the garlic salt. Layer the sausage, tomatoes, and cheese mixture in each zucchini half. Bake for 40 minutes, then broil for 5 minutes to brown the cheese. Serves 4.

Three Beans, Venison Sausage, and Rice

6 cups rice
12 cups water
salt
1 lb. venison Kielbasa sausage
1 tsp. red pepper (optional)

2 lbs. ground beef
¼ onion, minced
2 (15 oz.) cans kidney beans, drained
1 (15 oz.) can pinto beans, drained
1 (15 oz.) can pork and beans

Cook the rice in salted water according to package directions. Cut the venison Kielbasa into 1" chunks and quarter the chunks. Place the sausage in a large skillet and cook over medium-high heat until lightly browned. Season with red pepper. Reserve the grease and transfer to the cooked rice pot. In the same skillet, sauté the ground beef and onion for 5 minutes. Mix into the rice; reduce the heat to medium and cook for 5 more minutes. Drain well and add to the pot. Stir the kidney beans, pinto beans, and pork and beans into the pot. Add a little water if necessary and simmer over low heat until heated through. Serves 14 to 16.

Baked Venison Sausage and Onion Casserole

1 lb. freshly ground venison sausage
1 onion, thinly sliced
1½ cups shredded Cheddar cheese

4 slices bread, crusts removed
6 eggs, lightly beaten
2 cups milk

Preheat the oven to 375° F. Brown the sausage in a skillet, drain, and place in a square casserole dish. Lay the onion slices on top of the sausage. Sprinkle with the cheese. Place the slices of bread on top of the cheese so that they completely cover the cheese and do not overlap. Mix the eggs and milk in a bowl and slowly pour over the top of the bread. Bake for 45 minutes. Serves 6.

Fighting red deer stags sometimes
lock their antlers together and cannot
separate. When this happens, both
will starve to death.

Hutsput Dutch Stew with Venison Sausage

¼ cup butter
2 lbs. beef roast, sliced ½" thick
2 cups cold water
3 lbs. potatoes, peeled and quartered
3 medium onions, diced

3 lbs. carrots, peeled and diced
1 tsp. salt
½ tsp. pepper
1 lb. smoked venison sausage, sliced ½" thick

Heat the butter in a large pot until melted and sear the roast on all sides until brown. Add water to just cover the roast, place the lid on, and simmer for about 1 hour. Add the potatoes, onions, carrots, salt, and pepper. Cover and simmer for about 1 hour more. Lay the smoked sausage on top during the last 15 minutes of cooking. Remove the meat and vegetables. Gently mash the vegetables together and spoon onto a serving plate. Place the roast and sausage slices on top. Serves 4 to 6.

Sauerkraut and Venison Sausage Balls

1½ lbs. bulk venison sausage
1 onion, finely chopped
1 cup flour
½ tsp. dry mustard
4 drops Tabasco sauce
½ cup milk
1 Tbsp. dried parsley

1 (16 oz.) can sauerkraut, drained, finely chopped
¼ cup butter
2 eggs, slightly beaten
¼ cup cold water
¾ cup unseasoned bread crumbs

Preheat the oven to 400° F. Place the ground venison sausage and onion in a skillet and cook until the sausage is brown. Drain and stir in the flour, mustard, and Tabasco sauce. Whisk in the milk. Stir constantly and continue cooking for 5 minutes. Remove from the heat and mix in the parsley and sauerkraut. Place the butter in a 9" × 13" baking dish, and melt in the preheated oven. Mix together the eggs and cold water. Shape the sausage mixture into 1" balls, dip into the egg and water mixture, and then roll in the bread crumbs. Place the sausage balls in the baking dish in a single layer. Bake for approximately 30 minutes or until brown. Turn after 15 minutes. Serves 6.

Simmered Red Cabbage, Apple, and Venison Sausage

1 small head red cabbage, shredded
1 apple, cored and diced
3 tsp. salt, divided
1 Tbsp. lemon juice
½ cup water
1 small onion, chopped

1 Tbsp. butter
⅛ tsp. pepper
1 Tbsp. red wine vinegar
1 lb. Kielbasa venison sausage, cut into
   1" pieces

Place the cabbage in a large pot and add the apple, 2 tsp. of the salt, the lemon juice, and the water. Bring to a boil, reduce the heat to a simmer, cover, and cook for about 15 minutes until the cabbage wilts. Sauté the onion in the butter until just beginning to brown. Add the onion to the cabbage along with the remaining salt, pepper, vinegar, and venison sausage. Cover and cook for 20 to 30 minutes until the sausage is cooked through. Spoon the cabbage into a large serving bowl and top with the sausage. Serves 4 to 6.

Apple and Smoked Venison Sausage Skillet Dinner

12 oz. smoked venison link sausage, cut
   diagonally into 1" pieces
8 medium red potatoes
1 cup water
1 medium onion
2 small red cooking apples

2 Tbsp. butter, divided
¼ cup apple cider vinegar
3 Tbsp. sugar
½ tsp. caraway seeds
2 Tbsp. parsley

Place the venison sausage, potatoes, and water in a large pot, cover tightly, and cook over medium-high heat for 8 minutes, stirring occasionally. Cut the onion into wedges; core and cut each apple into wedges. Drain the sausage and potatoes, and cut the potatoes into large pieces. In a large skillet, melt 1 Tbsp. of the butter and cook and stir the onion and apples until the apples are just tender. Remove from the skillet. Heat the remaining 1 Tbsp. of butter, add the potatoes, cover, and cook over medium-high heat until tender/brown, stirring occasionally. Mix together the vinegar, sugar, and caraway seeds. Reduce the heat; return the sausage, apple mixture, and vinegar mixture to the skillet and cook until heated through, stirring gently. Sprinkle with the parsley and serve. Serves 4.

Slow-Cooker Lentils and Venison Sausage

1 (16 oz.) pkg. dry lentils
1 (16 oz.) can diced tomatoes, drained
2 (14 oz.) cans beef broth
1½ cups water

1 carrot, chopped
2 lbs. Polish Kielbasa venison sausage,
  sliced ½" thick
1 celery stalk, chopped

Briefly rinse the lentils. In a Crock-Pot, combine and mix together all the ingredients. Cook on the low setting for 6 to 7 hours. Stir well before serving. Serves 10 to 14.

Sautéed Smoked Venison Sausage and Zucchini

1 lb. smoked venison sausage links, sliced
  1" thick
1 Tbsp. butter
2 zucchini, cut lengthwise and then in half
1 Tbsp. dehydrated onion flakes

½ tsp. garlic salt
¼ tsp. dried oregano leaves
¼ tsp. black pepper
2 tomatoes, chopped

Brown the venison sausage in a skillet over medium heat. Remove the sausage and set aside. Add the butter, zucchini, and onion to the skillet and cook until the zucchini is tender. Return the browned sausage to the skillet and add the garlic salt, oregano, and pepper. Cook until all ingredients are heated through. Remove to a serving dish and sprinkle the chopped tomatoes over the top. Serves 4.

In Iceland, Domino's Pizza has a reindeer sausage pie on its menu.

Americans consume seven billion hot dogs between Memorial Day and Labor Day.

Spicy Spanish Venison Sausage Sauté

1 Tbsp. vegetable oil
½ cup chopped green bell pepper
⅓ cup chopped celery
¼ cup chopped onion
1 lb. smoked venison sausage links, sliced
2 cups water

1 (10 oz.) can diced tomatoes with green chili peppers
1 (6.8 oz.) pkg. Spanish-style rice mix
¼ cup sliced stuffed green olives
⅛ tsp. pepper

Heat the vegetable oil in a large skillet over medium heat; sauté the green bell pepper, celery, and onion until wilted. Add the venison sausage, water, tomatoes with green chilies, Spanish rice mix, olives, and pepper. Mix well and simmer for 20 minutes, stirring occasionally. Serves 4.

Spicy Hot Sweet-and-Sour Smoked Venison Sausage

1½ lbs. smoked venison sausage links, sliced ½" thick
1 green bell pepper, sliced into ¼" strips
1 red bell pepper, sliced into ¼" strips
1 onion, thinly sliced

2 Tbsp. butter
salt and pepper to taste
2 Tbsp. sweet-and-sour sauce
⅛ tsp. red pepper (optional)
1 dash Tabasco sauce (optional)

Place the sausage in a large skillet and sauté on both sides until browned. Drain the fat and set the sausage aside. In the same skillet, add the green bell pepper, red bell pepper, onion, and butter, and sauté for 10 minutes or until all the vegetables are tender. Add the venison sausage and stir together. Season with salt and pepper. Add the sweet-and-sour sauce, red pepper, and Tabasco sauce. Reduce the heat to low and simmer for 5 to 10 minutes. Serve 4 to 6.

Much of our modern hunting and shooting terminology is based on fourteenth and fifteenth century Anglo-French hunting manuals.

Szechwan Venison Sausage Lettuce Wraps

1 Tbsp. vegetable oil
1 lb. bulk venison sausage
2 tsp. McCormick Szechwan Seasoning
1 (8 oz.) can sliced water chestnuts, drained and chopped
1 cup shredded carrots

½ cup green onions
½ cup chopped toasted walnuts
3 Tbsp. dry sherry
1 head lettuce, leaves separated, rinsed, and drained

Heat the vegetable oil in a large skillet; add the sausage and sprinkle with the Szechwan Seasoning. Break up the sausage while cooking. Add the water chestnuts, carrots, green onions, walnuts, and sherry. Cook and stir for 2 to 3 minutes. To serve, spoon about ½ cup of the sausage mixture into the center of each lettuce leaf, fold up and tuck in the sides, and roll like a burrito. Serves 4.

18

Sandwiches, Breads, and Pies with Venison Sausage

Although we do not normally associate venison sausage with sandwiches, breads, and pies, the combination will add a unique touch to many occasions.

The Greeks and Italians have traditionally combined sausage with bread; an English holiday favorite is a Christmas cake made with sausage.

Venison sausage sandwiches are a summer favorite. For a special occasion, try the first recipe—Crêpes with Venison Sausage and Cream Cheese Sauce.

Woven Venison Sausage Pie

¾ cup all-purpose flour
½ cup plus 2 Tbsp. butter
2 Tbsp. water
shortening
12 oz. bulk venison sausage

2 Tbsp. ketchup
⅛ tsp. Italian seasoning
2 tomatoes, peeled and sliced
1 yellow onion, chopped
2 hard-boiled eggs, chopped

Preheat the oven to 375° F. In a large bowl, mix the flour, butter, and water to make a firm dough; knead until smooth and silky. Roll out the dough into a 12" square and place on a greased cookie sheet. Mix the venison sausage, ketchup, and herbs. Place the filling in the center of the pastry and spread so that there are 4" of dough on each side. Place the tomatoes, chopped onion, and eggs on top of the venison sausage filling. Cut 1" strips from the sides of the pastry and weave over the top. Bake for 30 to 40 minutes until the pastry is beginning to brown. Serves 4.

Crêpes with Venison Sausage and Cream Cheese Sauce

½ lb. ground venison sausage, crumbled
½ to ¾ cup chopped green onions
1 cup shredded sharp Cheddar cheese
2 Tbsp. butter
4 large eggs, beaten
8 oz. cottage cheese, puréed in a food
   processor until smooth

8 to 10 crêpes
1 cup heavy cream
1 Tbsp. dry white wine
1 large green onion, finely chopped
¼ tsp. Dijon mustard
red pepper
½ cup shredded sharp Cheddar cheese

Preheat the oven to 350° F. In a large skillet, cook the venison sausage over medium heat for about 15 minutes until brown. Remove the sausage to a medium bowl. Reserve 2 Tbsp. of the drippings. Add the green onions to the skillet and cook over medium-high heat until just tender. Add the green onions to the venison sausage. Stir in the Cheddar cheese.

In a separate skillet, melt the butter over very low heat. Add the eggs and cook slowly until just beginning to set. Remove from the stove and allow to slightly cool. Stir the puréed cottage cheese into the eggs. Fold the egg mixture into the venison sausage mixture. Place ⅓ cup of filling down the center of each crêpe and roll up. Place the crêpes in a baking pan with the seam down and cover with foil. Bake for 20 minutes or until heated through.

While the crêpes are baking, make the cream cheese sauce. In a medium saucepan, mix together the cream, wine, and green onions. Reduce to ¾ cup, or until the sauce lightly coats the back of a spoon. Stir in the mustard and red pepper. Stir in the Cheddar cheese until melted. Spoon over the baked crêpes and serve. Serves 4 to 5.

Saganaki with Greek Venison Sausage

A traditional Greek sausage dish made with venison.

2 Tbsp. olive oil
2 lbs. Kefalotyri cheese or any soft-firm, tart
   white cheese
1 tsp. dried oregano

4 oz. Loukanika venison sausage or other
   dry link sausage, sliced thin
1 lemon
hot heavy bread

Preheat the oven to 400° F. Grease a small (6") au gratin pan with the olive oil. Slice the cheese ¼" thick and layer in the pan. Sprinkle with the oregano. Bake for 10 minutes until the cheese melts. Remove the pan from the oven and top with the Loukanika venison sausage slices. Broil for 3 to 5 minutes. Squeeze lemon juice over the top and serve over hot bread. Serves 4.

Italian Venison Sausage
and Spicy Italian Vegetable Sandwiches

2 lbs. sweet Italian venison sausage
12 oz. Giardiniera, drained
1 cup fresh Italian parsley leaves
1 large tomato, halved, seeded, thinly sliced
½ red onion, very thinly sliced
olive oil

red wine vinegar
coarse salt
pepper to taste
4 lettuce leaves
4 crusty rolls, split

Divide the sweet Italian venison sausage into four equal portions and form into patties. Heat a skillet and cook the patties on each side until done. Place the Giardiniera salad and parsley leaves in a food processor and pulse into a fine relish. Toss the sliced tomato and onion with a little oil and vinegar. Season to taste with salt and pepper. Cover the inside of each roll bottom with chopped relish and top with sausage, tomato and onion slices, and a lettuce leaf. Cover each with a roll top and serve with a vegetable salad. Serves 4.

Note: Giardiniera is Italian pickled cauliflower, carrots, and peppers. It is available in the Italian foods section of your local market.

Syrian Sausage Pita Sandwich with Venison

2 lbs. (6 links) Syrian Venison Sausage
   (page 90)
butter
olive oil

6 individual pita rounds
6 Tbsp. yogurt, divided
1 bunch coriander, chopped

Sauté the sausage in a mixture of half butter and half olive oil until brown on all sides, turning occasionally. Open a pita bread round, then slip in a sausage, 1 Tbsp. of the yogurt, and 2 Tbsp. of the chopped coriander. Serves 6.

Antlers are rarely used to defend against predators. Their main purpose appears to be in the settlement of mating disputes.

Italian Venison Sausage and Pepper Rolls

3 qts. spaghetti sauce
4 lbs. Italian venison sausage links
5 green peppers, cut into ¼" strips
3 red peppers, cut into ¼" strips
3 large onions, cut into ¼" strips
1 cup olive oil

3 garlic cloves, chopped
1 Tbsp. chopped fresh basil
1 Tbsp. chopped fresh oregano
5 Italian or other heavy dinner rolls,
    sliced open
10 slices mozzarella cheese

Pour the spaghetti sauce in a large pot and bring to a gentle boil. Add the venison sausage and simmer for 1 hour, stirring occasionally. After the sausage has cooked for an hour, add the peppers and onions. Stir in the olive oil, garlic, and herbs. Slow-boil for another hour. The sausages are ready when the internal temperature reaches 180° F. Cut the rolls open, add the sausage, peppers, and onions, and cover with cheese. Place the sandwiches on a flat pan and put them in a 350° F oven until melted. Watch closely—the cheese melts quickly. Serves 10.

Cheesy Pita Bread with Venison Sausage

½ lb. small venison sausages, cooked
1 (2 oz.) jar stuffed green olives, chopped
2 hard-boiled eggs, chopped
1 tsp. mustard
2 Tbsp. mayonnaise

½ cup chili sauce
½ lb. sharp Cheddar cheese, shredded
½ cup diced onions
4 pita rounds
Heavy-duty aluminum foil

Cut the venison sausages into ¼" cubes. Combine and mix well with the olives, eggs, mustard, mayonnaise, chili sauce, cheese, and onion. Cut the pita rounds in half. Open the pockets and fill each with the filling. Wrap each half in foil and refrigerate. Heat a grill, place the foil-wrapped sandwiches on it, and heat for 10 minutes. Uncover and continue heating until the pita bread is crisp and the filling is hot. Serves 4.

Scottish red deer (*Cervus Elephus*) was the staple diet of the ancient Scots, along with salmon and oysters.

Italian Venison Sausage Pie

2 lbs. mild Italian venison sausage
1 large onion, chopped
1 lb. potatoes, cut into ½" cubes
½ cup raisins
1 tsp. anise seeds
1 tsp. dry sage
¼ tsp. cinnamon
1⅓ cups beef broth, divided

3 apples, peeled and sliced
1 cup apple juice
2 Tbsp. cornstarch
flour
1 sheet frozen puff pastry, thawed
1 egg, beaten
1 Tbsp. fresh sage leaves

Preheat the oven to 375° F. Brown the venison sausage over medium heat. Remove the sausage and place in a mixing bowl. Reserve 2 Tbsp. of drippings. Stir the onion, potatoes, raisins, anise, sage, and cinnamon into the skillet with the fat and cook over medium heat until the onion is just clear. Add 1 cup of the broth, the apples, and the apple juice. Cover and simmer until the potatoes are tender, 5 to 10 minutes. Mix the cornstarch and remaining broth. Add to the pan and stir over high heat until the sauce boils. Stir in the venison sausage and pour into a shallow 2 quart baking dish. Cool to room temperature.

On a floured board, roll the puff pastry 2" longer and wider than the top of the dish. Brush egg on the outside of the dish along the top. Lay the puff pastry over the dish and press it against the edges. Trim any excess pastry from around the edges of the dish. Set the dish on a cookie sheet. Brush the top of the pastry with beaten egg and bake until the crust is well browned, about 40 minutes. Garnish with fresh sage leaves. Serves 8.

Baked Broccoli and Venison Sausage in Pastry Shells

6 baked pastry shells
1 lb. cooked venison sausage, crumbled
1½ cups cooked and chopped broccoli
6 eggs, lightly scrambled

½ cup grated Cheddar cheese
1 cup canned cheese soup
Parmesan cheese
¼ cup chopped green onions

Preheat the oven to 350° F. Fill the pastry shells with a layer each of sausage, broccoli, and eggs. Sprinkle each filled pastry shell with Cheddar cheese and bake for 10 minutes. Prepare the cheese soup per directions on the can. Place the baked pastry shells on individual serving plates and ladle over with cheese soup; sprinkle with Parmesan cheese and green onions. Serve at once. Serves 6.

Italian Roll Sandwiches with Venison Sausage and Sliced Onions

1 lb. venison sausage links
1½ Tbsp. chopped fresh rosemary
1 onion, thinly sliced

1 green bell pepper, cut into ¼" strips
6 Italian rolls, sliced open

Boil the venison sausage in water until cooked, drain, and cut into chunks. Place the rosemary in a skillet over medium heat until just beginning to brown. Add the onion and cook until soft and just clear. Add the green pepper and cook until soft. Add the sausage and cook until browned. Divide the filling among 6 Italian rolls; it can also be served over pasta or rice. Serve with potato salad or coleslaw. Serves 4 to 6.

Grilled Venison Sausage Tortilla Wraps

1 lb. small venison link sausages
8 flour tortillas, wrapped in foil
7 oz. guacamole
1 head romaine or other lettuce, shredded

7 oz. sour cream
7 oz. salsa, divided

Place the venison sausages on a preheated grill and cook for 10 to 12 minutes, turning occasionally, until thoroughly cooked. During the last 2 minutes of cooking, lay the foil-wrapped tortillas on the grill to warm. When warm, remove the tortillas; spread each with guacamole and top with lettuce, a spoonful of sour cream, and salsa. Add the venison sausage and roll. Serve with the remaining salsa and a cold sliced cucumber and onion salad. Serves 4.

Native Americans followed deer trails. Early settlers walked along these same paths. Wagon trains followed the paths made by the early settlers. Roads were built over wagon trails—and our interstate highways were built along existing paved roads.

Baked Venison Sausage and Corn Bread

shortening
1 lb. bulk venison sausage
1 onion, chopped
2 eggs, lightly beaten
1½ cups buttermilk
1½ cups self-rising cornmeal mix

1 (15 oz.) can cream-style corn
½ cup sour cream
¼ cup vegetable oil
2 cups shredded sharp Cheddar cheese
½ cup milk

Preheat the oven to 425° F. Grease a 10" ovenproof dish. In a medium skillet, brown the sausage and onion; drain well. In a large bowl, combine the eggs, buttermilk, cornmeal mix, corn, sour cream, and oil. Pour half of the cornmeal mixture into the greased dish and sprinkle with the sausage mixture and cheese. Pour the remaining cornmeal batter over the top. Bake for 30 to 40 minutes. Let stand for 10 minutes before serving. Serves 4 to 6.

Grilled Venison Chorizo Sausage Burritos

nonstick cooking spray
1 green bell pepper
1 red bell pepper
1 yellow bell pepper
6 small venison Chorizo sausage links
1 (15 oz.) can black beans

¾ cup chunky salsa
6 (12") flour tortillas
½ head lettuce, shredded
2 cups sour cream
2 cups guacamole

Preheat a grill and spray with nonstick spray. Place the whole bell peppers on the grill and cook until evenly charred; turn occasionally. Place the peppers in a cold-water bath and allow to cool. Place the venison Chorizo sausages on the grill and cook on all sides. Move to the side and allow to cook through, about 10 minutes. Heat the black beans in a small saucepan over medium heat until heated through. Remove from the heat and drain off the liquid. When the peppers are cool, peel off the skins, remove the seeds and stems, and chop. Transfer the peppers and beans to a medium bowl, stir in the salsa, and set aside. When the sausages are done, slice into ½" thick pieces and stir into the pepper mixture. Wrap the tortillas in aluminum foil and place on the grill to warm. Spoon the sausage filling onto each tortilla and sprinkle lettuce on top. Spoon on sour cream and guacamole. Serves 6.

Broiled Venison Sausage Pizza Sandwiches

1 lb. sweet Italian venison sausage
5 Tbsp. olive oil, divided
2 large onions, sliced
1 garlic clove, pressed
1 (8 oz.) can tomato sauce
salt and pepper to taste

red pepper flakes to taste (optional)
¼ cup sliced stuffed green olives
1 (1 lb.) loaf French bread, sliced
 horizontally
6 oz. mozzarella cheese, shredded

Remove the venison sausage from its casings and sauté in 2 Tbsp. of the olive oil until browned. Drain to remove excess oil. Remove from the skillet and set aside. In a skillet, heat the remaining 3 Tbsp. of olive oil, add the onions and garlic, and sauté until the onions are just clear. Add the tomato sauce, salt, pepper, and red pepper. Simmer for about 5 minutes on low. Combine the sausage, onion mixture, and sliced olives. Toast the French bread lightly under the broiler. Top with the sausage mixture and sprinkle on grated mozzarella. Broil for about 3 minutes until the cheese melts. Watch carefully—the cheese will burn very quickly. Remove from the broiler, slice each piece of bread diagonally, and serve. Serves 6 to 8.

Stir-Fried Venison Sausage and Cabbage Pita Sandwiches

1½ lbs. ground venison sausage
1 medium head cabbage, shredded
1 small onion, chopped
1 Tbsp. red pepper flakes
1 Tbsp. sugar

salt to taste
½ cup water
⅓ cup sour cream
1 (8 oz.) pkg. pita bread, halved

In a wok or skillet, brown the venison sausage, drain, and set aside. Mix together in the wok or skillet the cabbage, onion, red pepper flakes, sugar, salt, and water. Cover and steam for approximately 20 minutes or until the cabbage is tender. Stir occasionally. Return the venison sausage to the wok or skillet with the cabbage mixture. Add the sour cream and mix well. Stuff into pita bread halves and serve hot. Serves 6.

Apple Turnovers with Venison Sausage

2 medium baking apples
12 oz. venison sausage
2 Tbsp. sorghum molasses or maple syrup

½ cup flour
2 sheets frozen puff pastry dough
flour

Peel and core the apples and cut into small slices. Over medium heat, brown the apples and venison sausage in a skillet, allowing the sausage to crumble. Cook for 5 to 10 minutes until the sausage is fully browned and the apples are soft. Pour off all the grease and pat with paper towels. Stir in the syrup and chill until the mixture is cool to the touch. Thaw the puff pastry dough and cut each sheet of dough into six pieces. Flour a rolling surface and roll each piece of dough into a 6" to 7" square. Stir the sausage mixture and spoon a generous portion onto the middle of each square. Fold in half and seal the edges. Chill the turnovers until the dough is cool to the touch. Preheat the oven to 400° F and bake the turnovers on a cookie sheet for 15 minutes or until golden brown. Serves 6.

Three-Cheese and Venison Sausage Bread

1 (16 oz.) pkg. hot bread roll mix
parchment paper
2 lbs. bulk venison sausage
1 lb. venison or other Pepperoni, finely
   chopped
5 Tbsp. grated Parmesan cheese
3 cups shredded mozzarella cheese
2 cups shredded Cheddar cheese

4 eggs, beaten
1½ tsp. dried parsley
2 tsp. garlic powder
1 tsp. Accent (MSG)
1 tsp. dried minced onion
½ tsp. dried oregano
flour
2 eggs, beaten

Prepare the roll mix according to package directions, letting it rise only once for about 1 hour. Preheat the oven to 350° F. Line a large baking sheet with parchment paper. In a large skillet, brown the venison sausage and Pepperoni and drain well. In a large bowl, combine the cooked sausage mixture, Parmesan, mozzarella, Cheddar, 4 beaten eggs, parsley, garlic powder, Accent, onion, and oregano. Stir until well combined. Divide the risen dough into two equal portions. On a floured board, roll out one piece into a rectangle about 1" thick. Spread half of the filling over the dough. Starting at the wide side, roll and pinch the seam and ends closed. Repeat with the remaining piece of dough. Place the rolls on the baking sheet. Brush generously with 2 beaten eggs. Use natural wooden toothpicks to help hold the seam shut. Bake for 1 hour. Serves 4.

Christmas Venison Sausage Cake

1 tsp. ground cinnamon
1 tsp. ground nutmeg
½ tsp. ground cloves
2 cups self-rising flour
1 lb. venison sausage, crumbled
1 cup cold coffee
1 cup dark brown sugar, packed
1 cup white sugar
2 eggs, beaten

½ cup raisins
½ cup golden raisins (sultanas)
1 cup chopped walnuts
¾ cup rum, divided, plus extra
1 can white cake frosting
1 jar maraschino cherries, drained
10 to 15 mint leaves
sweetened whipped cream

Preheat the oven to 350° F. Mix together the cinnamon, nutmeg, cloves, and flour in a bowl. Add the sausage, coffee, sugars, and eggs to the dry ingredients. Add the raisins and nuts. Pour into an ungreased angel food cake pan. Bake for 1 hour or until a toothpick comes out clean. When cool, remove the cake, soak a small hand towel with ½ cup of the rum, and wrap the cake with it. Place the cake in a tin, pour over with the remaining ¼ cup of rum, and refrigerate for several weeks or months. Every 2 weeks, pour over with ¼ cup of rum. To serve, cover with white frosting and garnish with whole cherries and mint leaves. Serve each slice with a spoonful of sweetened whipped cream. Serves 10 to 15.

19

Venison Sausage Soups, Stews, Gumbos, and Chowders

What would a gumbo be without sausage? . . . unremarkable to say the least.

Soups and gumbos take on a whole new character and aroma when they are allowed to rest and mellow in the refrigerator overnight.

Hearty soups with chunks of venison sausage and large pieces of broken heavy bread make us think about sitting by a warm fire on a cold night, talking about good things, dreaming about the past, and wondering about the future.

Hearty soups make us want to remember our roots and the people who lived in simpler times. But this may only be part of the dream. There may have been no simpler times—only times when we lived differently than we do today.

Sweet Potato and Andouille Venison Sausage Soup

½ lb. Andouille venison sausage, diced
¼ cup butter, divided
1¼ cups chopped onion
1 tsp. dried thyme
1½ lbs. sweet potato puree

¼ cup praline liqueur
7 cups chicken broth
½ cup brown sugar, packed
⅜ cup heavy cream

Cook the diced venison sausage in a skillet with 2 Tbsp. of the butter for 5 minutes. Add the onion and cook until soft. Add the thyme and sweet potatoes and cook for 5 minutes. Add the liqueur, broth, and brown sugar. Cover and simmer over low heat for 45 minutes or until the sweet potatoes are tender. In a blender, purée the soup in batches. Return the purée to the pan, stirring in the cream and remaining 2 Tbsp. of butter. Warm but do not boil. Serve immediately. Serves 6 to 8.

Note: You can also substitute 1½ pounds of cubed pumpkin for the sweet potato puree.

Cajun Venison Sausage Soup

4 lbs. Andouille or sweet Italian venison
   sausage
6 Tbsp. cooking oil, divided
1 large onion, diced
3 celery stalks, diced
2 carrots, peeled and diced
2 potatoes, peeled and diced
6 ripe tomatoes, cored and cubed

3 (32 oz.) cans tomato juice
1 cup Cajun seasoning
1 Tbsp. cayenne pepper
1 cup cornstarch
⅔ cup water
2 cups whipping cream
salt and pepper to taste

Cut the venison sausage into small ½" pieces, brown in 2 Tbsp. of the cooking oil, and set aside. Heat the remaining ¼ cup of oil in a soup pot and cook the onion, celery, carrots, potatoes, and tomatoes until tender. Add the tomato juice, Cajun seasoning, cayenne pepper, cooked sausage, and drippings. Bring the mixture to a gentle boil. Whisk the cornstarch into the water and stir into the soup until thickened. Remove from the heat; add the heavy cream, salt, and pepper. Makes 1 gallon.

Cabbage and Tomato Venison Sausage Soup

2 lbs. Italian sausage links
2 cups dry white wine
2 garlic cloves, minced
1 medium onion, finely chopped
5 cups chopped cabbage

1 (28 oz.) can tomatoes (liquid reserved),
   cut into large pieces
1 cup water
1 (4 oz.) can green chili peppers, seeded
   and chopped

Prick the Italian venison sausages with a sharp fork several times. Cut the sausage into 1" pieces. Place the sausage pieces in a large mixing bowl; add the wine and garlic, mixing well. Marinate for 1 hour. Drain the sausage and reserve the marinade. In a large pot, cook the sausage and onion until the meat is brown and the onion is just clear. Drain off the fat. Add the reserved marinade. Bring to a boil, reduce the heat, cover, and simmer for 20 minutes. Stir in the cabbage, undrained tomatoes, water, and green chili peppers. Cover and simmer for 20 minutes, stirring occasionally. Serves 8 to 10.

Italian Sausage Soup

1 lb. Italian venison sausage
1 garlic clove, minced
2 (14 oz.) cans beef broth
1 (14½ oz.) can Italian-style stewed tomatoes
1 cup sliced carrots
salt and pepper to taste
1 (14½ oz.) can great northern beans,
undrained
2 small zucchini, cubed
2 cups packed fresh spinach, rinsed and torn
¼ tsp. pepper
¼ tsp. salt

In a large pot, brown the Italian venison sausage and garlic. Stir in the beef broth, tomatoes, and carrots, and season with salt and pepper. Reduce the heat, cover, and simmer for 15 minutes. Stir in the beans with their liquid and the zucchini. Cover and simmer for another 15 minutes or until the zucchini is just tender. Remove from the heat and add the spinach. Cover and allow the heat from the soup to cook the spinach for 5 minutes. Serves 6.

Vegetable and Black Bean Venison Sausage Stew

3 (15 oz.) cans black beans, drained and rinsed
1½ cups chopped onion
1½ cups chicken broth
1 cup sliced celery
1 cup chopped red bell pepper
4 garlic cloves, minced
1½ tsp. dried oregano
¾ tsp. ground coriander
½ tsp. ground cumin
¼ tsp. ground red pepper
6 oz. cooked venison link sausages, sliced thin

Combine all the ingredients in a Crock-Pot, cover, and cook on low for 6 to 8 hours. Remove about 1½ cups of the bean mixture from the Crock-Pot and puree in a food processor or blender. Return the purée to the Crock-Pot and stir in. Cover and cook on low for an additional 15 minutes. Serves 6.

In general, the older the buck, the less he moves when disturbed.

Slow-Cooked Cajun Venison Sausage and Rice Stew

½ lb. venison Kielbasa sausage, sliced ¼"
   thick
1 (14½ oz.) can diced tomatoes, undrained
1 medium onion, diced
1 medium green bell pepper, diced
2 celery stalks, thinly sliced
1 Tbsp. beef bouillon granules

1 Tbsp. steak sauce
3 bay leaves, halved
1 tsp. sugar
¼ to ½ tsp. Tabasco sauce, or to taste
1 cup uncooked instant rice
½ cup water
½ cup chopped fresh parsley

Combine the sausage, tomatoes, onion, bell pepper, celery, bouillon, steak sauce, bay leaves, sugar, and Tabasco sauce in a Crock-Pot. Cover and cook on low for 8 hours. Remove the bay leaves; stir in the rice and water. Cook for an additional 25 minutes. Stir in the parsley and serve. Serves 5.

Vegetable and Venison Kielbasa Potato Soup

1 (15½ oz.) can dark kidney beans, rinsed
   and drained
1 (14½ oz.) can diced tomatoes, undrained
1 (10½ oz.) can condensed beef broth,
   undiluted
½ lb. venison Kielbasa sausages, cut into ½"
   cubes

1 large baking potato, cut into 1½" cubes
1 medium green bell pepper, diced
1 medium onion, diced
1 tsp. dried oregano leaves
½ tsp. sugar
1½ tsp. ground cumin

Combine all the ingredients, except cumin, in a slow cooker. Cover and cook on low for 8 hours. Stir in the cumin and serve. Serves 6 to 7.

Since ancient times, deer have been important in the economy of man. Red deer became the basis of specialized Mesolithic economies throughout Eurasia.

Slow-Cooked Spicy Venison and Rice Stew

1 tsp. cooking oil
2 lbs. spicy Italian venison sausage, casings removed
2 garlic cloves, minced
2 tsp. ground cumin
4 onions, chopped

4 green bell peppers, chopped
3 jalapeño peppers, seeded and minced
4 cups beef broth
2 (6¼ oz.) pkgs. long-grained and wild rice mix

Heat the cooking oil in a large skillet. Add the venison sausage and break up while cooking. Cook for about 5 minutes or until browned. Add the garlic and cumin and cook for 30 seconds. Add the onions, bell peppers, and jalapeño peppers. Sauté for about 10 minutes until the onions are just clear. Pour the mixture into a Crock-Pot, stir in the beef broth and rice, and cook on low for 4 hours. Serves 10 to 12.

Chocolate Mole Stew with Venison Sausage

1 Tbsp. olive oil
¼ lb. side of bacon, cubed
2 lbs. 1" thick venison steak, cut into 1" cubes
1 large onion, chopped
4 garlic cloves, chopped
1 Tbsp. flour
1 cup dry white wine
½ cup beef stock or canned broth
½ tsp. ground thyme

1 bay leaf, halved
2 Tbsp. minced fresh parsley
½ tsp. dried oregano leaves
salt and pepper to taste
½ tsp. unsweetened chocolate, minced
2 large potatoes, peeled, cubed, and boiled
2 lbs. Italian venison sausage links, sliced ¼" thick

Warm the olive oil in an ovenproof dish and sauté the bacon pieces until just beginning to brown. Add the venison and brown on all sides. Mix in the onion and garlic and continue to sauté until the onion is just clear. Whisk the flour into the wine and mix into the dish. Stir in the beef stock, thyme, bay leaf, parsley, and oregano. Season to taste with salt and pepper. Cover and simmer over low heat for 2 hours. Scrape the bottom occasionally to prevent sticking. Mix in the chocolate and potatoes, cover, and simmer for another 10 minutes. Brown the sausage pieces. To serve, place the stew in a large serving bowl and cover with the venison sausage pieces. Serves 4 to 6.

Split Pea and Smoked Venison Sausage Soup

½ lb. smoked venison sausage, sliced ½"
  thick
1 (16 oz.) pkg. dried split peas, rinsed
3 medium carrots, sliced ¼" thick
2 celery stalks, sliced ¼" thick

1 medium onion, chopped
¾ tsp. dried marjoram leaves
1 bay leaf, halved
2 (14½ oz.) cans reduced-sodium chicken
  broth

Heat a small skillet over medium heat. Add the venison sausage and cook for 5 to 8 minutes or until browned. Drain well. Combine the sausage and remaining ingredients in a Crock-Pot. Cover and cook on low for 4 to 5 hours or until the peas are tender. Turn off the heat. Remove the bay leaves. Cover and let stand for 10 minutes. Serves 6.

Smoked Polish Venison Sausage Gumbo

1 cup chicken stock or broth
1 (14½ oz.) can diced tomatoes, undrained
¼ cup flour
2 Tbsp. olive oil
¾ lb. Polish venison sausage, sliced ½" thick
1 medium onion, diced
1 green bell pepper, diced
2 celery stalks, chopped

1 carrot, peeled and chopped
2 tsp. dried oregano leaves
2 tsp. dried thyme leaves
⅛ tsp. cayenne pepper
1 cup uncooked long-grained white rice
2 cups water
3 Tbsp. chopped fresh parsley

Combine the chicken broth and tomatoes in a Crock-Pot. Sprinkle the flour evenly over the bottom of a small skillet. Very carefully cook over high heat, without stirring, for 3 to 4 minutes or until the flour just begins to brown. Reduce the heat to medium and stir for about 4 minutes. Stir in the oil until smooth. Carefully whisk the flour mixture into the Crock-Pot. Add the venison sausage, onion, bell pepper, celery, carrot, oregano, thyme, and cayenne pepper. Stir well. Cover and cook on low for 4 to 5 hours or until the juices are thickened. About 30 minutes before the gumbo is ready to serve, prepare the rice by cooking it in 2 cups of boiling water in a medium saucepan. If the gumbo thickens while standing, stir in additional broth. Serve the gumbo over rice. Serves 4.

Quick French Cassoulet

Cassoulet is a traditional way to eat sausage in France. The real French Cassoulet takes hours to prepare and cook; this version is ideal for people in a hurry.

½ lb. dried white beans
1 large carrot
2 garlic cloves
1 medium onion, peeled
2 Tbsp. olive oil, divided
3 Tbsp. mixed fresh herbs, tied in a small
   bag

4 pork chops, without bones
6 oz. beef stock
4 large venison sausage links
4 lamb chops, with bones
parsley
1 large piece pork belly or slab bacon

Soak the beans overnight. Drain well. Roughly chop the carrot and sliver the garlic. Stick the pieces of garlic into the peeled onion. Heat 1 Tbsp. of the oil in a large casserole dish and gently cook the carrot and garlic for a few minutes on top of the stove. Add the beans, onion, herbs, pork chops, and enough beef stock to moisten. Cook over gentle heat for 1 hour until the beans are soft. Meanwhile, heat the remaining oil in a pan and brown the venison sausage and lamb chops. When the beans are ready, add the meat and more stock if needed. Simmer for another hour. Serves 4.

Portuguese Bean Soup with Venison Sausage

½ lb. Chorizo venison sausage, chopped
¼ cup olive oil
2 carrots, chopped
5 celery stalks, chopped
1 cup chopped onion
5 tomatoes, chopped

3 small potatoes, peeled and chopped
1 (15 oz.) can kidney beans, drained
3 qts. chicken stock or canned broth
1½ Tbsp. red pepper (optional)
½ cup tomato paste
salt and pepper to taste

Place the sausage in a large skillet and sauté until brown. Drain, crumble, and set aside. In a soup pot, heat the olive oil and sauté the carrots, celery, and onion. Add the tomatoes, potatoes, kidney beans, and chicken stock, and bring to a boil. Mix in the red pepper and tomato paste. Reduce the heat and simmer for 20 minutes. Add the sausage and season with salt and pepper to taste. Serves 10.

Marinated Venison Sausage Stew à la Provence

6 oz. olive oil
1 medium onion, sliced
½ head celery, cut into 1" pieces
1 medium carrot, sliced
½ cup dry white wine
½ cup white wine vinegar
4 stalks of parsley, chopped
4 green onions, chopped
3 garlic cloves, chopped
1 tsp. dried thyme leaves
2 bay leaves, halved
1 tsp. rosemary
8 black peppercorns
⅛ tsp. salt
2 lbs. venison steak, cut ¾" thick
1 lb. Italian venison, cut ½" thick

2 Tbsp. fat drippings
¼ to ½ cup dry white wine, if needed
2 Tbsp. chopped fresh thyme
2 Tbsp. chopped fresh rosemary
2 Tbsp. chopped fresh oregano
2 Tbsp. chopped fresh marjoram
3 garlic cloves, minced
¼ lb. smoked bacon, cubed
4 carrots, quartered
¾ lb. mixed black and green pitted olives
salt and pepper to taste
1 qt. oysters, drained
3½ tomatoes, chopped
egg noodles for 6
grated Parmesan cheese
parsley sprigs for garnish

Heat the olive oil and lightly sauté the onion, celery, and sliced carrot. Add the remaining ingredients through ⅛ tsp. salt and simmer for 30 minutes. Remove from the stove, set the marinade aside, and allow to cool. Place the venison steaks, venison sausage, and marinade in a large resealable bag and refrigerate for 24 hours. Remove the venison and reserve the marinade.

Preheat the oven to 275° F. In a skillet, sauté the venison and sausage in the fat drippings until just brown on all sides. When brown, remove to a large glass cooking dish and pour in the reserved marinade. If needed, add additional wine. Stir in the remaining ingredients, except oysters and tomatoes. Cover with aluminum foil and bake for 3 hours or until the venison is tender. Mix in the oysters for the last 10 minutes of cooking. Before serving, skim off the fat and sprinkle with the tomatoes. Serve over egg noodles, sprinkle with Parmesan cheese, and garnish with sprigs of parsley. Serves 6.

In summer, mule deer bucks retire as soon as the sun shines where they are feeding and go to the dense shade of some grove to bed down for the day.

Split Pea and Lentil Soup
with Sicilian Venison Sausage

1 lb. Sicilian or mild Italian venison
    sausage, broken into small pieces
¼ cup vegetable oil
3 qts. mirepoix (1 qt. each diced onion,
    celery, and carrots)
¼ cup chopped garlic
1 gal. beef stock or broth

1 ham hock
3 cups lentils
1 cup split peas
2 Tbsp. chopped fresh thyme
2 Tbsp. chopped fresh rosemary
salt and pepper to taste

Brown the venison sausage in a soup pot. Remove from the pot and drain on paper towels. Discard the grease. Sauté the mirepoix in the same pot with the garlic in a small amount of vegetable oil until limp. Add the stock and ham hock. Bring to a simmer and add the lentils, split peas, and herbs. Simmer until the lentils and peas are tender. Add the cooked sausage. Season with salt and pepper. Makes 1 gallon.

Corn Chowder with Venison Sausage

6 cups peeled and cubed potatoes
1 tsp. salt
½ tsp. dried marjoram
3 cups water
1 lb. bulk venison sausage

1 onion, chopped
1 (15¼ oz.) can whole kernel corn
1 (14¾ oz.) can creamed corn
1 (12 oz.) can evaporated milk

Combine the potatoes, salt, marjoram, and water in a soup pot. Boil until the potatoes are just tender. Brown the sausage and onion in a skillet over medium heat. Drain off any excess fat and add the sausage mix to the potatoes. Stir in the cans of corn and the evaporated milk. Heat through and serve. Serves 6.

The "stuffed paunch of an ass" was a
delicacy of ancient Athens.

Louisiana Wild Duck
and Smoked Venison Sausage Gumbo

1 (5 lb.) wild or domestic duck, dressed and
   skinned
2 celery stalks with leaves, cut ¼" thick
1 large carrot, cut ¼" thick
1 large onion, quartered
1½ cups flour
1 tsp. cayenne pepper
1 tsp. paprika
¾ tsp. dry mustard
¾ tsp. white pepper
¾ tsp. black pepper
½ tsp. salt

1 cup cooking oil
2 cups chopped green bell pepper
2 cups chopped onion
2 cups chopped celery
2 Tbsp. minced garlic
1¼ lbs. chopped smoked venison link
   sausage
1 (16 oz.) pkg. frozen sliced okra
2 bay leaves, halved
cooked long-grained rice for 10
filé powder
French bread

Place the duck in a large pot, cover with water, and bring to a boil. Skim off the foam as it cooks. Add the celery pieces, carrot, and quartered onion. Cover and slow-simmer for 1 hour. Remove the duck and reserve 8 cups of liquid. Discard the vegetables. Set the duck and reserved liquid aside to cool. Scrape the meat from the bones and chop into bite-sized pieces.

Combine the flour and next 6 ingredients. Heat the cooking oil in a large pot. Add the flour mixture and cook over medium heat, stirring constantly, until the roux is chocolate colored, about 30 to 45 minutes. Caution: You must stir constantly to prevent the flour from burning. If the flour burns, discard and begin again. Reduce the heat to medium low; add the bell pepper, onion, celery, and garlic. Cook, stirring constantly, until the vegetables are tender. Gradually mix in the reserved broth. Add the chopped duck meat, venison sausage, okra, and bay leaves. Bring to a boil, reduce the heat, and simmer for 1 hour. Discard the bay leaves. Serve with hot cooked rice, filé powder, and hot French bread. The gumbo can be frozen and served at a later time. Serves 10.

Easy access to spices was one of the major
motivators for the voyage that Columbus
made to find a newer and safer route to
the East Indies.

Sicilian Venison Sausage Soup

1 tsp. olive oil
½ lb. Italian venison sausage, cut ¼" thick
1 large onion, diced
⅛ tsp. fennel seeds
3 carrots, peeled and sliced
2 celery stalks, sliced
1 (28 oz.) can crushed tomatoes

¼ cup chopped fresh parsley
2 Tbsp. chopped fresh basil
4 cups chicken stock or broth
½ cup small macaroni
salt and pepper to taste
½ cup freshly grated Parmesan cheese

Heat the olive oil in a large pot over medium heat. Stir in the sausage, onion, and fennel and cook until the sausage is brown. Stir in the carrots and celery, and continue to cook and stir until the vegetables begin to soften, about 5 minutes. Stir in the tomatoes, parsley, basil, and chicken broth. Bring to a boil, reduce the heat, and simmer for 20 minutes or until the vegetables are tender. Stir in the pasta, salt, and pepper and cook for about 10 minutes more until the pasta is tender. Place in a large serving bowl and top with Parmesan cheese. Serves 6.

Cajun Chicken and Venison Sausage Gumbo

1 large chicken, cut into pieces
salt and black pepper to taste
½ cup cooking oil
¾ cup flour
1 large onion, chopped
3 celery stalks, chopped
1 green bell pepper, chopped
4 garlic cloves, minced
2 qts. chicken stock or canned broth
1 tsp. thyme

1 tsp. oregano
1 Tbsp. Worcestershire sauce
Tabasco sauce to taste
cayenne pepper to taste
1 lb. venison Andouille sausage or any
  smoked venison sausage
cooked long-grained rice for 10 to 12
1 cup chopped green onions
filé powder

Season the chicken with salt and pepper. Warm the oil in a large pot and brown the chicken. Remove the chicken, cover, and set aside. Add the flour to the hot oil. You must keep stirring constantly until the flour begins to brown or it will burn and have to be discarded. When the flour begins to turn a chocolate color, immediately add the onion, celery, bell pepper, and garlic, and cook until the onion turns just clear. Slowly add the chicken stock, stirring to dissolve the roux. Add the thyme, oregano, Worcestershire sauce, Tabasco sauce, and cayenne pepper. Add the chicken pieces to the pot and mix well. Cook over low heat for 30 minutes or until the chicken is tender. Add water as needed to adjust the thickness. Add the venison sausage and cook for 15 minutes more. Serve over cooked rice, sprinkling with chopped green onions and a dash of filé powder. Serves 10 to 12.

Danish Pea Soup with Venison Sausage

1 lb. yellow split peas, washed and drained
2 lbs. smoked slab bacon
3 medium carrots, scraped
1 celery root, peeled and quartered
4 medium leeks, white part

2 medium onions, halved
½ tsp. dried thyme
1½ tsp. salt
¼ tsp. black pepper
1 lb. venison link sausage, cooked

Place the split peas in a large pot with 6 cups of water, cover, and cook over low heat for 1½ hours or until tender. In another pot, place the bacon, carrots, celery root, leeks, onions, thyme, salt, and pepper. Cover with water, place on the lid, and simmer for 40 minutes or until the vegetables are tender. Remove the bacon slab, allow to cool, and slice. Remove the vegetables, add the peas along with enough of their liquid to make a soup, and reheat. Place the soup and vegetables in a large soup bowl and serve with bacon and sausage on the side. Serves 6 to 8.

Black Bean and Italian Venison Sausage Soup

3 Tbsp. butter
1 cup chopped carrots
1 cup chopped onions
1 cup chopped celery
2 Tbsp. minced garlic
salt and pepper to taste
⅛ head chopped thyme

2 Tbsp. chopped fresh basil
⅛ head marjoram
1 cup Italian dry red wine
2 qts. chicken stock or broth
10 oz. black beans
1¼ lbs. cooked Italian venison sausage

Sauté the vegetables with the spices in the butter. Remove and set aside. Deglaze the pan with wine and reduce by two-thirds. Add the vegetables and reduction to a stock pot. Add the chicken stock, beans, and venison sausage. Cook over low heat until tender. Makes 1 gallon.

The longest sausage on record measured more than a mile long—5,917 feet. It was cooked in Barcelona, Spain, on September 22, 1986.

Hawaiian Portagee Bean Soup

A rich, classic soup of the Pacific Islands, drawing on their Portuguese roots.

¾ lb. Portuguese venison sausage or any
    other garlic-flavored sausage, sliced ¼"
    thick
1 large onion, coarsely chopped
2 large carrots, coarsely chopped
4 cups chicken broth
½ lb. tomatoes, peeled and diced
1 Tbsp. tomato paste

2 smoked ham hocks
3 potatoes, peeled and cubed
2 bay leaves
1 tsp. paprika
cayenne pepper to taste
salt and pepper
2 (15 oz.) cans red beans (with liquid)

In a large pot, sauté the sausage along with the onions and carrots until the onion is just clear. Add the remaining ingredients, except the beans, and bring to a boil. Reduce the heat and simmer for 2 hours. Shortly before serving, remove the ham hocks and scrape off the meat. Discard the fat and bone. Chop the meat and stir into the pot along with the beans and liquid. Heat for a few minutes and serve. Serves 6 to 8.

Venison Sausage, Corn, and Pepper Chowder

2 Tbsp. butter
1 onion, chopped
2 garlic cloves, minced
1 red bell pepper, chopped
1 green bell pepper, chopped
2 cups chicken stock or broth
1 lb. red potatoes, cut into 1½" cubes

¼ tsp. white pepper
¼ tsp. cumin
3½ cups whole-kernel corn
¼ lb. venison Kielbasa, halved and sliced
⅓ cup milk
⅓ cup heavy cream

Melt the butter in a large pot over medium heat. Add the onion, garlic, and bell peppers, and cook until just tender. Stir in the stock, potatoes, white pepper, and cumin, and bring to a boil. Reduce the heat and simmer for 20 minutes or until the potatoes are tender. Place half the whole-kernel corn in a blender and purée until smooth. Mix the puréed corn, remaining whole corn, venison Kielbasa, milk, and cream into the soup. Simmer for another 20 minutes. Serves 6.

20

Hors d'Oeuvres and Appetizers for Every Venison Sausage Taste

When you think about hors d'oeuvres and appetizers, one of the first things that might come to mind is sausage or charcuterie. The reason is that ground meats can be made into many different types of finger foods that are easy to prepare and travel well. Venison sausage is no different.

In formal dining, hors d'oeuvres and appetizers are similar in that they both are served as a precursor to the meal and are intended to excite the appetite. The technical difference is that hors d'oeuvres are offered as a prelude to the meal and are often served from a separate buffet or passed by the wait staff, whereas appetizers are served at the table as a first course.

In informal dining, hors d'oeuvres and appetizers serve different purposes. They may constitute the complete meal for many informal social gatherings, or they may be brought by the individual guests and served as a focal point in the activity.

Whether it be:

- *Hot and Creamy Venison Sausage Dip*
- *Yam and Venison Sausage Spread*
- *Mushroom and Venison Sausage Strudel Appetizers*
- *Pumpkin and Venison Sausage Tarts*
- *Greek Loukanika Venison Sausage Balls*

You will find a venison appetizer to go with any occasion. If you have a favorite recipe that calls for commercial sausage, substitute the appropriate venison sausage.

Baked Venison and Cheese Sausage Balls

1 lb. bulk venison sausage   1 lb. Cheddar cheese, shredded
2 cups biscuit mix

Preheat the oven to 350° F. In a large bowl, combine the sausage, biscuit mix, and cheese. Form into walnut-sized balls and place on baking sheets. Bake for 15 to 20 minutes or until golden brown. Serves 6 to 8.

Pumpkin and Venison Sausage Tarts

2 cups flour
½ tsp. ground sage
¼ tsp. salt
⅔ cup shortening
5 Tbsp. cold water, divided
flour
¼ lb. bulk venison sausage
2 Tbsp. minced onion

2 eggs, slightly beaten
1 cup canned pumpkin
¼ cup milk
2 Tbsp. sugar
⅛ tsp. salt
⅛ tsp. ground cinnamon
fresh sage leaves for garnish

Preheat the oven to 325° F. Stir together the flour, ground sage, and 1/4 tsp. of salt. Cut in the shortening until the pieces are the size of small peas. Sprinkle 2 Tbsp. of the cold water over part of the mixture and gently toss with a fork. Push to the side of the bowl. Repeat with the remaining cold water, 1 Tbsp. at a time, until all is moistened. Shape the dough into a ball. On a lightly floured surface, roll the dough ⅛" thick. Cut circles with a 3" to 3½" round cutter (depending on the size of the tart or individual brioche pans used). Line 2½" to 3" round fluted tart pans or individual brioche pans with the pastry circles. Trim off any excess dough. Place the pans in a baking pan and set aside.

To make the filling, cook the venison sausage and onion in a small skillet until the sausage is lightly browned and crumbly. Break up the sausage into fine pieces as it cooks. Remove the sausage and drain on paper towels. Set aside. Stir together the eggs, pumpkin, milk, sugar, salt, and cinnamon. Stir into the sausage mixture. Spoon a slightly rounded Tbsp. of the mixture into each pastry-lined pan. Bake for 15 to 20 minutes or until the filling is set. Remove the tarts from the oven and let cool in the pans for 15 minutes or until firm. With a wooden toothpick, carefully loosen the tarts from the pans. Cool on wire racks. Wrap and chill for at least 2 hours.

To serve, place the tarts on a baking sheet. Reheat in a 350° F oven for 8 to 10 minutes or until heated through. Garnish by placing sage leaves on top of each tart. Serves 24.

Appetizer Balls with Venison Sausage and Mashed Potatoes

1½ lbs. fresh venison sausage, crumbled
½ cup unseasoned bread crumbs
½ cup mashed potatoes
1 egg, lightly beaten
1 tsp. brown sugar, packed
1 tsp. salt
¼ tsp. black pepper
⅛ tsp. ground ginger

¼ tsp. freshly ground nutmeg
¼ tsp. allspice
⅛ tsp. ground cloves
¼ cup butter
fresh parsley
lime or lemon
tangerine or small oranges

Mix together all the ingredients, except the butter, parsley, and fruit. Wet your hands and roll the sausage mixture into 1" balls. Melt the butter in a skillet and brown the sausage balls on all sides. Cover and simmer until cooked through. To serve, arrange on a serving tray with natural wooden toothpicks and garnish with parsley and citrus slices. Makes about 60 sausage balls.

Chorizo Venison Sausage and Baked Phyllo Rolls with Cilantro Salsa

2 green onions, cut 1" long
1 cup packed fresh cilantro leaves
1 (7 oz.) can salsa verde
6 sheets phyllo dough
¼ cup butter, melted

½ lb. bacon, cooked crisp
4 small Chorizo venison sausages, fully
    cooked and cut lengthwise
12 dates, cut lengthwise
shortening

Preheat the oven to 400° F. In a food processor, pulse together the green onions and cilantro until finely chopped. Add the salsa verde and pulse several times until the salsa is well blended. Scrape into a bowl and set aside.

Spread out one sheet of phyllo dough and brush with melted butter. Layer another sheet of phyllo directly on top of the first. Brush the second sheet of phyllo with butter. Along one edge of the phyllo, lay a single row of cooked bacon. Place the venison Chorizo halves on top of the row of bacon. Lay a row of dates, end to end, on top of the venison Chorizo. Carefully roll the phyllo dough over the filling to form a single long roll. Repeat the process with the remaining pieces of phyllo until you have 3 rolls. Cut the rolls across into 2" pieces; keep the pieces together in a roll.

Put the sliced rolls on a greased cookie sheet and bake for about 12 minutes or until golden and crisp. Stand the pieces up on a serving platter and top each with cilantro salsa. Serve warm. Serves 6 to 8.

Baked Chunky Applesauce
and Venison Sausage Appetizers

2 lbs. Italian venison sausage
¾ cup brown sugar, packed

1 cup chunky applesauce
1 onion, chopped

Preheat the oven to 325° F. In a large skillet, fry the venison sausage until browned. Drain well. Cut the sausage into bite-sized pieces. In a small casserole dish, combine the sausage, brown sugar, applesauce, and onion. Bake for 45 minutes. Serve with natural wooden toothpicks. Serves 8.

Italian Venison Sausage Rolls

2 (1 lb.) loaves frozen bread dough
1 lb. Italian venison sausage, cooked and
   drained

2 eggs, lightly beaten
½ lb. shredded mozzarella
3 Tbsp. grated Parmesan cheese

Preheat oven to 400° F. Roll the bread dough out into a rectangular shape. Spread the cooked and drained Italian venison sausage onto each roll. Layer the mozzarella and Parmesan over the sausage. Pour the eggs over the cheeses. Roll the dough loaves and seal the edges with water. Place on a cookie sheet and let rise for 30 minutes. Bake for 20 to 25 minutes. Serves 16 to 20.

French Bread Appetizers
with Venison Chorizo Sausage

1 loaf French bread, cut in half lengthwise
1 lb. venison Chorizo sausage, cubed
¼ cup minced onion
2 garlic cloves, minced
1 (4 oz.) can green chilies, minced
1 cup prepared salsa

2 cups shredded Monterey Jack cheese
1 cup sliced black olives
1 cup chopped artichoke hearts
1 tsp. cumin
1 tsp. salt

Preheat the oven to 350° F. Remove the soft inner bread from the loaf halves. Sauté the venison Chorizo, onion, and garlic until the onion is just clear. Add the remaining ingredients and mix thoroughly. Spoon the venison filling into the French bread halves and place on an ungreased baking sheet. Bake for 30 minutes or until the bread is crisp and the filling is hot and bubbly. Remove the loaves from the oven and allow to cool. Slice the loaves across into appetizer-sized servings. Serves 6 to 8.

Hot Venison Sausage Tamales

boiling water
24 prepared corn shucks
1 lb. ground venison
¼ cup chili powder
½ lb. hot or mild bulk venison sausage
cayenne pepper to taste

2 Tbsp. salt, divided
6 cups masa or cornmeal
1 cup lard or vegetable shortening
boiling water
cotton twine

Pour boiling water over the dried corn shucks and soak to make pliable. Combine the ground venison, chili powder, venison sausage, cayenne pepper, and 1½ tsp. of the salt in a large bowl and set aside. Mix the cornmeal, remaining salt, and lard in a mixing bowl and stir in enough boiling water to hold the ingredients together. Place 1 heaping Tbsp. of the cornmeal mixture on a soaked corn shuck and pat out to the desired length. Place 1 Tbsp. of the venison mixture down the center of the cornmeal patty. Fold over both ends of the corn shuck and then roll the tamale to close. Tie securely with a piece of cotton twine. Repeat with the remaining cornmeal mixture and meat mixture.

Stand the tamales on end in a large pot. Add enough water to come within 1" of the tamale tops. Bring to a boil, reduce the heat, and simmer for 40 minutes. The tamales may be frozen. Makes 23 to 25 tamales. Serves 6 to 8.

Venison Sausage–Stuffed Mushroom Appetizer

24 fresh mushrooms
1 cup packed bulk venison sausage

½ lb. jalapeño cheese, grated

Clean the mushrooms and remove the stems. Place the mushrooms round-side-down on a cookie sheet, stuff with the venison sausage, and sprinkle with the grated cheese. Place the mushrooms under the broiler for 6 to 8 minutes or until the sausage is crisp. Serve immediately. Makes 24 stuffed mushrooms.

In Vermont, an estimated 115,000 deer are harvested annually.

Stuffed Puff Pastry Venison Sausage Canapés

1 lb. ground venison sausage
1 onion, finely chopped
2 celery stalks, finely chopped
1 Tbsp. chopped fresh parsley

pepper to taste
½ (17½ oz.) pkg. frozen puff pastry,
  refrigerator thawed

Preheat the oven to 300° F. In a medium bowl, mix together the ground venison sausage, onion, celery, parsley, and pepper. Roll out one sheet of the puff pastry to ⅛" thick. Evenly spread on half the sausage mixture. Beginning at one of the shorter sides, roll up the pastry. Moisten the seam with water and seal the edge with a moist fork. Slice the roll into 1" pieces. Repeat with the second pastry sheet and remaining sausage mixture.

On a large baking sheet, stand the sausage rolls on end. Bake for approximately 20 minutes. After 10 minutes, turn the sausage rolls over and bake until the pastry is golden brown. Drain on paper towels and serve warm. Serves 16.

Breaded Venison Sausage–Stuffed Mushrooms

1 lb. bulk sausage, honey flavored or hot
  and spicy
3 Tbsp. chopped fresh parsley
2 cups seasoned bread crumbs

30 large fresh mushrooms
hot jalapeño cheese
shortening
olive oil

Preheat the oven to 350° F. Brown the venison sausage and drain on paper towels. Mix the sausage with the parsley and seasoned bread crumbs and set aside. Wash the mushrooms and pat dry. Stuff the mushrooms with the sausage mixture and place 1 tsp. of the cheese on each one. Lightly grease a cookie sheet and place the mushrooms on it. Brush lightly with olive oil and bake for about 10 minutes. Makes 30 stuffed mushrooms.

> As many as 500,000 people hunt deer each fall in Ohio. Deer hunting contributes an estimated $200 million to Ohio's economy.

Mushroom and Venison Sausage Strudel Appetizers

½ lb. bulk hot sausage
½ lb. mushrooms, chopped
½ tsp. crumbled dried thyme
1 Tbsp. Dijon mustard

¼ cup sour cream
flour
1 (8 oz.) pkg. refrigerated crescent rolls
flour

Preheat the oven to 350° F. Place a rack in the center of the oven. Make the filling by sautéing the venison sausage in a skillet. Break up the sausage while cooking. Drain off the fat. Add the mushrooms and thyme, and sauté over high heat until all liquid has evaporated and the mushrooms begin to brown. Cool and stir in the mustard and sour cream.

To make strudels, remove half of the rolls and place on a lightly floured board. Press the perforations together to seal. Turn over and seal the perforations on the other side. Gently roll out to a 15" × 4" rectangle. Pile half of the filling down the center of the pastry. Roll tightly and crimp the edges. Lay, seam-side down, on an ungreased baking sheet. Repeat with the remaining filling and rolls. Bake for 14 to 18 minutes or until golden. Remove from the oven and cool slightly. Cut into 1" pieces. Makes approximately 28 appetizers.

Sweet-and-Sour Venison Sausage Appetizers

2 rings venison Kielbasa or other venison
   link sausage
1 lb. bacon
natural wooden toothpicks

1 (8 oz.) jar sweet-and-sour sauce
2 cups ketchup
2 cups brown sugar

Preheat the oven to 350° F. Cut the sausage into 1¼" chunks. Cut the bacon strips in half, wrap each sausage chunk with a bacon strip, and seal with a toothpick. Place the sausages on a cookie sheet and bake for 30 minutes. Mix together the remaining ingredients and spoon over the sausage. Bake for an hour until the sauce gels on the sausage. Makes approximately 30 appetizers.

Reindeer are now raised successfully in most parts of the U.S., including Texas, Alabama, and Oklahoma.

Danish Venison Meatballs with Dill Sauce

Meatballs

½ lb. lean veal, cubed
½ lb. lean pork, cubed
¼ lb. venison, cubed
¼ lb. ham, cooked and cubed
1 medium onion, chopped
½ tsp. salt

½ tsp. black pepper
1 egg
1 tsp. baking soda
1½ cups unseasoned bread crumbs
⅓ cup cream
oil

Dill Sauce

2 Tbsp. mayonnaise
1½ Tbsp. cream

¾ tsp. minced dried dill
½ tsp. caraway seeds

Grind the meats together and mix in the remaining ingredients, except oil. Cover and place in the refrigerator for 1 hour. Shape the sausage into 36 balls and flatten. Fry, 8 at a time, in about 1" of hot oil until brown on both sides. Drain and spoon over with Dill Sauce. Serves 4.

Cheese and Venison Sausage Biscuit Appetizers

½ cup spicy or mild bulk country venison
   sausage
2 cups flour
1 Tbsp. baking powder
¾ tsp. salt
¾ tsp. sugar
¼ cup butter

¼ cup shortening
½ cup grated sharp Cheddar cheese
¾ cup buttermilk
½ tsp. baking soda
flour
shortening

Preheat the oven to 450° F. Fry the venison sausage over medium-high heat for 5 minutes, breaking the meat as it cooks. Drain the sausage through a colander and place on paper towels to cool. In a large bowl, sift together the flour, baking powder, salt, and sugar. Cut in the butter and shortening. Mix the sausage and grated cheese into the dough. Whisk together the buttermilk and baking soda, pour into the flour mixture, and stir until a soft dough forms. Turn onto a lightly floured surface and knead gently for 10 to 20 seconds. Roll to a thickness of ½". Cut into 1½" biscuits and arrange on a lightly greased cookie sheet. Bake for 10 to 15 minutes, until lightly browned. Serve warm. Serves 2 to 4.

Fresh Venison Sausage Roll

2 (1 lb.) loaves frozen white bread dough
1 Tbsp. vegetable oil
1 lb. ground venison sausage
1 lb. ground spicy venison sausage
½ large green bell pepper, chopped

1 (6 oz.) can mushrooms, drained
2 cups shredded mozzarella cheese
1 egg
2 Tbsp. water

Rub the frozen bread dough with vegetable oil, cover, and allow to thaw overnight at room temperature. Preheat the oven to 350°F. Place the sausage in a large skillet and cook over medium-high heat until brown. Drain, crumble, and set aside. Roll out one loaf of bread and place on an ungreased cookie sheet. Leave a 1" border around the edges bare. Layer the bread with the cooked sausage, bell pepper, mushrooms, and cheese.

Roll out the second loaf of bread, lay on top of the first loaf, and press around all the edges to seal. In a small bowl, beat together the egg and water. Brush the surface with the egg wash. Bake for 25 to 30 minutes or until golden brown. Serves 12.

Hot and Creamy Venison Sausage Dip

1 lb. ground spicy bulk venison sausage
5 green onions, finely chopped, divided
1 cup sour cream

½ cup mayonnaise
¼ cup grated Parmesan cheese
1 (2 oz.) jar chopped pimientos

Preheat the oven to 350° F. Place the spicy venison sausage in a large, deep skillet. Cook over medium-high heat until brown. Drain the sausage and remove to a large bowl. Stir in four of the chopped green onions, sour cream, mayonnaise, Parmesan cheese, and pimientos. Transfer the sausage mixture to a medium baking dish and bake for 20 to 25 minutes or until the dip begins to bubble and is lightly browned. Sprinkle with the remaining green onion. Serve hot with chips. Makes 3 cups.

> Dry sausage was born as a result of the discovery of new spices, which helped to enhance flavor and preserve the meat.

Greek Loukanika Venison Sausage Balls

1 lb. ground pork
½ lb. ground venison
¼ cup dry red wine
1 Tbsp. chopped parsley
¼ cup grated cheese

1 Tbsp. grated orange peel
anise flavoring to taste
salt and pepper to taste
hot pepper flakes to taste

Combine all ingredients and grind through a fine disc. Roll into 1" to 1½" balls and broil until well done. Serve hot.

Skewered and Broiled Venison Sausage

Sausage
3 lbs. smoked venison sausage links, cut
    diagonally into ½" slices

steel or bamboo skewers

Caramelized Onions
6 Tbsp. butter
2 lbs. onions, thinly sliced

1 tsp. sugar
salt and pepper to taste

Horseradish and Apple Sauce
2 cups sour cream
¼ cup prepared finely ground horseradish

¼ cup minced apple
2 tsp. crushed caraway seeds

For the Sausage. Preheat the broiler or grill. If using bamboo skewers, presoak them in water for 30 minutes. Thread the venison onto the skewers and cook thoroughly. Turn several times. Serve with Caramelized Onions and Horseradish and Apple Sauce.

For the Caramelized Onions. Melt the butter and cook the onions until just clear. Add the sugar and simmer until golden brown. Season with salt and pepper.

For the Horseradish and Apple Sauce. Mix all the ingredients and refrigerate for at least 2 hours. This sauce can be made a day or two ahead.

Spicy-Hot and Creamy Venison Sausage Dip

1 lb. ground venison sausage
1½ cups chopped onions
1 (10 oz.) can diced tomatoes with green
   chili peppers, drained

1 (8 oz.) pkg. cream cheese
1 (16 oz.) container sour cream
1 Tbsp. red pepper flakes (optional)

Place the venison sausage in a large skillet and cook until brown. Drain the sausage and stir in the onions. Cook until the onions are just clear. Mix in the tomatoes with green chili peppers. Stirring occasionally, allow the mixture to simmer for 10 minutes. Mix in the cream cheese and sour cream. Season with the red pepper flakes. Serves 6.

Sauerkraut and Venison Sausage Balls

1 lb. spicy ground venison sausage
1 onion, diced
1 (2 oz.) pkg. dried beef, shredded
1 (16 oz.) can sauerkraut, drained and
   minced
1 tsp. prepared mustard
1 Tbsp. dried parsley

1 (8 oz.) pkg. cream cheese, softened
1 tsp. garlic salt
2 qts. oil for frying
1½ cups flour
1¼ cups milk
1 egg, lightly beaten
2 cups seasoned bread crumbs

Place the spicy ground venison sausage, onion, and dried beef in a deep skillet. Cook over medium-high heat until the sausage is brown and the onion is just clear. Drain and remove to a large bowl. Mix the sauerkraut, prepared mustard, parsley, cream cheese, and garlic salt into the sausage mixture. Cover and chill in the refrigerator for 2 hours.

Heat the oil in a deep-fryer to 375° F. Place the flour in a small bowl. Whisk the milk and egg together in a second small bowl. Place the seasoned bread crumbs in a third bowl. Roll the chilled sausage mixture into 1" balls. Dredge the sausage balls one at a time in the flour, then dip in the egg and milk mixture and roll in the bread crumbs. Deep-fry the sausage balls in small batches until brown. Drain on paper towels and serve warm. Makes 30 to 40 appetizers.

Crescent Rolls with Spicy Venison Sausage

1 lb. ground spicy or mild venison sausage
1 (8 oz.) pkg. cream cheese, softened
2 (8 oz.) pkgs. refrigerated crescent rolls
1 egg white, lightly beaten
1 Tbsp. poppy seeds

Preheat the oven to 350° F. In a medium skillet, lightly brown the venison sausage and drain. While the sausage is still warm, add the cream cheese and stir until the cheese is melted and the mixture is creamy. Set aside and allow to completely cool. Separate the crescent rolls and arrange into two rectangles. Form a log of sausage mixture lengthwise down the center of each rectangle. Fold over the long ends of the pastry to cover the sausage log. Place on an ungreased cookie sheet, seam down. Brush with the egg white and sprinkle with the poppy seeds. Bake for 20 minutes until the crust is golden. When completely cooled, slice into 1½" pieces. Serves 20.

Cheese-Wonton and Venison Sausage Canapés

shortening
1 lb. ground Italian venison sausage
½ cup shredded Monterey Jack cheese
½ cup shredded Colby cheese
1 cup salsa
24 (3½" square) wonton wrappers
¾ (16 oz.) container sour cream
1 bunch green onions, chopped

Preheat the oven to 350° F. Lightly grease a miniature muffin pan. Place the ground Italian venison sausage in a skillet, cook, and drain. Stir the Monterey Jack cheese and Colby cheese into the warm sausage and allow to melt. Stir in the salsa. Gently press wonton wrappers into the greased miniature muffin pan so that the edges extend past the top edges. Place a heaping Tbsp. of the sausage mixture into each wonton wrapper. Bake for 10 minutes or until wonton edges begin to brown. Transfer the baked wontons to a serving platter and spoon 1 Tbsp. of sour cream on each. Sprinkle on the chopped green onions. Makes 24 canapés.

> The red deer have proved to be the most exciting and successful introduction of a major livestock animal in the last century.

Stuffed Jalapeño and Venison Sausage Appetizers

¾ lb. ground venison sausage
2 (8 oz.) pkgs. cream cheese, softened
30 jalapeño chili peppers

1 lb. bacon, slices cut in half
natural wooden toothpicks

Preheat the oven to 375° F. Place the ground venison sausage in a skillet and cook. Drain the sausage and place in a medium bowl. Mix in the cream cheese. Cut the jalapeños in half lengthwise and remove the seeds. Stuff each half with the venison sausage and cream cheese mixture. Wrap with half slices of bacon and secure with toothpicks. Place the appetizers in a shallow baking pan. Bake for 20 minutes or until the bacon is brown. Makes 60 appetizers.

Yam and Venison Sausage Spread

½ cup whole-wheat flour
1 cup whipping cream
3 eggs, beaten
4 medium beets, peeled and cut into ¼"
    strips

¼ cup chopped chives
1 lb. bulk venison sausage, broken up
¼ cup ground allspice
2 Tbsp. baking soda
1 Tbsp. yam or sweet potato extract

In a medium bowl, mix the flour and whipping cream. Allow the mixture to stand in the refrigerator for 1 hour or until thickened. Stir the eggs, beets, chives, and venison sausage into the flour and heavy cream. Mix in the allspice, baking soda, and yam or sweet potato extract. Pour the mixture into a medium saucepan and bring to a boil. Stirring frequently, cook until the liquid has reduced, about 20 minutes. Makes 2 cups.

The smallest deer are the pudu of the Andes, which are about 30 cm (12 inches) tall and weigh 6.8 kg (15 pounds).

Mini Biscuits with Venison Sausage Topping

1⅔ cup flour
⅓ cup yellow cornmeal
2 tsp. baking powder
¼ tsp. baking soda
¼ tsp. salt
½ cup shortening
⅔ cup buttermilk or sour milk

flour
½ lb. bulk venison sausage
¼ cup sliced green onion
1 garlic clove, minced
2 Tbsp. tomato paste
1 Tbsp. water
6 slices American cheese

Preheat the oven to 450° F. Sift together the flour, cornmeal, baking powder, soda, and salt. Cut in the shortening until the mixture resembles coarse crumbs. Make a well in the center and add the buttermilk all at once; stir with a fork until the dough is just moistened. Turn the dough out onto a lightly floured board. Quickly knead 10 to 12 times or until the dough is nearly smooth. Roll out to ¼" thick. Cut out into 1¾" biscuits. Place the biscuits on an extra-large ungreased baking sheet. Reroll the dough until all biscuits are cut out. Bake for 8 to 10 minutes or until the biscuits are lightly browned.

Meanwhile, sauté the venison sausage, green onion, and garlic in a skillet until the sausage begins to brown, stirring well to break up any large chunks. Thoroughly drain off the fat. Stir in the tomato paste and water. Heat through. Cut each slice of cheese into quarters and halve each quarter to make 48 triangles. Spoon 1 tsp. of the sausage mixture onto each biscuit. Top with a cheese triangle. Return to the oven for 1 to 2 minutes or until the cheese melts. Serve hot. Makes 48 appetizers.

Ro-tel Venison Sausage Dip

1 lb. fresh venison sausage
1 (8 oz.) pkg. cream cheese, softened

2 cans Ro-tel (canned tomato and chili mixture)

Cook and drain the venison sausage. Add the remaining ingredients. Melt over low heat and stir all the ingredients together. The dip can be served either hot or cold with chips or hard bread or crackers. Serves 8 to 10.

The Key deer of Florida are usually less than 76 cm (2.5 feet) tall and weigh 23 kg (50 pounds).

Thoringer Venison Sausage Fondue

1½ lbs. Thoringer or other quick-cured
   venison sausage
2 (11 oz.) cans condensed Cheddar cheese
   soup

1 cup beer
1 (4 oz.) can chopped mild green chilies,
   drained
¼ cup cooking oil

Slice the Thoringer venison sausage into ¾" pieces. Blend together the soup, beer, and chilies, and heat in a double boiler over medium heat. Transfer to a fondue pot or chafing dish to keep warm. Sauté the venison sausage pieces in the cooking oil over medium-high heat until browned. Serve the sausage pieces with the hot sauce and chips. Serves 6.

21

Other Venison Sausage Dishes and Delights

Other Venison Sausage Dishes and Delights are recipes that don't fit into any one category, but can be a pleasant surprise on the menu for many occasions.

One favorite is Sweet Potatoes with Pecans and Venison Sausage Patties. This recipe is a blend of venison with the southern staples of sweet potatoes and pecans. It is this combination that makes this dish so good and simple to prepare. It is especially good for family gatherings during the holidays.

A favorite around the hunting camp is Venison Sausage and Gravy.

If you want to add an international flavor to a meal, try:

- *Yum Moo Ya with Small Venison Sausage*
- *Hot Tamale Venison Pie*
- *Venison Bratwurst Sausages in Beer*
- *Polynesian Venison Sausage Kabobs on Rice*

Baked Apples with Venison Sausage

3 large tart apples
1 cup fresh venison sausage

1 tsp. salt
2 Tbsp. brown sugar, packed

Preheat the oven to 375° F. Cut a slice from the tops of the apple. Scoop out the cores and pulp, leaving shells ¾" thick. Cut the pulp from the cores and chop it. Combine the chopped apple with the sausage. Sprinkle the apples with the salt and brown sugar. Overfill the apples with the sausage and apple mixture. Bake for 15 minutes or until tender. Serves 6.

Italian Venison Sausage Patties
with Mozzarella Cheese Topping

nonstick cooking spray
2 tsp. olive oil, divided
1 lb. bulk Italian venison sausage
1 egg, lightly beaten
1 lemon peel, grated

6 Tbsp. Italian bread crumbs
2 cups plain tomato sauce
3 basil leaves, chopped
⅛ tsp. fresh minced oregano
4 slices mozzarella cheese

Preheat the oven to 325° F. Spray a large nonstick skillet with cooking spray and add 1 tsp. of the olive oil. Combine the venison sausage with the egg and lemon peel; mix lightly. Sprinkle the bread crumbs on a shallow plate. Shape a quarter of the meat mixture into a flat patty and press into the crumbs, lightly coating both sides. Make 3 more coated patties with the remaining sausage and bread crumbs.

Brown the patties in a skillet over moderate heat for about 2 to 3 minutes. Add the remaining tsp. of oil and turn to brown the other side evenly. Remove the patties and set aside. Mix the tomato sauce with the basil and oregano. Place the patties on a cookie tray, pour sauce over each patty, and lay a piece of cheese on each. Place the sausage patties in the oven until the cheese begins to melt. Serves 4.

Simmered Rabbit and Italian Venison Sausage

1 lb. Italian venison sausage links
1 rabbit, cut into pieces
3 garlic cloves, minced
1 onion, chopped
1 red bell pepper, thinly sliced
1 green bell pepper, thinly sliced
1 (16 oz.) can Italian tomatoes, drained

½ tsp. red pepper flakes (optional)
2 Tbsp. tomato paste
¼ cup Chianti or other dry red wine
1 Tbsp. minced fresh basil
zest of 1 orange
½ orange, juiced
½ tsp. salt, or to taste

Prick the sausages several times with a sharp fork and sauté until the links are just browned on all sides. Remove the sausages, allow to cool, and slice into 1" long pieces. Sauté the rabbit pieces in the same skillet until just brown on the outside; set aside. Pour off all but a small amount of the drippings and sauté the garlic, onion, and bell pepper until just tender. Return the sausage to the pan and add the tomatoes, pepper flakes, tomato paste, Chianti, basil, zest, orange juice, and salt, and simmer for 10 minutes. Return the rabbit to the skillet, cover, and simmer for 25 to 30 minutes or until the rabbit is done. Serves 4.

French Potato Salad with Smoked Venison Sausage

1½ lbs. smoked venison sausage links
2 lbs. small red potatoes, cooked, pared,
   and sliced
3 Tbsp. white vinegar
⅓ cup olive oil

½ tsp. salt
¼ tsp. black pepper
⅓ cup sliced green onions with tops
2 Tbsp. capers
lettuce leaves

Grill the sausage until done and slice on the diagonal into ¼" thick pieces. Whisk together the vinegar, oil, salt, and pepper. Gently spoon the potatoes into the oil mixture and add the sausage. Place lettuce leaves on individual serving plates and spoon on the sausage and potatoes. Top with green onions and capers. Serves 4.

Easy Smoked Venison Sausage Crock-Pot

1 lb. smoked venison sausage
1 (15 oz.) can Hunt's Italian sauce or any
   good spaghetti sauce

cooked rice or spaghetti for 6

Cut the smoked venison sausage diagonally into ½" thick slices and place in a Crock-Pot. Pour over with sauce, cover, and cook on low for 6 hours. Serve over hot rice. Serves 6.

In well-protected areas where the habitat is good, deer numbers will increase beyond what the habitat can support. The only way to control a deer herd and keep it within its food supply is to harvest does and fawns equally with bucks.

Microwaved Fresh Venison Breakfast Sausage Patties

1 lb. bulk ground venison sausage
3 Tbsp. finely chopped fresh parsley
1 Tbsp. finely chopped green onion
1 large garlic clove, finely chopped
½ tsp. ground sage
½ tsp. ground marjoram
½ tsp. salt

½ tsp. pepper
¼ tsp. ground thyme
¼ tsp. ground nutmeg
¼ tsp. paprika
¼ cup whole-wheat flour or oat bran
½ tsp. cooking oil

Mix together all the ingredients, except flour and oil. Shape into patties and roll in the flour. Preheat a microwave-safe dish on high for 5 minutes. Coat the hot dish with the cooking oil and quickly add the patties. Microwave on high for 2 minutes. Turn the patties and microwave for another 1 to 2 minutes or until done. Serves 4.

Apple and Venison Sausage Stuffing

2 cups water
7 Tbsp. butter, divided
2 large bags corn bread stuffing crumbs
1 lb. bulk venison sausage
1 large onion, chopped fine

3 cloves garlic, minced
2 stalks celery, chopped fine
1 cup chopped walnuts
3 medium apples, cored and sliced

Heat the water in a large pot and melt ¼ cup of the butter. When the butter is melted, stir in the corn bread stuffing and set aside. Heat a large sauté pan over medium-high heat and melt 1 Tbsp. of the butter. Add the venison sausage and break up. Sauté until lightly browned and cooked. Remove the venison sausage and allow to drain on paper towels. In the same pan, melt the remaining butter and sauté the onion, garlic, and celery until the onion is just clear and the celery is just crisp. Add the walnuts and sauté for 1 minute. Add the apples and sauté for 1 minute more. Remove from the heat. Combine the corn bread stuffing with the sautéed vegetables and stuff a turkey. Do not stuff a turkey and place in the refrigerator overnight; stuff just before placing in the oven. Serves 8.

Note: Turkey stuffing can also be baked separately. Fill a 9" × 13" × 2" pan with the venison sausage stuffing, cover with foil, and bake in a preheated 350° F oven for 30 minutes. Remove the foil and bake for another 15 minutes.

Polynesian Venison Sausage Kabobs on Rice

2 precooked Polish venison sausages or
   other precooked sausage
4 green peppers, cut into 1" pieces

2 cups large cubed pineapple
1 cup sweet-and-sour sauce
cooked rice for 4

Cut each venison sausage into 1" long pieces. On a skewer, alternate chunks of pineapple and green peppers with the venison sausage. Place the skewers on a grill until heated thoroughly. Baste with the sweet-and-sour sauce. Serve over cooked rice. Serves 4.

Molded Egg and Venison Rolls

cooking oil
4 hard-boiled eggs, cooled
2 lbs. fresh bulk venison sausage
¼ cup small pecan pieces

1½ cups seasoned bread crumbs
2 eggs, lightly beaten
½ cup milk

Preheat the oil in a deep fat fryer to 375° F. Divide the sausage into four equal portions and flatten out into thin and wide patties. Lay a hard-boiled egg in the center of each patty and wrap the sausage around and completely over the egg. Mix together the pecan pieces and bread crumbs in a bowl. In a separate bowl, whisk the eggs and milk together. Roll each covered egg first in the pecan mixture, then in the egg mixture, and then again in the pecan mixture. Hold each egg in your hands and gently firm the pecans onto the sausage. Deep-fry until the sausage begins to brown. Serves 4.

Spicy Polish Venison Sausage Dinner

1 lb. Polish venison sausage links
¼ cup butter
1 medium onion, chopped
1 green pepper, chopped
nonstick cooking spray

1 cup water
1 cup chutney
1 medium apple, finely chopped
mashed potatoes for 6

Cut the venison sausage into 1" pieces. Melt the butter in a large skillet. Add the chopped onion and pepper, simmer until just soft, and remove from the skillet. Spray the skillet with nonstick spray, add the sausage, and brown until slightly crisp. Add the pepper, onion, and water. Let the mixture come to a boil. Stir in the chutney and chopped apple, and bring to a boil again. Remove from the heat and serve over mashed potatoes. Serves 6.

Turkey Stuffing with Venison Sausage and Celery

8 cups ½" cubed bread
1 lb. bulk venison sausage
¾ cup diced onion
2 Tbsp. butter
1 to 2 cups chopped celery
1 Tbsp. mixed dried fresh herbs

1 tsp. finely minced thyme
1 tsp. finely minced rosemary
1 tsp. finely minced tarragon or marjoram
¾ cups chopped pecans or 1 cup cubed
    apple
1 tsp. pepper

Place the cubed bread on a tray and allow to air-dry. Place the bread in a large mixing bowl. Fry the venison sausage, break into small pieces, drain, and set aside. Sauté the onion in the butter until just clear. Add the onion to the bread and mix in the remaining ingredients. The stuffing should be quite dry. Do not stuff a turkey and place in the refrigerator overnight; stuff the turkey just before placing in the oven. Stuffs an 8 to 10 lb. turkey.

Venison Sausage and Gravy

1 lb. bulk venison sausage
3 Tbsp. bacon grease or cooking oil
¼ cup flour

3 cups cold milk
½ tsp. salt
¼ tsp. black pepper

Brown the venison sausage in a skillet until done. Break up the sausage into small pieces. Set aside, leaving the drippings in the skillet. Mix the bacon grease into the sausage drippings. Reduce the heat to medium. Whisk the flour into the milk and mix into the hot grease. Stir constantly until the flour begins to turn golden brown. When the mixture is smooth, thickened, and begins to bubble, return the sausage to the skillet. Season with salt and pepper. Reduce the heat and simmer for about 15 minutes. Serves 8.

Worldwide, reindeer meat production is on the order of 25,000 to 30,000 tons. But the industry's main importance is the traditional livelihood it provides for minority groups of northern Eurasia.

Venison Bratwurst Sausages in Beer

boiling water
1 lb. venison Bratwurst sausages
¼ cup flour
3 Tbsp. bacon drippings
1 onion

10 oz. brown ale or any darker beer
2 Tbsp. flour
¼ cup milk
salt and pepper to taste

Steep the venison Bratwurst sausages for a few minutes in boiling water to remove any surplus fat. Dry the sausages and roll in the flour. Gently brown the sausages in the bacon drippings for a few minutes. Cut the onion into rings and add along with the ale to the sausages. Cover the pan and simmer until the onion is soft. Whisk the flour into the milk and slowly stir into the gravy. Season with salt and black pepper. Serves 4 to 6.

Wurstsalat Swiss Salad with Venison Summer Sausage

1 bundle red radishes, sliced
2 carrots, sliced
½ cucumber, cubed
4 potatoes, cooked and cubed
1 onion, chopped
1 garlic clove, minced
¼ lb. Emmentaler cheese, cubed
¼ lb. Gruyère cheese, cubed
¼ lb. Tilsiter cheese, cubed
½ lb. venison summer sausage, sliced ¼" thick

¼ tsp. salt
black pepper
1 Tbsp. prepared mustard
¼ tsp. dried basil
¼ tsp. dried thyme
1 tsp. lemon juice
¼ cup white vinegar
5 Tbsp. olive oil
2 hard-boiled eggs, sliced
2 tomatoes, quartered and sliced
1 green onion, chopped

Toss together the vegetables, cheeses, and venison summer sausage. Mix together the remaining ingredients, except the eggs, tomatoes, and onion. Pour the sauce over the meat and cheese. Lay on the eggs and tomatoes. Sprinkle with green onion. Serves 4.

Yum Moo Ya with Small Venison Sausage

½ lb. small venison sausage links
¼ onion, thinly sliced
12 cilantro sprigs, minced
3 Thai chili peppers, minced

1 Tbsp. *nuoc mam* (fish sauce)
1 tsp. sugar
juice of ½ lime, or to taste

Pan-fry the venison sausage, allow to drain, and cool. Slice the sausage into bite-sized slices. Add an amount of sliced onion that is equal to the amount of sausage. Mix together the sausage, onion, cilantro, chili peppers, half of the fish sauce, and the sugar in a bowl. Add three-quarters of the lime juice and taste. Add more lime juice or fish sauce, depending on your taste. This dish should taste a little hot and well balanced between the lime and the fish sauce. Serve warm or cold. Serves 2 to 4.

Apple, Mushroom, and Venison Sausage Corn Bread Stuffing

2 (8½ oz.) pkgs. dry corn muffin mix
1 lb. breakfast venison sausage links, thinly sliced
½ lb. fresh mushrooms, sliced
1 cup chopped celery
1 cup chopped onion

2 garlic cloves, chopped
1 Granny Smith apple, peeled, cored, and chopped
8 slices white bread, cut into ½" cubes
salt and pepper to taste

Prepare the corn muffin mix according to package directions. Cook, allow to cool, and crumble. Preheat the oven to 350° F. Place the sausage in a large skillet. Cook over medium-high heat until browned. Drain and set aside. In the skillet, slowly cook and stir the mushrooms, celery, onion, and garlic until just soft. In a large bowl, mix the crumbled corn muffins, sausage, mushroom mixture, apple, bread, salt, and pepper. Transfer the mixture to a medium baking dish and bake for 45 minutes or until lightly browned. Do not stuff a turkey and place in the refrigerator overnight; stuff the turkey just before placing in the oven. Serves 8 to 10.

Bourbon-Cooked Venison Sausage

1 lb. small venison sausage links   ⅜ cup cocktail sauce
½ cup brown sugar, packed   ½ cup bourbon

In a large skillet, combine the venison sausages, brown sugar, cocktail sauce, and bourbon. Bring the mixture to a simmer and cook until the sausages are heated through. Serves 6.

Roasted Venison Sausage Links

1 lb. venison sausage links

Preheat the oven to 400° F degrees. Use a sharp fork to pierce holes along each venison sausage. Place the sausages on a rack in a roasting pan. Roast for 25 minutes. Serves 2.

Portuguese Chourico with Venison Sausage

2 lbs. venison Chorizo sausage, crumbled   1 cup dry red wine
2 green bell peppers, seeded and chopped   1 cup water
2 onions, chopped   2 Tbsp. minced garlic
1 (6 oz.) can tomato paste   cooked rice for 8

Mix the sausage, green pepper, onion, tomato paste, wine, water, and crushed garlic together in a Crock-Pot. Cover and cook on low for 8 hours. Uncover the pot and cook for an additional 2 hours. Serve over rice. Serves 8.

When frightened, a deer may remain
motionless, waiting for the danger to pass.

Crown Roast with Venison Sausage Stuffing

3 Tbsp. butter
1 (5½ lb.) venison or pork crown roast
¾ lb. bulk venison sausage
1 onion, chopped
4 cups dry French bread crumbs
1 (7 oz.) can steamed chestnuts, chopped
2½ cups chicken broth, divided
½ cup chopped parsley
2 tsp. dried sage leaves

2 tsp. dried thyme leaves
salt and pepper to taste
1½ cups dry vermouth
3 slices bacon
3 Tbsp. butter, softened
1½ Tbsp. flour
salt and pepper to taste
butter

Preheat the oven to 350° F. Grease one 8" × 8" × 2" glass baking dish with 1 Tbsp. of the butter and set aside. Cover a roasting rack with aluminum foil and place in the roasting pan. Place the crown roast, bone-ends up, on the foil-lined rack. Bake for 1 hour.

Prepare the stuffing by melting the remaining 2 Tbsp. of butter in a large skillet over medium-high heat. Add the venison sausage and onion; cook until the sausage is crumbled and fully cooked. Remove from the heat. Stir in the bread crumbs, chestnuts, ½ cup of the chicken broth, parsley, sage, thyme, salt, and pepper. Mix well. Boil the remaining 2 cups of chicken broth and the vermouth in a large saucepan until reduced by half. Fry the bacon until crisp. Drain, crumble, and set aside. In the same skillet, over medium-high heat, melt the softened butter. Add the flour; mix and cook until golden brown. Add the broth mixture and boil until slightly thickened, about 5 minutes. Add the bacon; season with salt and pepper.

Remove the crown roast from the oven, fill the center with stuffing, and cover the stuffing with foil. Transfer the remaining stuffing to a buttered baking dish. Place the crown roast and extra stuffing in the oven. Insert a thermometer into the center of the stuffing and bake until the temperature reaches 160° F, about 1 hour. Baste the crown roast occasionally with drippings. Transfer the crown roast to a serving platter and cover. Decorate the ends of the bones with paper tufts.

To serve, slice down between the bones and serve with the stuffing and gravy. Do not stuff a roast and place in the refrigerator overnight; stuff the roast just before placing in the oven. Serves 6.

Oyster Venison Sausage Stuffing

1 lb. bulk venison sausage
16 oz. unseasoned dry bread stuffing mix
1 lb. oysters chopped, liquid reserved
2 cups chopped celery
1 onion, chopped

¼ cup butter, melted
1½ cups chicken broth
salt and pepper to taste
Creole seasoning to taste

Cook the venison sausage in a skillet and crumble. In a large bowl, combine the dry bread stuffing with the sausage and pan juices. Stir in the oyster pieces and liquid, chopped celery, onion, and butter. Add the broth a little at a time until the dressing is moist, but not soggy. Season to taste with salt, pepper, and Creole seasoning. Refrigerate until cold. Stuff the turkey just prior to roasting. After stuffing the turkey, place the remaining stuffing in a baking dish and cook along with the turkey until crusted and brown. Do not stuff a turkey and place in the refrigerator overnight; stuff the turkey just before placing in the oven. Makes 1 gallon.

Sweet Potatoes with Pecans and Venison Sausage Patties

1 lb. bulk venison sausage
3 lbs. sweet potatoes
2 Tbsp. butter

⅓ cup brown sugar, packed
¾ cup chopped pecans
1 tsp. ground cinnamon

Preheat the oven to 350° F. Form the sausage into round patties and cook over medium-high heat until brown on both sides. Drain and set aside. Wash the sweet potatoes, prick with a sharp fork, and place on a baking sheet. Bake for 1 hour or until soft. Set aside to cool. Cut the cooled sweet potatoes into 2" cubes and place in a 2½ quart casserole dish. Add the sausage, butter, brown sugar, pecans, and cinnamon. Mix thoroughly, cover, and bake for 30 to 40 minutes until bubbly. Serves 4 to 6.

Hot Tamale Venison Pie

2 cups masa or cornmeal
6 cups boiling water
1 lb. ground venison
4 pieces ground smoked bacon
1 white onion, chopped
½ green bell pepper, chopped

2 Tbsp. bacon fat
2 cups canned tomatoes
salt and pepper to taste
chili powder to taste
shortening

Preheat the oven to 400° F. Sift the cornmeal slowly into rapidly boiling water, stirring constantly. Cook for 5 minutes. Mix the ground venison and bacon, and brown with the onion and green pepper in hot fat. Add the tomatoes. Season with salt, pepper, and chili powder. Simmer for 10 minutes. Fill a greased baking dish with alternate layers of the cornmeal mush and the meat mixture. Bake for 20 minutes. Serve hot. Serves 4 to 6.

Appendix
Sources For Sausage-Making Supplies And Equipment

Check Local Sources First

For local sources of sausage-making supplies, equipment, and cures, look in your Yellow Pages under "Butcher's Equipment & Supplies."

Morton cures can sometimes be found at local butcher supply stores or in the salt or canning and freezing sections of supermarkets, discount shopping centers, and rural grocery stores. The best time to look for these cures is just before the spring vegetable canning season.

Mail-Order and Other Sources

Allied Kenco Sales
26 Lyerly, No. 1
Houston, TX 77022
Toll-free: 800-356-5189
Phone: 713-691-2935
Email: aks@alliedkenco.com
Website: www.alliedkenco.com
Sausage-making supplies, equipment, and cures.

Bradley Technologies Canada, Inc.
2118–21320 Westminster Highway
Richmond, BC
Canada V6V 2X5
Toll-free: 800-665-4188
Phone: 604-270-3646
Email: info@bradleysmoker.com
Website: www.bradleysmoker.com/products.asp
Home-style hot-/cold-smoker with automatic smoke generator.

The Brinkmann Corporation
4821 Simonton Road
Dallas, TX 75244
Toll-free: 800-468-5252, ext. 430
Website: www.thebrinkmanncorp.com/default.asp
Smokers/cookers.

Butcher & Packer Supply Company
1468 Gratiot Avenue
Detroit, MI 48207
Toll-free: 800-521-3188
Email: al@butcher-packer.com
Website: www.butcher-packer.com
Sausage-making supplies, equipment, and cures.

Cabela's
812 13th Avenue
Sidney, NE 69160–9555
Toll-free: 800-237-4444
Website: www.cabelas.com
Sausage-making supplies, equipment, and sporting goods.

Chaney Instrument Company
965 Wells Street
P.O. Box 70
Lake Geneva, WI 53147
Toll-free: 800-777-0565
Email: info@chaney-inst.com
Website: www.chaneyinstrument.com/products/timers.html
Acu-Rite dial and digital cooking/oven thermometers.

Craft's Custom Meats
5205 I-55 South
Jackson, MS 39212
Phone: 601-346-0120
*Custom deer/meat processing and
sporting goods.*

DeWied International, Inc.
5010 East I.H. 10
San Antonio, TX 78219
Toll-free: 800-804-5834
Phone: 210-661-6161
Email: hq@deweidint.com
Website: www.dewied.com
Offices in the United States, Canada,
Mexico, Argentina, Germany,
Finland, France, and China.
*Manufacturer and distributor of
sausage casings worldwide.*

Doug Care Equipment
P.O. Box 802072
Santa Clarita, CA 91380
Toll-free: 888-278-0377
Phone: 661-297-0377
Email: sales@dougcare.com
Website: www.dougcare.com
Commercial sausage equipment.

Eldon's Jerky and Sausage Supply
HC75 Box 113-A2
Kooskia, ID 83539
Toll-free: 800-352-9453
Phone: 208-926-4949
Email: customerservice@eldonsausage.
com
Website: www.eldonsausage.com/
index.html
*Sausage-making supplies, equipment,
and cures.*

Harbor Freight Tools
3491 Mission Oaks Boulevard
Camarillo, CA 93011–6010
Toll-free: 800-423-2567
Email: tech@harborfreight.com
Website: www.harborfreight.com
Meat grinders and stuffers.

HuntingNet.com
The Ultimate Hunter's Website
11964 Oak Creek Parkway
Building B, Unit G
Huntley, IL 60142
Phone: 847-659-8200
Email Addresses:
General Inquiries: feeback@hunting.
net
Subscriptions: subscriptions
@hunting.net
Advertising Opportunities: sales
@hunting.net
Website: www.hunting.net

KitchenAid
P.O. Box 218
St. Joseph, MI 49085
Toll-free: 800-541-6390
Email: Info-countertop@countertop.
kitchenaid
Website: www.kitchenaid.com
Combination mixer, grinder, and stuffer.

L.E.M. Products, Inc.
P.O. Box 244
Miamitown, OH 45041
Phone: 513-353-4004
Email: info@lemproducts.com
Website: www.lemproducts.com
*Sausage-making supplies, equipment,
and cures.*

Linemaster Switch Corp.
29 Plaine Hill Road
P.O. Box 238
Woodstock, CT 06281–0238
Toll-free: 800-974-3668
Phone: 860-974-1000
Email: sales@linemaster.com
Website: www.linemaster.com
Grinder foot-control switch.

Morton Salt Central Regional Office
290 Springfield Road—Suite 290
Bloomingdale, IL 60108–2217
Phone: 630-924-5516
Website: www.mortonsalt.com/recp/
    speb1recp.htm
Morton Meat Cures

Northern Tool & Equipment Co.
P.O. Box 1499
Burnsville, MN 55337–0499
Toll-free: 800-221-0516
Website: www.northerntool.com
Meat grinders and stuffers.

Rebel Butcher Supply
106 Flowood Drive
Flowood, MS 39208
Phone: 601-939-2214
Email: mike@rebelbutcher.com
Website: www.rebelbutcher.com
*Sausage-making supplies, equipment,
    and cures.*

Road Runner Distributing Co.
4432 South 70th East Avenue
Tulsa, OK 74145
Toll-free: 800-331-2676
Email: rrmerit@swbell.net
Website: www.roadrunner-merit.com
*Sausage-making supplies, equipment,
    and cures.*

S & D Deer Processing
1114 Honeysuckle Lane
Utica, MS 39175
Phone: 601-885-6474
Custom deer processing.

The Sausage Maker, Inc.
1500 Clinton Street, Building 123
Buffalo, NY 14206
Toll-free: 888-490-8525
Phone: 716-824-5814
Email: sausmaker@aol.com
Website: www.sausagemaker.com
*Small commercial smokers; sausage-
    making supplies and equipment.*

Smoky Hollow Products Ltd.
25 Delano Park
Cape Elizabeth, ME 04107–1901
Phone: 207-799-0570
Email: smoky@smokyhollow.com
Website: http://members.bellatlantic.
    net/~cfmitch/index3c.html
Double-barrel smoker.

Summers Sausage Company
P.O. Box 34
12644 North State Road 245
Lamar, IN 47550
Phone: 812-529-8456
Email: summersenterprises
    @yahoo.com
Website: www.summerssausage
    company.com
*Deer processing; sausage-making
    supplies, equipment, and cures.*

Tilia, Inc.
P.O. Box 194530
San Francisco, CA 94119–4530
Phone: 415-543-9136
Email: customerservice@tilia.com
Website: www.tilia.com
FoodSaver vacuum machine and bags.

Tony Chachere's Creole Foods of Opelousas, Inc.
P.O. Box 1639
Opelousas, LA 70571–1639
Toll-free: 800-551-9066
Email: creole@tonychachere.com
Website: www.tonychachere.com
Creole seasonings.

Tor-Rey
3920 Westhollow Parkway
Houston, TX 77082
Toll-free: 800-867-7391
Phone: 281-564-3150
Email: gmanager@tor-ray.com
Website: www.tor-rey.com
Small commercial meat-processing equipment.

Van's Deer Processing
777 Highway 468
Brandon, MS 39042
Phone: 601-825-9087
Custom deer processing and sporting goods.

Wal-Mart Supercenters
Website: www.walmart.com
FoodSaver vacuum machine and bags.

Zupancich Brothers, Inc.
303 East Sheridan Avenue
Ely, MN, 55731
Phone: 218-365-3188
Email: info@zups.com
Website: www.zups.com/mkpl/ creating.html
Sausage-making supplies, equipment, and cures.

Cooking and Oven Conversion Tables

Whether you are accustomed to using American, imperial, or metric measurements, it is not always necessary for you to spend time trying to convert the individual measurements into the units that you are familiar with. Most cookery supply shops around the world sell measuring accessories that have more than one measurement scale.

If you will be using recipes which call for a measurement system that you are not familiar with, you may wish to purchase measurement tools that are used in the recipe. You can also use these tables to make your own conversions.

Oven temperature conversions are simple when you use a thermometer that registers the temperature in both Fahrenheit and Celsius. The Oven Temperature Conversion Table will also allow you to make a quick conversion. The exception is for those cooks who use an Aga stove and oven. If you own one of these fine stoves, you are already skilled in judging the temperature on the cooking heads and in the separate ovens. Oven heat controls are not as accurate as you may think. It is not uncommon for home ranges to have an error in excess of 50° to 100°. An inexpensive oven thermometer will take all the guesswork out of correctly setting the temperature of your oven.

If you wish to work out your own specific measurement and temperature conversions, these Internet pages will automatically make the calculations/ conversions for you:

- http://www.allrecipes.com/cb/ref/convert/conversions.asp
- http://foodgeeks.com/resources/conversioncharts.phtml#fm
- http://www.onlineconversion.com

Weight–Volume–Length Conversion Formulas

To Convert	Multiply	By
ounces to grams	the ounces	28.350
grams to ounces	the grams	.035
liters to British quarts	the liters	.880
liters to American quarts	the liters	.950
deciliters to ounces	the deciliters	3.380
milliliters to ounces	the milliliters	.338
British quarts to liters	the quarts	1.140
American quarts to liters	the quarts	1.057
inches to centimeters	the inches	2.540
centimeters to inches	the centimeters	.390

Basic Metric–U.S. Cooking Conversions

Metric Measures Conversion		U.S. Measures	
28.35 g	= 1 oz.	1 Tbsp.	= 3 tsp.
100 g	= 3.53 oz.	1 cup	= 16 Tbsp.
453.6 g	= 1 lb.	1 cup	= 8 oz.
1 kg	= 2.21 lbs.	1 pt.	= 2 cups
1.25 ml	= ¼ tsp.	1 qt.	= 4 cups
2.5 ml	= ½ tsp.	1 qt.	= 32 oz.
5 ml	= 1 tsp.	1 gal.	= 4 qts.
15 ml	= 1 Tbsp.	1 gal.	= 128 oz.
118 ml	= ½ cup	1 lb.	= 16 oz.
237 ml	= 1 cup	1 lb.	= 2 cups butter
946 ml	= 1 qt.	¼ lb.	= ½ cup butter
1 lt	= 4 cups	¼ lb.	= 1 stick butter
1 lt	= 1,000 ml	¼ lb.	= 8 Tbsp. butter

Approximate U.S.–Metric Equivalents—
Dry and Liquid

U.S. Measures	Metric	U.S. Measures	Metric
¼ tsp.	1.23 ml	2 Tbsp.	29.57 ml
½ tsp.	2.36 ml	3 Tbsp.	44.36 ml
¾ tsp.	3.70 ml	¼ cup	59.15 ml
1 tsp.	4.93 ml	½ cup	118.30 ml
1¼ tsp.	6.16 ml	1 cup	236.59 ml
1½ tsp.	7.39 ml	2 cups or 1 pt.	473.18 ml
1¾ tsp.	8.63 ml	3 cups	709.77 ml
2 tsp.	9.86 ml	4 cups or 1 qt.	946.36 ml
1 Tbsp.	14.79 ml	4 qts. or 1 gal.	3.79 lt

Gram–Ounce Conversions

Grams		Ounces	Grams	Ounces
500 g	1 livre	17⅗ oz.	60 (56.6) g	2 oz.
454 g	1 lb.	16 oz.	50 g	1¾ oz.
250 g		8⅞ oz.	30 (28.3) g	1 oz.
150 g		5¼ oz.	25 g	⅞ oz.
125 g		4½ oz.	21 (21.3) g	¾ oz.
115 (113.2) g		4 oz.	15 (14.2) g	½ oz.
100 g		3½ oz.	7 (7.1) g	¼ oz.
85 (84.9) g		3 oz.	3½ (3.5) g	⅛ oz.
80 g		2⅘ oz.	2 (1.8) g	¹⁄₁₆ oz.

All-Purpose Flour Conversions

U.S.		Grams
7 cups	2.2 lbs.	1,000 g
3½ cups		500 g
3⅓ cups	1 lb.	454 g
1¾ cups		250 g
⅔ cup		100 g
⅓ cup		50 g
¼ cup		35 g
3 Tbsp.		25 g
1 Tbsp.		7½ g

Salt and Sugar Conversions

U.S.	Grams
⅔ cup	125 g
¼ cup	50 g
⅓ cup	65 g
2½ cups	454 g (1 lb.)
1 Tbsp.	13–15 g
1 tsp.	5 g

U.S. Cups–Deciliters Conversions

U.S. 8 oz. Cups	Deciliters	U.S. 8 oz. Cups	Deciliters
⅛ cup	.30 dl	1⅛ cups	2.66 dl
¼ cup	.59 dl	1¼ cups	2.96 dl
⅓ cup	.79 dl	1⅓ cups	3.16 dl
½ cup	1.18 dl	1½ cups	3.55 dl
⅔ cup	1.58 dl	1⅔ cups	3.95 dl
¾ cup	1.78 dl	1¾ cups	4.10 dl
1 cup	2.37 dl	2 cups	4.73 dl

U.S. Cups–Milliliters Conversions

U.S. 8 oz. Cups	Milliliters	U.S. 8 oz. Cups	Milliliters
⅛ cup	29.59 dl	1⅛ cups	266.27 dl
¼ cup	59.17 dl	1¼ cups	295.86 dl
⅓ cup	78.99 dl	1⅓ cups	315.68 dl
½ cup	118.34 dl	1½ cups	355.03 dl
⅔ cup	157.99 dl	1⅔ cups	394.67 dl
¾ cup	177.51 dl	1¾ cups	414.20 dl
1 cup	236.59 dl	2 cups	473.37 dl

Approximate Metric Equivalents by Volume

U.S.	Metric
¼ cup	60 milliliters
½ cup	120 milliliters
1 cup	230 milliliters
1¼ cups	300 milliliters
1½ cups	360 milliliters
2 cups	460 milliliters
2½ cups	600 milliliters
3 cups	700 milliliters
4 cups (1 qt.)	.95 liter
1.06 quarts	1 liter
4 quarts (1 gal.)	3.8 liters

Metric	U.S.
50 milliliters	.21 cup
100 milliliters	.42 cup
150 milliliters	.63 cup
200 milliliters	.84 cup
250 milliliters	1.06 cup
1 liter	1.05 quarts

Approximate Metric Equivalents by Weight

U.S.	Metric
¼ ounce	7 grams
½ ounce	14 grams
1 ounce	28 grams
1¼ ounces	35 grams
1½ ounces	40 grams
4 ounces	112 grams
5 ounces	140 grams
8 ounces	228 grams
10 ounces	280 grams
15 ounces	425 grams
16 ounces (1 lb.)	454 grams

Metric	U.S.
1 gram	.035 ounce
50 grams	1.75 ounces
100 grams	3.5 ounces
250 grams	8.75 ounces
500 grams	1.1 pounds
1 kilogram	2.2 pounds

U.S. Measurement Equivalents

pinch/dash (dry)	less than ⅛ tsp.	⅛ cup	2 Tbsp.
dash (liquid)	a few drops	¼ cup	4 Tbsp.
3 tsp.	1 Tbsp.	¼ cup	2 fluid oz.
¼ Tbsp.	¾ tsp.	⅓ cup	5 Tbsp. + 1 tsp.
½ Tbsp.	1½ tsp.	½ cup	8 Tbsp.
2 Tbsp.	1 fluid oz.	1 cup	16 Tbsp.
4 Tbsp.	¼ cup	1 cup	8 fluid oz.
5⅓ Tbsp.	⅓ cup	1 cup	½ pint
8 Tbsp.	½ cup	2 cups	1 pint
8 Tbsp.	4 fluid oz.	2 pints	1 quart
10⅔ Tbsp.	⅔ cup	4 quarts (liquid)	1 gallon
12 Tbsp.	¾ cup	8 quarts (dry)	1 peck
16 Tbsp.	1 cup	4 pecks (dry)	1 bushel
16 Tbsp.	8 fluid oz.	1 cord (128 cf)	8' L × 4' H × 4' W

Oven Temperature Conversion Table

To convert Fahrenheit to Celsius: subtract 32, multiply by 5, and divide by 9
Example: $125° F - 32 = 93 \times 5 = 464 \div 9 = 52° C$

To convert Celsius to Fahrenheit: multiply by 9, divide by 5, and add 32
Example: $60° C \times 9 = 540 \div 5 = 108 + 32 \times 5\ 140° F$

(°F)	(°C)	American: Oven Terms	English: "Regulo" Gas Mark	French: Oven Terms
120	49			
125	52			
130	54			
135	57			
140	60	cold	#0	¼
145	63			
150	66			
160	71			*fras*
170	77			
200	93	low		
212	100		#1	1
221	105			
225	107			
230	110			
240	116			*doux*
250	121			
265	130	medium low		
284	140		#2	2
290	143			
300	149			*tiède*
302	150			
310	154		#3	3
325	163	medium		*modéré*
335	168		#4	4
350	177			*modéré à chaud*
355	179	moderate		
358	181		#5	5
375	190	medium hot		
380	193			
390	200		#6	6
400	205			*chaud*
410	210	hot	#7	7
425	218			*très chaud*
428	220		#8	8
445	229	very hot		
450	232			
470	243		#9	*très chaud plus*
475	246	ext. hot		9
490	253			
500	260			
510	265			*rotir*
525	274			
550	288	max. temp		*grilloir*

Index